W9-BVK-110

Dalí & I

Stan Lauryssens

Dalí & I

The Surreal Story

THOMAS DUNNE BOOKS

St. Martin's Press ❧ New York

THOMAS DUNNE BOOKS.
An imprint of St. Martin's Press.

DALÍ & I. Copyright © 2008 by Arendsoog Ltd. All rights reserved. Printed in the
United States of America. For information, address St. Martin's Press, 175 Fifth Avenue,
New York, N.Y. 10010.

www.thomasdunnebooks.com
www.stmartins.com

Design by Kathryn Parise

LIBRARY OF CONGRESS CATALOGING-IN-PUBLICATION DATA

Lauryssens, Stan, 1946–
    Dali & I : the surreal story / Stan Lauryssens.—1st ed.
        p. cm.
    Dali and I
    ISBN-13: 978-0-312-37993-3
    ISBN-10: 0-312-37993-5
    1. Lauryssens, Stan, 1946– 2. Art dealers—Belgium—Biography. 3. Impostors
and imposture—Belgium—Biography.   4. Dalí, Salvador, 1904–1989—Forgeries.
5. Art—Forgeries—Economic aspects. I. Title. II. Title: Dali and I.
    N8660.L38A3 2008
    709.2—dc22
    [B]   2008012729
First Edition: July 2008

10 9 8 7 6 5 4 3 2 1

Acknowledgments

I'd like to thank David Sacks, Daniel Brunt, Jason Reitman, Michael R. Newman, Andrew Niccol, and John Salvati. I owe you, guys. You've made the dream come true.

Author's Note

This is a work of nonfiction. Events and actions have been retold as I remember them, though names and identifying characteristics of certain people mentioned in the book have been changed. Conversations presented in dialogue form have been re-created based on my memory of them, but they are not intended to represent word-for-word documentation of what was said; rather, they are meant to reflect the substance of what was said.

Part I

McDali

This is how it started: I was twenty-two and worked in a Belgian cheese factory. I'm not a poet and I can't sing, yet I wrote poetry and sang in a rock band at night while I spent my days in the underground cold store, making holes in wheels of Emmentaler cheese. One day, I got a phone call from the editor of Antwerp's weekly *Panorama* magazine. He'd seen me on-stage and read my poetry and wondered if I would be interested in a job switch. Of course I was. Wouldn't you be?

Panorama asked me to become the weekly's correspondent in Hollywood. In an attempt to boost the magazine's circulation and sell more printed paper, the editors had hit upon the idea of splashing the finest film stars of the day—a very young Al Pacino, Faye Dunaway, Robert Redford, Barbra Streisand, Paul Newman—on the cover. As I understood it, I had to interview the Pacinos and Dunaways of this world, then and there, in Hollywood. Would you have hesitated a single second? I didn't. I'd made enough holes in Emmentaler wheels. I immediately quit the cheese business and signed my contract as the magazine's correspondent in Hollywood.

There was one problem, though: *Panorama* didn't have the necessary funds to send me to California. We worked out a compromise. They gave me an old desk, a chair, a manual typewriter, a stack of *Variety* and *Hollywood Reporter* back issues—this was the early seventies, well before the Internet and Google—and a pair of scissors with a pot of glue, and asked me to cook up, invent, fabricate, or dream up interviews that would read as if I wined and dined with the stars of the silver screen every day of the week. Instead of languishing next to my swimming pool on Melrose Place, I would be slaving under the leaking roof of an editorial office on an Antwerp backstreet.

I was good at my new job, and for years I fabricated "live" interviews and wrote glamorous cover stories about leading ladies Barbara Hershey, Karen Black, Anita Ekberg, and Anne Bancroft, as well as actors like Nick Nolte and Robert De Niro, among others. Week after week, I found my name on the printed page under the pumped-up byline FROM OUR MAN IN HOLLYWOOD, which pleased me enormously. One week I concocted a story about Kojak, the week after that, I fantasized about Salvador Dalí. Though not a movie star, Dalí was as famous as Kojak and had more facial hair.

This is how I did it: I collected exhibition catalogs, old *Life* and *Paris Match* articles, Reuters dispatches and secondhand art books and hit upon the idea of situating Dalí in Hollywood, where he was helping Walt Disney create the most scandalous and scabrous animated porn cartoon ever—or so I had people believe. It was all fiction and fantasy and a figment of my imagination. Dalí looked good on the magazine's cover, in close-up, rolling his bulging, fishy eyes. His famous waxed mustache had never been in better shape.

To see which covers—and which film stars—were the best-sellers, I regularly made the rounds to newsagents and booksellers that had the magazine on display. I soon learned that, on a cover, a female star is superior to a male star for sales—Mia Farrow beats Woody Allen and Ali MacGraw beats Steve McQueen—while a *blond* female star far outsells a dark-haired beauty. Faye Dunaway and Farrah Fawcett beat Liza Minelli and Audrey Hepburn ten times over.

But the biggest surprise was still to come. To my amazement, the balding, mustachioed, wrinkled Salvador Dalí, weary with age, far outsold superstars Warren Beatty, Raquel Welch, Ursula Andress, Dustin Hoffman, Woody Allen, and even Elizabeth Taylor, the all-time beauty queen.

That's when I got my first lesson in life.

Dalí *sells*.

Another unexpected phone call. The president of Money Management Counselors urgently needed to see me, seven o'clock sharp. No discussion. I knew that MMC was the brainchild of an American financier who—all through the sixties—sold bonds to American soldiers stationed in Germany. Other MMC investment branches included works of art, diamonds, and real estate in Dallas and Canada.

I had never met a president, so I agreed to meet him at the Century Center Hotel, in the dining room, right at seven. As could be expected from the president—any president—of a multimillion-dollar company, he was already spooning heaps of beluga caviar on buttered toast when I arrived at his preferred table. A waiter in evening dress brought me an ivory spoon, butter, some very thin slices of lemon, an extra rack of white toast, and half a kilo of choice caviar.

The president told me he was a financier. He was also a play-boy. He was restructuring his company's art-investment branch. "It's all about making money, and I'm fed up with all these con artists trying to fool the art world," he said. "I want *you* to run our fine art–investment branch and supply our wealthiest clients with the finest artworks available."

"Why me?" I asked. "I know nothing about art."

"You know Salvador Dalí," the president replied. "You inter-viewed him in Hollywood, didn't you? Boy oh boy, that was one hell of an interview!"

Then and there, I got my *second* lesson in life.

Anyone—even presidents—can be taken for a ride.

From one day to the next, I became an art consultant and investment broker. I couldn't believe my luck. My job de-scription was simple: Talk as much cash as I could out of the greedy suckers of this world. I read. I studied. I traveled to Sotheby's and Christie's in London and New York. I bought my first Dalí in Paris. A 1937 futuristic ink drawing representing what looked like a mass of swirls and ovals or fried beans. I didn't ask for a certificate of authenticity—supposedly, the drawing had been commissioned for *American Weekly*, a rather famous magazine in the forties—and I sure as hell didn't check the credentials of the snooty gallery owner who sold it. For all I knew, there might have been a warrant out for his arrest. Why else would he sell a genuine Dalí at half price, if it was true that—as he'd explained to me—the famous Paris auctioneers of the Hôtel Drouot had estimated its retail value to be almost double the asking price? It was a bargain and I went for it. You see? That's how unsuspecting and inexperienced I was.

I paid and took possession of the framed drawing and then had a stroke of beginner's luck. Unknown to the seller, the Dalí drawing was reproduced in an official museum catalog, in black-and-white, on a half page. The next day, I tripled the price I had paid for it, hung the swirls and ovals and fried beans on the wall in my brand-new executive office in the President Building in Antwerp, and although I'd never actually done this before, I sold the drawing to the first "art investor" who walked through the door.

That's how a local undertaker carrying a plastic shopping bag became my first client.

I told him it must be a sad way to earn your money when your clients have all died.

"That's life," the undertaker replied. "Today you're on this side; tomorrow you may be on the other side. A dead person is a wooden plank and I'm the carpenter. I plane and polish and when it looks more or less decent, I bury the plank. If you think of it, the deceased are not my clients. I've got only one client: the good Lord in Heaven, he who governs life and death. As long as I've got the good Lord on my side, there will be dead people around."

I asked him to sit down.

He was wearing the uniform of his profession: dark gray suit, white shirt, gray tie, and highly polished black shoes. He sat perfectly motionless, his back straight as a rod, the plastic shopping bag in his lap, never once crossing his long legs.

"My bank manager said I should talk to you," the undertaker said. Only his mouth seemed to move. "What can *you* do that my bank manager can't?"

"Launder your money," I said.

"What have you got to sell?"

"Nothing."

"Nothing?"

"I'm not a salesperson. I'm an art dealer, and my only client is Salvador Dalí. I'm selling works of art not for their artistic value or their sheer beauty but purely as an investment. The art market is global and has been growing by thirty percent a year for the last five years. New money from China, India, and Russia is joining the chase and pushing prices up. One day, I will resell for you, at a profit."

"How much profit do you guarantee?"

"The sky is the limit."

"At long term?"

"There is no long term. We'll all be dead planks tomorrow."

"I've got ten thousand dollars for you," the undertaker said.

I shrugged. "Dalí is not a clearance sale," I replied.

"Fifty thousand. What have you got for fifty thousand?"

"Nothing. I told you: Dalí is not a clearance sale."

"Make it a hundred thousand."

"Now you talk like a man."

"If Dalí dies," the undertaker chuckled, "I will gladly fix some wax on his mustache. He'll be as good as new."

"When will I get your money?" I asked.

"Now," the undertaker said, and shot into action, emptying the plastic bag on my brand-new mahogany desk. Suddenly the desktop overflowed with British pounds, greenbacks, French francs, German marks, kroner, pesetas, and an assortment of Belgian, Swiss, and Russian currency.

"Where did you get all this?" I asked while trying to act natural, stifling my laughter.

The undertaker apologized. "People die everywhere, all the time. Being in the service of the good Lord in Heaven is an international business, you know," he replied, and briskly walked out, carefully clutching his little Dalí masterpiece.

So began my introduction to the world of art. My first sale had come so easy to me, no effort at all. Beginner's luck. I thought I would be on a high for weeks. The scene in my brand-new office reminded me of the title of a Woody Allen film I had seen a few years previously, *Take the Money and Run,* a classic presented as a documentary on the life of an incompetent petty criminal called Virgil Starkwell, played by Woody Allen. I felt like an incompetent petty criminal myself. I had taken the money, but now that it was time to run, I didn't run. Though I was unsure of the morality of what I had just done, bluffing the undertaker out of his hard-earned cash, my MMC president was delighted. He shot me a wide smile. Next day, he took me to his own personal tailor, who fitted me with a custom-made suit while enjoying an afternoon coffee.

"You're a natural, Stan! Fantastic," the president exclaimed.

"I'm puzzled. Why do these rich people buy art?" I asked. "To beautify their lives?"

"Fuck beauty!"

"To add to their cultural . . . pastiche?"

"Don't make me regret hiring you, Stan!"

I sighed. "I don't know . . . do they really buy as . . . as an investment?" I asked.

The MMC president nodded and smiled.

"How far can I go?" I asked.

"The only limit to what you can charge is what the buyer is willing to pay," the president told me. "If you're good, there's no price limit. None. Rich people need to flaunt their wealth without appearing to be vulgar. I mean, they can't hang their cash on the wall, can they? Always remember that (a) rich men respect you when you don't bullshit them, (b) the wives are your secret weapon, and (c) don't show pity, take the money without remorse, and take as much as you can. Always remember that every great fortune in the world is built on a life of crime."

"Okay. Time to go to work," I said.

The MMC president cocked his head. "Now we're talking."

"I need more Dalí paintings," I said resolutely.

Easy come, easy go. I pocketed the undertaker's money, and smartly dressed in my new clothes, I hired a private plane and flew to London. A small Dalí oil on paper titled *Don Quixote* was pictured in a Sotheby's sales catalog. It represented a man stepping out of the ocean, foaming waves sloshing around his legs. He didn't have a torso; he had a ship's mast and bulging sails instead. Why it was called *Don Quixote* was a mystery to me. I told you, I was simpleminded: I relied on the sales catalog and took it for granted that the oil on paper was a genuine Dalí stage design for the *Mad Tristan* ballet that opened in New York in December 1944. At the famous auction house in New Bond Street there was a packed sales room, but no hands or sales paddles went up. No one was bidding but me. In the end, I paid starting price for what I thought was a charming little gem.

The hired plane—a Cessna, if I remember well—had been waiting for me at London Airport. I tucked the Dalí under my shirt and walked through Her Majesty's Revenue & Customs. Back in my mahogany-and-leather office, I displayed the oil on paper in exactly the same spot where Dalí's fried beans had—with a little help from the good Lord in Heaven—brought me such good luck.

It wasn't long before the next investor knocked on my door and walked in, flush with money.

He had big ruddy hands—to me, his hands looked as if they'd been soaked in hot soapy water for a week or two—and came to the meeting wearing white rubber boots and a white apron sprinkled with blood. He told me he had started off as a small-time butcher, and although he now owned a nationwide chain of butcher shops, he still loved hacking and sawing dead carcasses into steaks and cutlets.

"I make so much money that it fills my Chinese vase to the rim," he said.

"A Chinese vase? What Chinese vase?"

"The one in my bedroom. Antique, Chinese, traditional. That's where I hide my money," the butcher said. "Gray market money, unofficial money, black money not reported to the government for tax purposes. Illegal and 'funny' money. I'm anxious to get rid of my hidden fortune. I don't trust the government or my banker, you know."

He glanced at *Don Quixote* on the wall.

"A masterpiece?" he asked.

"Um, okay . . . Uh . . . Well, this is certainly a fine example of Dalí's work . . . ," I replied. "It deals with common elements in the artist's oeuvre, as you can see: the sea . . . the ocean . . . which symbolizes his desire to return to the womb . . . a landscape . . . bulging sails as the universal symbol of the future . . . various deformities."

"Would you advise me to buy it?"

"Certainly."

"Why on earth? It's ugly."

"Because . . . because it's a Dalí!"

The butcher raised an eyebrow. "What does it cost?"

"Stupid question," I said.

"Why?"

"How much cash have you got in your Chinese vase? That's a better question."

"Fifty thousand," he quickly replied.

"Fifty thousand what? Dollars or Japanse yen or Russian rubles without any monetary value?"

"American dollars."

"*Only* fifty thousand?"

"Fifty thousand every month, at the end of each month."

"Empty your vase," I said, "and I'll give you this Dalí masterpiece."

"Who says it's a masterpiece?"

"I do."

"If I buy now, when will I make a profit?"

"A British investment magazine has calculated that the art of Salvador Dalí has gone up 25.94 percent per year between 1970 and 1975, and that's only for starters. When Dalí dies, prices will skyrocket."

When it came to Dalí, I already knew my sales talk by heart.

These days, we all wear jeans. Back then, I didn't. In the seventies, when I was working for MMC, I dressed like a banker: striped shirt, stylish tie (no Windsor knot), a three-piece suit made to measure, leather belt, and leather-soled suede shoes. I behaved like a banker, too. I collected money and gave nothing in return. In life, it's important to dress the part. The undertaker did, the butcher did, my president did, and so did I. One day, I had taken off my jacket. In shirtsleeves, I was dozing in my snug leather office chair when a young man and his pretty wife walked in, both dressed in well-tailored jeans. He was carrying a suitcase and introduced himself as a manufacturer and wholesaler of counterfeit luxury goods—primarily Gucci and Louis Vuitton handbags, but also Dior lipstick, executive Fendi luggage, Prada shoes, Chanel dresses, and Armani and Ralph Lauren jackets. He explained his business to me: he bought the cheapest fabrics in low-cost countries like China and India and had them stitched together in sewing studios in Africa, mainly in Tunisia, Nigeria, and Senegal. He was in praise of Tunisian women, who are pretty good seamstresses, especially competent in stitching labels on all kinds of Chinese and Indian-made goods. You name it, they did it.

"How old are you?" I asked the designer-handbags manufacturer. I myself was now in my early thirties.

"Twenty-nine," he said. "Why do you want to know?"

"Are the police after you?"

"No comment."

"The denim you're selling, is it the real thing?" I asked. "Or a clever forgery like fake Louis Vuitton handbags and fake Cartier watches and bottles of fake Dom Pérignon champagne?"

"None of your business," he snapped.

It's a good thing to know when to shut up. I shut up.

"Good. Now will you listen to me?" the handbag manufacturer asked.

"I'll listen."

"You're the talk of the town. You're an expert on Dalí, they say. You're a moneymaker. I'd like to buy a Salvador Dalí painting. Not a drawing, not some diddlydoo on paper, no—I want a *real* oil on canvas. Big, impressive, a museum piece. We're rich. We've got money to spend. We live in Germany, in the Rhine Valley, in a castle with turrets and a drawbridge. Though I can drive only one at a time, I've got four cars. A silver Mercedes 500 SL, a mud-splattered four-by-four Land Rover, a new Porsche, of course, and a Fiat Punto for my wife's shopping. My wife's name is Catherine, by the way."

I tried a joke. "If you're as rich as you say you are," I said, "you should buy Catherine a golden carriage drawn by four white horses instead of a Fiat Punto."

They didn't laugh. They didn't even smile.

Catherine was blond. An ice queen, I thought.

"What have you got to sell?" the handbag manufacturer asked.

I sighed.

I didn't have a Salvador Dalí oil on canvas.

I didn't have a Dalí drawing or some diddlydoo on paper either.

"We'll reverse roles. What have *you* got to pay?" I replied.

"One million. Dollars. In cash."

I coughed and choked and rocked with laughter. "You sure have to work hard to earn *that* kind of money," I stuttered.

"My dear friend," the handbag manufacturer replied, "*working* never earns you any money. To make it rich, you have to be a smart-ass."

"Well?" Catherine said suddenly. "Have you got a one-million-dollar Dalí for me?"

A client is a client. Never turn him away. I was sweating and racking my brain.

"Well? What are you waiting for?" the ice queen asked again.

"Show me your money," I said.

The twenty-nine-year-old snapped his suitcase open and spread an enormous amount of bundles on my desk, each one hard as a brick and held together with rubber bands. Some fell from my desk and dropped on the floor. Each brick contained hundreds of brand-new hundred-dollar banknotes in U.S. currency and even some frayed thousand-dollar bills. I'd never before in my life seen that much money. I'd never seen a thousand-dollar banknote either. In all honesty, I must have looked like someone who is hypnotized by a hissing cobra. I started shaking all over. I went cold inside.

Like a good salesman, I tried to hide my astonishment behind a poker face, until it was my turn to impress the handbag manufacturer. Racking my brain and buying time, I slid a VHS tape into the video player. On screen, in grainy black-and-white, a stream of rainwater is flowing down the gutter of a New York street. In the water, an old wooden crutch floats by, carried by the current. A second and third crutch follow the first. Suddenly the crutches are no longer there. In the cold and rain outside the St. Regis Hotel, gaggling reporters, TV crews, and autograph-hunters call out Dalí's name like a chorus.

REPORTERS:
Dalí! Dalí! Dalí!

REPORTER #1:
I am from *Time* magazine. *Time* magazine. Everyone says you're a genius?

We watched Dalí emerge from a yellow cab. In his sixties, as flamboyant and outrageous as ever, wearing a gold lamé jacket under a giraffe-skin fur coat and carrying his familiar gold-plated cane, his famous mustache waxed to pinpoints. As always, there is the familiar upturned twist in his mustache; otherwise he feels naked, like a woman without makeup, as he used to say. Dalí got on his knees (in the gutter!) and made the sign of the cross, his head bowed. Only then did he get up and address the waiting TV reporters and newspapermen while flashbulbs were going off.

SALVADOR DALÍ:
Dalí *izzz* no mo*rrr*e a geniu*zzz* zan Dalí!

REPORTER #2:

You compare yourself to God?

SALVADOR DALÍ:

If Dalí wazzz God zerrre would be no Dalí and *zat* would be a trrragedy!

REPORTER #3:

Some people say you make a mockery of modern art?

SALVADOR DALÍ:

You wish Dalí to give you hizzz autogrrraph? So you can sell it?

REPORTER #4:

What are you working on?

SALVADOR DALÍ:

At last someone azzzks. Dalí will tell you. Ze worrrld's lar-rrgest penis!

REPORTER #1:

That's news!

SALVADOR DALÍ:

Of courrrse it izzz! Zere izzz a universal fixation on penis length. Everrry penis is too shorrrt and no penis in ze world is as good as a dildo. Zerrreforrre, Dalí will build ze ultimate penis constructed of nylon mesh with a diameter*rr* of app*rrr*oxi-mately *two* meters.

REPORTER #2:
How long will this penis be?

SALVADOR DALÍ:
Dalí intends his penis to ci*rrr*cle ze planet!

REPORTER #4:
How will you get your penis across the oceans?

SALVADOR DALÍ:
Same way they lay telephone cable. When Dalí's penis i*zzz* finished, it will ejaculate ove*rr* the headqua*rrr*te*rrr*s of ze United Nations!

REPORTER#2:
Can you make money of this?

SALVADOR DALÍ:
Whatever Dalí touches tu*rrr*ns to gold. Dalí's penis i*zzz* no ex-cep-tion!

Dalí had a wonderful voice, and his English was very comi-cal. He rolled his *rrr*'s as in Spanish, with a sharp twist, exag-gerating his bad pronunciation and articulating every syllable, while throwing in a few Catalan vowels. He also referred to himself in the third person, as if he were talking about someone else. He pulled a wad of dollar bills out of his pocket and threw the money to the shouting reporters. Then he gave his mustache a playful twist.

"Whatever Dalí touches, turns to gold," I said. "The man says so himself. Yes, I'll give you a Dalí. The best Dalí you've ever seen."

Catherine looked around the office. "Where . . . where is it?"

Offhand I flipped through a Dalí museum catalog on my desk and let it fall open on the world-famous *Last Supper* oil on canvas, property of the National Gallery of Art in Washington, D.C. "Here it is," I said, and showed the couple the peaceful image on glossy paper. "Your Dalí." It looked impressive, I must say, on paper. I could hear my heart pounding. "It's yours. Did you notice the size of the painting—167 by 268 centimeters. That's huge, for a Dalí oil on canvas. Huge but a perfect size in your castle."

The fake designer handbag manufacturer turned to his wife. "Dalí will look great next to the Monet and Degas and the one Rubens we've got!" he said with a shrewd smile.

"Good. Good. When can we collect it?" Catherine asked impatiently.

"I'm sorry," I said. "If ever there was a Dalí masterpiece, it's this one. Unfortunately, you can't collect it—not yet. You'll have to be patient. The painting is on loan to a major American museum. When this show is over, it will travel to the Paul Ricard Foundation in Paris, the Glasgow Art Gallery and

Museum in Scotland, and the Minami Art Museum in Tokyo. Finally, it will end up for its first Spanish exhibition ever in the Dalí Museum in Figueres." I shook my head. "I agree, that's a long way to go. But please, don't worry. While you talk to me now, at this very moment, you're earning money. Imagine . . . your painting will be reproduced in color in museum catalogs all over the world. The *International Herald Tribune* and *Le Monde* and *Iwate Nichi-Nichi Shimbun* in Japan will write about it and praise its beauty. It will be on TV everywhere. Hundreds of thousands of art lovers will have seen and enjoyed it. You pay a million dollars now. By the time the international exhibitions are over, the value of your Dalí will have tripled."

They looked at each other in disbelief.

"You think so?"

"I don't *think;* I never do. I *know.*"

"When will that be?"

"Two, three years? Four, perhaps."

I could see greed as well as disappointment on their faces.

"Give it to us—now!" they hissed anxiously.

I had to do something. I had to gamble and do it quickly. I pocketed one bundle of crisp dollars and stacked the remaining bundles of U.S. currency in my top desk drawer, and over the desk, I gave Catherine the Dalí museum catalog with the image of the famous painting on glossy paper.

"What the fuck am I gonna do with a book?" the fake designer handbag manufacturer snapped.

With a wide sweep, I tore the *Last Supper* out of the Dalí museum catalog and handed the crumpled glossy to the new owners.

"Frame it," I said. "Enjoy it."

I was nervous as hell. A million dollars. A fortune, even in those days, and 10 percent of it was mine, on top of a generous personal-expenses allowance and my hefty salary that was fifteenfold what I'd made as *Panorama*'s "correspondent in Hollywood." I deposited my 10 percent commission in my Antwerp bank account. The rest of the money we wanted to get to a bank in duty-free Switzerland as soon as possible, where our headquarters was located close to Geneva Airport, in a posh office block. On the flat roof, the giant illuminated MMC logo could be seen from far away. Marketing, you know. The main MMC office within the building was in fact just one small room with only one telephone, a desk, and a couple of cheap Ikea chairs.

My president acted swiftly. He ordered thirty ham-and-cheese sandwiches from the best local delicatessen—female company typists and secretaries would be traveling, too—and made arrangements with a plane-rental company that catered to the local business community. Within half an hour, a sleek Learjet brought us from Antwerp Airport to Switzerland. Smuggling the money out of the country was easy as pie. I stuffed the bricks in a wheeled Samsonite suitcase and simply rolled them onto the plane, *crack-crack-crack* over the concrete tarmac. It's not a secret that private planes everywhere easily avoid border control regulations. All the pilot needs to provide customs is a signed declaration that, to the best of his knowledge, no person on board the aircraft is suffering from any contagious disease. The flight to Switzerland took us less than an hour. From the airport, we took a taxi to one of four hundred banks in Geneva and deposited the money in a Swiss numbered account. Needless to say, it disappeared forever.

An hour after arrival, we crammed into the single room of our headquarters, ready for lunch. Coffee and whiskey were brought in, but no sandwiches.

"Goddammit! We forgot the sandwiches!" a secretary shouted.

My MMC president merely smiled. "No problem," he said, and grabbed the telephone. He instructed our pilot to fly back to Antwerp immediately, take a taxi, get the ham-and-cheese sandwiches from the delicatessen, and bring them back to Geneva ASAP.

"Don't they sell ham-and-cheese sandwiches here in Switzerland?" I asked.

"Hey, man, what are you saying?" my president barked. "These sandwiches—they were paid for! We're not going to throw them away, are we?"

Private plane rental was a flat fee of thirty-five thousand dollars a day.

A little over an hour and a half later, the pilot brought us our lunch, in plastic wrap on a paper tray. The coffee was cold by that time, and the whiskey bottle was empty. The sandwiches were good. They were excellent. They were also the most expensive ham-and-cheese sandwiches I've ever eaten.

I was riding a roller coaster. Difficult to get off, even if I had wanted to. The high life was great fun, and investment money was rolling in. I bought myself a villa opposite the Middelheim Sculpture Park, a second expensive car, and a gold Cartier watch—yet still had money to spend. I clearly remember the first time I visited a prospective buyer who was not only interested in the art of Salvador Dalí, but also in diamonds and U.S. real estate. A financial adviser working for Money Management Counselors would accompany me. The guy went to fancy parties all over the world, seven nights a week, all over Europe, the United States, even Japan, in order to meet rich people. His whole purpose in life was to find people with too much money and win them over.

"Let's go," the financial adviser said, "we're going to squeeze his balls. You'll be astounded how much fun this is."

"Squeeze his balls? How do we do that?" I asked.

"Easy. Grab, squeeze and—snòk!—pull."

Pulling balls internationally became a sporting event. We were no longer salespeople, we were sportsmen, and I was Sportsman of the Year.

Every month, I stuffed half a million investment dollars in a duty-free shopping bag, got in my car, and drove all over

Europe, from Barcelona to Basel to Cologne to Amsterdam, exchanging dollars into Spanish pesetas, Swiss francs, German marks, and Dutch guilders at every border exchange office. That's what the police mean when they talk about money laundering. Only once, in France, the gendarmes stopped me. Luckily, I managed to talk myself out of a lot of trouble: the penalty for money laundering in France is ten years in prison, no suspended sentences allowed.

While in Paris, I picked up a very large Dalí oil on canvas, *Twist Dancing in the Studio of Velásquez,* very dark and brown and smudgy. It purported to represent several playing cards. If you looked at it and blinked your eyes several times very quickly, in rapid succession, the cards started doing the once-famous twist dance. At least, that was the idea. After I'd bought the painting, I blinked my eyes for weeks on end but never saw the playing cards dance. What inspired Dalí to paint *Twist Dancing in the Studio of Velásquez*? I wondered. The oil on canvas was dated 1962. That year, Chubby Checker's "The Twist" was in the number-one spot on the U.S. bestseller charts and won a Grammy for Best Rock Performance. Salvador Dalí had his finger on the pulse of the times; he knew how to be modern and keep up with the market.

After each shopping spree, I returned home with the trunk of my car stuffed with framed Dalí watercolors, small oils on canvas or copper, glass Daum sculptures, and bronze surrealist Dalí horses that weighed almost a ton each. *Twist Dancing* didn't fit in the trunk and had been shipped to the President Building. Even with my fresh haul, I needed more material. In order to make it big in the art world, I had to become a wholesale supplier. A drawing and a watercolor now and then wouldn't do. I was lucky: clients were waiting in line, many of them desperate to get rid of their hard-earned gray or black market money. They didn't want to pay their taxes, they didn't trust their bank, they were looking for help in getting rid of their money, and I volunteered and was pleased to help them empty their purse.

In an international art magazine, I read an article about a respected French businessman who had signed an exclusive print deal with Salvador Dalí and his wife, Gala. I dressed in an all-black suit and white button-down shirt and colorful tie. My pockets stuffed with banknotes of all denominations, I made an appointment and took an Intercity train to Paris.

For a businessman, even a French one, Gilbert Hamon's warehouse in the rue de Seine was hopelessly shabby. The place had fallen into disrepair. Instead of running a posh art gallery downstairs, on street level, he had a ramshackle shop selling secondhand refrigerators and scrap washing machines. Gilbert Hamon turned out to be short, chubby, moonfaced, and extremely friendly. His clothes were as shabby as his warehouse.

"I need Dalí," I told him. "Lots of Dalí."

"Did you bring some cash money?"

I emptied my pockets.

"How many prints do you need?"

"A hundred? A hundred and fifty? Three hundred? Is there a quantity problem?"

"Problem? What problem? No problem at all. There are no problems."

Gilbert Hamon took me to a barricaded strongroom in the back of his warehouse. Chains, locks, and bolts held a steel door in place. He produced a bunch of keys and unlocked the door, using at least five different keys, and pulled on a hanging light-bulb chain, illuminating the strongroom. It was the size of a small gym and unbelievably tidy. The windows overlooking the street were barred and blacked out. On old wooden pallets—EuroPallets, they were called—mountains of rectangular paper were heaped. *All* kinds of paper, but mostly Arches, Rives, and Japon. I knew that Arches is French mold-made paper. It has a warm white color and a smooth surface that hides dot patterns and is excellent for reproducing works of art. Like Arches, Rives is a velvety paper made in France, of 100 percent cotton, perfectly suited for lithography printing and even charcoal drawing. Each sheet is watermarked with an official factory blindstamp. Japon—French for "Japan"—is a thin, translucent rice paper with a satinlike texture. It will retain its freshness a hundred years from now, they say. Quality-wise, at least the paper on the EuroPallets was first rate.

"Here they are. My Dalí's," Hamon said. "Three hundred thousand of them. Is that enough for you?"

"W-w-what are they?"

"Lithographs," Hamon said. "Identical hand-signed art prints, executed on an old-style lithographic press. Numbered in a limited edition of nine hundred per image with twenty artist's proofs. Although theoretically one could continue to run an *endless* series of lithographs, the lithographic plate is defaced—destroyed—so that the image can never be printed again. Although they're mass produced—lithographs were the videotape of the nineteenth century—each image on each sheet of paper is in itself an original and is a close reproduction of an actual Dalí painting now in a major museum. I've got a thousand French francs apiece in mind. Wholesale. A hundred and fifty dollars approximately. Fine art galleries in Hawaii and California sell one such print for four thousand dollars to American doctors and dentists. Figure it out."

I took out my magnifying glass and had a closer look at the Himalayas of paper.

They weren't originals. No way. These so-called lithographs were not drawn on limestone and hand-reproduced on a lithography press, as in the old days. They were industrial prints—commercial chromos, actually—and run-of-the-mill four-color copies. Their print run could be in the millions instead of three hundred thousand.

For the art buyer, the difference between an original lithograph and a four-color reproduction is not simply a question of semantics. The former may have real commercial value. Regardless of the name and quality of the artist, the latter is always worth very little.

I'm not very good at mathematics and made a quick calculation. "Three hundred thousand prints multiplied by four thousand dollars for each print. That's a grand total of over a billion dollars wholesale!" I said, and grabbed my head. It was a dizzying amount of money.

"Right. Now show me some more cash," Hamon said quietly.

"What if I buy a *fake* Dalí print?"

"A *fake* Dalí print? Never heard of it. Doesn't exist. Every Dalí print has its certificate of authenticity hand-signed by myself. By Captain Moore, Dalí's secretary and business manager. Or by Dalí himself. With such certificates, even the fakest Dalí becomes a genuine Dalí."

"I'll take two hundred."

"Only two hundred?" Hamon was disappointed. "Be a man, make it two thousand," he said.

I sighed. "Okay, then."

"Well done," Hamon said. "You know, you came to the right address. I'm the only official Dalí print agent in Europe. On behalf of my company, Arts, Lettres et Techniques, I acquired world reproduction rights to more than fifty Dalí surrealist images. My associate is Dalí's confidant. He personally countersigned all my business contracts with Dalí. I'll tell you a secret. Not only is he Dalí's confidant, he also happens to be Gala's lover. You know Gala is Dalí's wife, don't you? As Dalí's officially recognized agent, I consider myself to be his worldwide representative as far as limited editions are concerned. Art dealers from America, Asia, Germany, France, and even from Dalí's native Spain have to knock on *my* door if they want a genuine Dalí print hand-signed by Dalí himself. Isn't that something?"

I rolled my eyes. "Dalí is seventy now," I said. "What happens when he becomes too old to hand-sign your prints?"

Hamon shrugged. "No problem," he said. "My contracts with Dalí stipulate that he can certify authenticity with a stamp bearing his thumbprint, reproduced in the bottom right-hand corner of each lithograph. According to the contracts, the thumbprint will be the equivalent of his signature. You know, you have to be smart to survive in the art business. A few years ago, I was only selling refrigerators and washing machines. Today I'm selling Dalí, too. Tell me, in all honesty: What's the difference between a Dalí and a washing machine? There is no difference. Business is business and a deal is a deal. Now give me some more money first. Talking to you takes time and time is money. Without money, there's no business."

I'm a lucky man, I thought. I'm lucky because my clients are not art buyers; they are investors. They wouldn't know the difference between a Dalí and a washing machine either.

I didn't negotiate the asking price. I quickly paid Hamon and we shook hands on the deal.

With a spring in my step, I walked along the EuroPallets, examining and selecting the prints on top. Each print represented a classic surreal Salvador Dalí image: melting clocks; a burning giraffe; long-legged horses and elephants, their legs thin and spidery, like a mosquito's. Though some of the colors were faded and certainly not so bright as in the original canvases, I recognized several Dalí masterpieces known the world over, reproduced in every Dalí art book: *Specter of Sex Appeal, Portrait of Gala, Dream Caused by the Flight of a Bee around a Pomegranate One Second before Awakening, The Great Masturbator, Swans Reflecting Elephants, The Persistence of Memory,* and the superb *Temptation of Saint Anthony,* Dalí's undisputed master-piece of 1946, the year I was born. Was he painting this while I was crying in my cradle? I was so captured by the quantity of prints on display in the strongroom—imagine, three hundred thousand in all—and the imaginative force of the surreal images, that—at first—I hadn't even noticed what I should have seen from the beginning.

"Oh, my God!" I shouted.

"What's the matter?"

"These prints! They're not signed!"

"It . . . It . . . It's not what you think," Gilbert Hamon stuttered. His moonface was swelling like a balloon. He pulled his collar and loosened his tie. "I beg you . . . do come back . . . tomorrow . . . please."

"Why should I?"

"Dalí is in Paris, to see his psychiatrist."

"What's Dalí's psychiatrist got to do with my prints?"

"Dalí is staying at the Hôtel Meurice. Room 108, the Royal Suite. Your prints . . . they will be hand-signed tomorrow, I promise."

Such a strange and confusing experience. I wanted to see for myself and walked over to the Hôtel Meurice, facing the Louvre Museum, the Jardin des Tuileries, and the chestnut trees. The hotel's Winter Garden was filled with exotic flowers blooming under a stunning art nouveau glass roof and all 121 rooms on seven floors were decorated in a style reminiscent of

Louis XVI. In the main salon, a man who looked like Beethoven was playing the grand piano with a slow and melancholic touch.

To be honest, I had heard and read enough weird tales about bogus prints that flooded the Dalí market. I had become suspicious. There were also circulating tales of Dalí getting up at the crack of dawn, spraying eau de cologne in his armpits, and tucking a twig of pale purple lavender behind each ear for the abundant perfume of the blossoms to quell the stench of his continuous farting. While sitting on the toilet, he would press the stem of the flowers between his fingers. The stem dripped a fluid that resembled sperm. I had read his rambling autobiography, I knew Dalí liked extravagance, but I wasn't sure my investor clients had the same taste. Although the Hô-tel Meurice boasts oversize en suite marble bathrooms, Dalí hardly ever washed and never took a shower or a bath. His vanity of vanities was his world-famous mustache. To keep it shipshape, Dalí rubbed its whiskers every morning with a mix-ture of beeswax, honey, rhubarb jam, and Hungarian pomade. Then he would sit on the white stone balcony for a light breakfast of roasted quail cooked whole—guts and feathers and all. He would bless the food on the table, hold the tiny birds by the beak and swallow them whole. These creepy stories that were all over the papers didn't seem to diminish Dalí's stature. They didn't seem to bother my clients either. Per-haps they didn't read newspapers.

It was rumored that right after breakfast Dalí signed preprinted paper for hours on end, netting him hundreds of thousands of dollars before midday, all cash, in neatly ironed hundred-dollar bills, while Captain Moore—his business manager—broke hundreds of pencils in half and sharpened them on both ends. Gala sat alongside Dalí, dabbing his face and feeding white grapes into his mouth, the floor covered with signed lithographs. Beads of sweat poured down Dalí's face. He had become a money factory, and it still wasn't enough. It was never enough. The Dalí art market was getting hotter by the day, and Dalí couldn't keep up with demand.

Was all this true?

Or was it just hearsay?

By the way, people also told me that Dalí farted to music.

No luck at the hotel. The night porter of the Hôtel Meurice hadn't seen Dalí for at least three months. At the moment, a royal head of state occupied Dalí's magnificent second-story suite.

The next day I returned to Gilbert Hamon's warehouse. My prints were hand-signed with Dalí's big, bold, flashy trademark signature. All two thousand of them. No questions asked. The art world is like a woman's love life, they say. Hear, see, and speak no evil. Within a fortnight, I sold all the prints in batches of hundreds per client and made a 300 percent net profit. It wasn't beginner's luck anymore. I was rapidly becoming a European Dalí expert. A surrealist aficionado. Insurance companies and even the court of justice increasingly relied on my expertise. I studied the financial markets and read *Forbes*, the

Financial Times, The Economist, and *The Wall Street Journal* as well as banking and investment magazines. I was well dressed, charming, courteous, and I exuded an air of confidence. In my search for ever more Dalí—big, small, cheap, as expensive as they get, it didn't matter so long as the Dalí name was on it—I hopped on planes and trains and crisscrossed the continent, traveling like a madman.

True, when in Paris, Dalí stayed in the five-star Hôtel Meurice. I didn't want to be second to Dalí. Since by now I had my pockets stuffed with cash, too, whenever in Paris I rented a suite at the super luxury Hôtel George V, all brocade and gold, in the eighth arrondissement only steps from the Champs-Élysées. My suite featured a private terrace overlooking the world's most romantic city, with a view of the Eiffel Tower.

Opposite the hotel was—and still is—the world-famous Le Crazy Horse de Paris cabaret, know for its stage shows *strip-tease à l'américaine* performed by seminude female dancers and showgirls sporting extravagant names such as Candy Capitol, Vanilla Banana, Melba Parachute, and Lova Moor. If you pronounce the last name slooooowly, I soon learned, it sounds like Love *Amour.*

I went to an early show and, quite by accident, I sat next to Alain Bernardin, the owner of the cabaret. Later that night, the three of us—Bernardin, Lova Moor, and I myself—went out for a late dinner of *boeuf bourguignon,* which sounds truly Parisian but is none other than hefty chunks of beef, onions, and garlic stewed in the contents of a bottle of dry red wine, preferably burgundy or Côtes du Rhône.

"Tell me, Stan, what do you do for a living?" Alain Bernardin asked.

"I'm an art dealer," I said.

"Really? An art dealer?"

"Yes. Well, that is to say, I'm an art consultant and investment broker. The other day, I bought two thousand Dalí prints from Gilbert Hamon, here in Paris. You know Hamon?"

"I'm not interested in middlemen," Bernardin said.

"Hamon is not a middleman," I replied. "He's got world reproduction rights to over fifty Dalí images."

"That's precisely what makes him a middleman," Bernardin said.

Lova Moor looked at him sideways. "We've got some original Dalís at home," she said. "Paintings. Oil on canvas. Bought them from our good friend John Peter Moore—*Captain* Moore—who is Dalí's business manager and private secretary."

"Forget the middlemen. You should talk to Captain Moore directly," Bernardin told me. "A man you can do business with."

"Captain Moore?" I said haughtily. "He sharpens Dalí's pencils, that's all he does."

"—and gets a flat ten percent commission on every print signed with one of those sharpened pencils," Lova Moor replied.

I knew by then a little about Captain Moore. Born in London in 1919, he claimed to have been a Royal Air Force fighter pilot in the Second World War. An officer, hence the name *Captain* Moore, by which he was generally known. After the war, he was private secretary to British film producer Alexander Korda—a spy posing as an international movie producer, his enemies claimed. He worked on *The Third Man* and other fifties movies and befriended Orson Welles. According to legend, Captain Moore met Dalí in Rome, where he delivered money to the artist for a purchase of a portrait of the actor Sir Laurence Olivier that Dalí had painted. Movie producer Korda had commissioned the painting. The former fighter pilot started running errands for Salvador Dalí and in no time he went on to become the artist's official business manager and private secretary.

"Dalí nicknamed him *el capitán del dinero,* which is Spanish and literally means 'the money captain,' " Lova Moor said.

"I'll call Captain Moore," Bernardin said. "First thing in the morning."

Remember, we're in the late seventies, before mobile phones.

"Does Dalí sometimes visit the Le Crazy Horse de Paris?" I asked.

Alain Bernardin and Lova Moor laughed. "Whenever Dalí is in Paris," Bernardin said, "he goes to Madame Arthur's French Fun House, where the boys in the band are the only boys who look like it. The rest is an all-male cast of transvestite singers. He also loves to see a Dolly Van Doll show. She's a Spanish hermaphrodite who is male and female within the same body."

The next day, although I could easily have walked, I took a taxi to Captain Moore's sumptuous art deco house in the rue de Longchamp between the Champs Élysées, the Arc de Triomphe and the Eiffel Tower, in the elegant sixteenth district. I was dressed to the nines, in my banker's uniform of striped shirt, stylish tie, a suit made to measure, leather belt, and suede shoes. For once I didn't have the cash in my pockets. That was becoming too dangerous. Instead I had sewn it in the lining of my jacket and the inside of my shirt and underwear and my trouser legs and had tucked the rest in my socks.

I expected a big, burly man, an army captain with a military bearing. Instead of big and burly, he was short and thin, with wavy hair and a David Niven mustache. Dalí's business manager was neat and tidy and extremely polite, with old-fashioned good manners. He had an elongated face, weathered skin, and a plummy voice. Because he wore a gray Prince de Galles suit with a herringbone motif, I thought he also somewhat resembled the Duke of Windsor. Or David Niven in miniature. After I had introduced myself, Captain Moore opened a drawer in a large flat-file cabinet, revealing a jumble of perhaps hundreds of ballpoint pens, glued together by yellowish stalagmite growths that looked eerily alive.

"What are these?" I asked.

"Dalí's pee-pee pens," Captain Moore said, laughing. "Dalí steals them from his hotel rooms and throws them all together in a drawer. Whenever he's in the mood, he opens the drawer and pees on the free pens. The minerals in his urine oxidize on the metal that coagulates, and they grow these fantastic stalagmites. Beautiful, isn't it?"

I was flabbergasted. "How is Dalí?" I asked.

Captain Moore shrugged. "Dalí is Dalí," he said.

"You don't like him?"

"He's my boss. I don't have to *like* him."

"Is Dalí in Paris now?"

"Now? At this time of the year? No, never. Dalí is in New York. Always, in winter."

"If Dalí is in New York," I said, "I wonder who signed the prints I bought from Gilbert Hamon."

Captain Moore laughed. "Ask Hamon," he said, and opened a bottle of pink champagne.

"I'd like to buy some original Dalís."

"Drawings?"

"Why not?"

"Have you got cash money on you?"

"Yes, of course."

"Dollars?"

"No, Swiss francs."

"Show me."

"Can I go to the toilet first?"

I had to undo the money from the inside of my shirt and my underwear and my trouser legs.

"Have you got a pair of scissors for me, please?" I asked.

That night, Captain Moore and I had dinner with the CEO of L'Oréal, the cosmetics multinational. My circle of high-ranking personal friends and powerful business acquaintances was widening rapidly, and everywhere I went, whomever I met, I was always the youngest of the bunch.

"One day, I'd like to meet Dalí," I told Captain Moore over dinner.

"Better not," he replied, "you'll be disappointed."

"Disappointed? Why?"

"Dalí is a sex maniac."

"A sex maniac? Dalí?"

"Yes."

I sighed. "Picasso, Modigliani, Magritte—they're all dead," I said. "I think Dalí is the greatest commercial artist alive. He's unique. He's making me rich, and not only me. Me, you, all of us."

"Perhaps he is," Captain Moore said. "He's also a sex maniac."

Again I sighed. I didn't know what to say. What *could* I say? I was a little boy once, playing in sand and mud. That boy was gone for good, and I missed him dearly. What was I doing there, at the dinner table, trying to play ball with these big shots? Wasn't it about time to jump out of this nasty business and quit before I was swallowed whole and eaten alive?

The L'Oréal CEO must have read my thoughts, for he looked straight at me. "Join the club, kid," he said, and slapped my back.

"If there's anything I can help you with, ring me," Captain Moore said.

In the next couple of months, he introduced me to Luis Romero, one of Dalí's "official" biographers, and to Catalan film director Antoni Ribas, who had a biopic about the life and loves of Dalí in preproduction, starring Robert De Niro as Dalí. A miscast, I thought. Charlotte Rampling for the Gala part was also miscast. The film was never made. Yet I devoured their stories of Dalí. The more I learned about him, the better my sales talk would be. I was hungry for every snippet of information and never forgot anything.

I sold Dalí's *Twist Dancing in the Studio of Velásquez* to L'Oréal.

The money was deposited in our secret Swiss bank account.

There was no name on the account, only a code, made up of letters and numbers.

I went to Spain to collect the drawings that I'd bought from Captain Moore. They turned out to be signed doodles, beautifully framed. Perhaps the frames were more expensive than the doodles. The signatures didn't look anything like the signatures in the right-hand corner of the Hamon prints. Since I planned to buy more Dalí originals from art dealers in Barcelona, I took the contents of the butcher's Chinese vase with me and locked the currency in a Spanish bank vault. A couple of months later, I'd forgotten whose money it was. I needed a second vault to stash more of my growing fortune.

I didn't speak the language when I first traveled to Barcelona. I needed an interpreter and asked the receptionist at my hotel if he could find me someone who was fluent in either French, English, or German—and Spanish, of course. Castilian, as they call their language. That's how I met Ana. She drove up to the hotel in a battered old canary yellow Ford Fiesta in the bright blue uniform of a hostess for conventions and seminars. She got out of the car—petite, with a dark, olive oil skin and chestnut eyes—clutching a dog-eared paperback.

"Stán? Stán Lau-Lau-Lauryss?" she asked in a tiny voice.

I nodded. I smiled.

"Wie gehts?" she said in German, and we shook hands. Her hands, too, were tiny.

"Don't you speak French?" I asked.

"Ah, oui, bien sûr."

"Alors, on parle français?"

"D'accord. Don't you like German?"

"I don't like Hitler."

She held the paperback upside-down, but I could still read its title. Malcolm Lowry's *Bajo el Volcán,* with an image of a deadly drunken man slumped over a table in a Mexican *taberna* on the jacket. *Under the Volcano,* that's an interesting book, I thought.

Ana introduced herself. She said she was Catalan. She was fluent in French and German, as well as in Catalan and Spanish, of course, her native languages. She spoke English well, too. For years, she had lived in Figueres, the small border town close to France best known as Dalí's birthplace. Figueres is also where the Dalí Museum is situated. Ana told me her family was on friendly terms with what remained of Dalí's family. A local lawyer named Ramón Guardiola handled Ana's real estate interests. I knew Guardiola was also the name of the former mayor of Figueres and first director of the town's Dalí Museum.

"I'm an art dealer," I told Ana. "I'm buying and selling Dalí all over the place. Dalí is all I handle. I know a lot about the man, probably more than he knows himself, but where does he come from? I want to understand the background of the most famous surrealist of all. What's his country like? I'd like you to show me."

"Have you been to Figueres?"

"No."

"Cadaqués?"

"No."

"Port Lligat?"

"No."

"The Ampurdán countryside?"

"Nope."

"The fishing villages of Cadaqués and Port Lligat are Dalí personified," Ana said. "Ampurdán is the background land-scape in so many Dalí paintings. It's a two-and-a-half-hour drive from Barcelona."

I remembered some titles of Dalí paintings I'd seen in my art books and museum catalogs: *Apparition of a Stereoscopic Face in the Ampurdán Landscape. Girl of Ampurdán. Landscape near Ampurdán. The Ampurdán Chemist Seeking Absolutely Nothing.* The paintings were sexy, weird, and their imagery looked dangerous.

"Let's go," I said.

"I charge per hour," Ana said. "Plus expenses."

"No problem." I was in love in about five minutes.

In her Ford Fiesta, we drove from Barcelona to Girona and Figueres and explored the wild and beautiful Ampurdán coun-tryside. The journey east from Girona and Figueres, in north-eastern Spain, took us across an immense open space with a tall sky and a fringe of soft green hills. Bright poppies flowered in abundance on the hills. Sprinkled across the landscape were charming old *fincas* and *masías* or farmhouses and haciendas in the simple local style, in earthy colors with austere pink staggered-stone rooftops and square towers that made them look like fortresses. We scrambled over the rocks that dominate the coastline. I sat down on a jagged ridge and reached into the crystal-clear water for a shell I wanted to give to Ana. The orange pincers of a hermit crab flicked my fingers away. In most people's eyes, this part of the world is the most beautiful Mediterranean setting. Boys were throwing pebbles into the sea.

Sitting on these rocks, I could just picture Dalí over there on the beach. In his tiny 1934 painting *The Specter of Sex Appeal,* the artist portrays himself as a child in a sailor suit on this same spot, looking up at a monstrously mutilated female body. A peculiarly shaped rock in the distance lent its silhouette to *The Great Masturbator,* a perversely surrealist 1929 composition of a woman dreamily caressing a man's impotent genitals. I suddenly realized that Dalí, in his formative years, was just a landscape painter. Ana explained that these sharp, edgy rocks were remains of a vast lava flow from an ancient volcano. The white hot lava river settled in a series of layers that were blasted, eroded, and exposed along the seashore, and fractured and perforated by huge gas bubbles, emanating from the hot pumice stone.

"Is that why you brought the book?" I asked.

"Which book?"

"*Under the Volcano.*"

She laughed. "No, no, that's a coincidence."

"I don't believe in coincidences."

I took Ana to a fancy restaurant at the end of a tiny, bumpy road over the hill above the rugged Rosas mountain on the Costa Brava, on a private beach with a striking view out to sea. Today, food critics the world over consider El Bulli to be the best and one of the most expensive restaurants anywhere, the talk of the food world, while every serious chef reckons that Ferran Adrià, the genius in the kitchen, is the most influential and gifted man in the culinary world. The bill wouldn't be a problem. I had enough credit cards in my wallet to last me a lifetime.

The place was empty. We were given a fork and a spoon—no knives in El Bulli, ever—and I ordered all twenty-seven courses of the gastronomic menu: tomato and seaweed jelly, cotton candy parmesan, freeze-dried Spanish omelet in a martini glass, fishy quicksilver pearls that looked like sardine eyes, liquid cro-quettes, chicken feet wrapped in sea lettuce, and oyster sperm with potato froth on a plate the size of a UFO. To be honest, it was a disaster. It took us six hours to go through the entire meal, and the more jellies and pearls and froth we ate, the hungrier we became.

"Do you like the food?" I asked Ana.

"It's different," she said.

"I hate it."

"The cook is not a cook," Ana said. "He's an artist."

"A chemist," I said.

"After this, I'd give my life for a slice of *pa amb tomàquet*," Ana said.

"What's that?"

"Toasted bread with a ripe tomato rubbed over it and seasoned with olive oil and salt. A simple Catalan delicacy."

Grudgingly, I paid the bill and we drove to the nearest bar in Rosas, where we grabbed a foil-wrapped cheese sandwich from the counter and wolfed it down.

"Ana?" I said. "Give me your telephone number."

"The hotel receptionist knows where to find me."

I laid a finger on her lips, leaned over, and kissed her.

To round off the day, we ate ice cream in all the colors of the rainbow and watched the sun set in the Mediterranean. I tried to look handsome while Ana rested her head on my shoulder. A triangle-shaped rock island emerged like a rhino horn from the sea, in the middle of the bay. Some clouds hung like frayed bedsheets in the dark blue sky. They seemed to be copied from a Dalí painting. This is the landscape of Dalí's childhood and adolescence, I thought. This is where he grew up and became the mad genius of surrealism, in this northeastern out-of-the-way region of Spain with its lovely summers and harsh, stone-cold winters.

A small biplane was circling the mountains and flying along the coastline, trailing a banner that read WELCOME TO DALÍ-LAND.

We were in the old Motel Ampurdán on the outskirts of Figueres. A stark white room, whitewashed walls, white bedsheets, a radio, a single night-light, and a Bible in Spanish plus Ana's paperback novel *Under the Volcano* on the bedside table. Ana and I didn't leave the motel room for two days and two nights.

"You're divine, Ana," I stammered.

"Don't forget, I'm Spanish. Love is in our blood."

On the third day, I fell out of bed. Ana turned on the radio. "T'estimo," a Lluís Llach love song in Catalan ("I Love You") about years that pass and the good-bye that will come. I didn't speak Catalan, and yet I understood every word.

"When our son is born, we'll name him Lluís," I whispered.

Ana smiled.

A girl from room service brought us a champagne breakfast for two. It wasn't champagne, it was *cava,* actually, the Spanish style of champagne. There were bread rolls with a vanilla custard filling in a basket, *pa amb tomàquet,* sweet *café con leche,* and fresh fruit: sliced pineapple, giant grapes, and wild forest strawberries the shape and color of droplets of blood. The wild strawberries were swimming in freshly squeezed orange juice.

Before she left, the girl looked around. "You know . . . ," she said, and paused. "Dalí and Gala often stayed in this room, on their way to Cadaqués after they came back from New York in springtime."

Ana raised her glass. "To Dalí," she said.

"To Gala," I answered.

"To our son, To Lluís," we said together.

"You liked the book?" I asked.

"What book?"

"*Under the Volcano.*"

"Oh, that one. I don't know, I didn't read it. It's not mine. A friend left it in my car. I meant to bring it back."

In addition to a home in Figueres, Ana also owned a house in the mountain village of Agullana, on the slope of the Pyrenees, near the Catalonian municipality of La Jonquera and the French border, some fifteen kilometers north of Figueres. She said we would go there; she wanted to show me something. We drove to Agullana. Suddenly I was lost in time. There was no electricity and no tap water in the village, only drinking wells, and there were no shops. Except for the candles and stained-glass windows in the stark Roman church, there was no color in the village either. All forms were simplified to blocks, sliced and diced in harsh, angular shapes, and everything—the slate gray houses and gray pebble streets—was monochromatic. We had arrived in the Middle Ages.

The next village on the map was Céret, on the other side of the Pyrenees. That's where Picasso invented cubism. More than for the invention of cubism, Céret is known for its cherries—the village produces its own cherry beer, cherry wine, cherry pie, cherry candy, and even a cherry burger—as well as its fragrant Cavaillon melons. In Agullana there were no Cavaillons, and no cherries either. The village was gray and somber like a cubist painting and broken down. It looked like a collage of rough surfaces. In the local café, known as the *cooperativo*, villagers were drinking sour wine and *carajillo*—strong black coffee laced with sweet Spanish brandy—and playing table football. The rod that was supposed to hold the goalkeeper was missing. Weathered wooden football players were painted white and *blaugrana*, Real Madrid and F. C. Barcelona club colors.

"Gooooo*oal!*" the villagers shouted.

Ana stopped her car at a modest stone house along a quiet dirt road and knocked on the rough, unpainted wooden door. From the yard, I could hear fattened pigs squealing like hell and several cocks crowing furiously. The overwhelming stench of manure and dunghills was everywhere. I pinched my nostrils and felt like Al Pacino when Don Michael Corleone in *The Godfather Part III* visited the Sicilian village of his forefathers. Nothing could be further away from the life I'd lived up to that moment. The door was ajar, and we stepped inside, where a very old man wearing a flat black cap was lying on a very old bed, fully dressed and snoring like a diesel engine. His face was like a mask. Hens were trampling over the mattress, trying to find the best spot to lay their eggs. Under the bed, rabbits slept in straw nests. The room had no flooring, just packed black earth. The moment we came in, the old man jumped up and poked at the fire in the hearth. Then he cut some oranges in half, threw them in a sizzling pan, and added a few spoonfuls of rough candy sugar to them.

"Would you care for some homemade orange marmalade on toast?" the old man asked, and skewered some old bread on a wooden stick.

Ana introduced the old man as Josep. He was seventy, she told me.

He looked like two hundred.

After Josep ate his breakfast, we followed him to a partly restored traditional stone house on two levels at the edge of the village, perched in the hills. While not isolated, it was very private. The house had tile floors and a fireplace in every room. A wrought-iron pergola led to a separate enclosed courtyard. Around us, gnarled vineyards stretched as far as I could see, over the hills and into the mountains. Beyond them was a striking view of the eastern Pyrenees and the snow-covered Canigó, a mountaintop almost three thousand meters high. We passed through a garden gone wild, where there grew an old pomegranate tree with knotty roots, heavy with thick-skinned grapefruit-size berries with a sour, tangy taste.

The house hadn't been lived in for years. It was dark, cold, damp, and smelled of mothballs. I looked into the cupboards and found old suits, long out of fashion, men's shirts, worn-out shoes and slippers, and even men's underwear, musty, mended, and yellowed with age. On a bedroom shelf, I noticed hundreds of trophy cups among dolls and baby toys. The silver of the trophy cups was blackened and had lost its shine. I went into the bathroom. On a grimy shelf under the pockmarked mirror, I noticed a shaving brush caked with soap scum, an old metal screw-on Gillette razor, and an open bottle of aftershave. The liquid had evaporated. The furniture in the rooms had seen better days. There were oil paintings everywhere—a raven, a severed hand on the beach, a skull, a still life depicting rotting pomegranates and two butterflies too close to the sun, their fragile wings melting like butter—and a poster and framed black-and-white photographs with a scribble and a distinctive pen-and-pencil signature scrawled over the image. Mold had settled on the frames. Ana was nowhere to be seen. What was this all about?

Josep saw me admiring the paintings.

"Ana's father painted them," he said. "He was more than an amateur and better than a Sunday painter, I guess. I can still see him sitting here, at his easel, a thick wad of old newspaper under his slippers to catch the splattered paint. Poor man. Did you see the wrought-iron pergola outside? He designed it. He was good in what he did, but he didn't enjoy life. He smoked like a chimney. He painted. He had a heart attack and then he was dead. When he was eight, he painted fairy-tale images on the lid of a hat box, as did Señor Dalí. They were boyhood friends and went to the same evening art school in Figueres, but nobody was interested in Ana's father as an artist."

EXTRAORDINARIA CORRIDA DE TOROS EN HOMENAJE A SALVADOR DALÍ, read the poster.

I climbed on a chair and had a closer look at the photographs. An old black American car, like the ones in a 1950s Hollywood film, is driven into the Plaza de Toros in Figueres, where the "extraordinary bullfight" has taken place. Dalí is standing on the passenger seat, in a tuxedo, a walking cane in hand, with bulging eyes, his waxed mustache almost touching the sky. Dead bulls lying all around the ring, banderillas sticking out of their backs and gore oozing from multiple wounds in their neck and shoulder muscles. The sand in the arena is drenched with blood. Some of the bulls have their ears cut off. Dalí is greeting the immense, ecstatic crowd with a wave of his cane.

"A bullfight paying homage only to Salvador Dalí, of course," Josep said, and I could see the anger in the old man's eyes. "Although he only designed the poster, that's all he did. Well, *designed* . . . he threw a blob of black paint on it."

Ana's father sat in the driver's seat of the old black American car, a cigarette in the corner of his mouth. His hair shiny with brillantine, he looked like a Don Juan past his prime. He wasn't laughing. He wasn't enjoying the ride. He was humiliated; you could see that.

There were more photographs. Dalí stepping out of the car. Dalí blessing the dead bulls. Dalí welcoming the applause, basking in the glory. Ana's father was in every single photograph, always smoking, always next to Dalí, never taking center stage.

I tried to decipher the pen-and-pencil scribble. *To Eleuteri, my dear old friend,* it said—in Catalan, *el teu gran amic, per sempre,*—followed by the giant familiar Dalí signature that covered the whole photograph and almost obliterated Ana's father from each and every picture.

"Where's Ana?" I asked Josep.

"Don't you know?"

"I don't."

"Come," Josep said. "Come with me, I'll bring you there."

We walked up the slope of the mountain. The grapes on the vines were brown, wrinkled, and tiny, like dried raisins, and unbelievably sweet. Everything around the house was wrinkled, knotted, and gnarled: the vines, the olive trees with the tiniest of fruit, and the hundreds of cork oak trees all over the slope, whose bark had been stripped off for hundreds of years and used as the raw material for bottle stoppers. Josep trampled through the vineyard, past a natural spring dripping ice-cold water from the mountain, up to a small cemetery hidden from view behind a high stockade of flint stones.

"After the death of her daughter, Ana severed ties with her in-laws," Josep said.

"Daughter? Which daughter?"

"Don't you know?"

"No. I don't. I don't know Ana that well. We met only a couple of days ago."

Josep was a gentle giant. He shook his heavy head. There was no emotion on his masklike face. "Sad story," he said. "So sad. Ghosts from the past, they always come back, always come back to haunt you. Ana was married, you know. She has a nine-year-old son, his name is Eleuteri, like his grandfather. Teri, we call the boy affectionately. He lives with his grandmother in Barcelona. Ana's husband was a champion rally pilot. He was good. Man, how good he was, until he died in a race, in Portugal, I believe. Ana also had a little daughter. Carola, her name was. The girl was two when her father died. Six months after the funeral, Ana was driving her yellow Volkswagen on the motorway, the girl sleeping in the baby car seat. There was an accident. Nothing special, just some splintered headlights and a dented fender. After she had dealt with the insurance formalities, Ana drove on. When they arrived in Barcelona, the girl in the baby car seat wasn't sleeping anymore. The little girl was dead. Unknown to Ana, her daughter had her neck broken in the accident."

I sighed.

Such a heartbreaking story.

At the outermost corner of the cemetery, the mountain precipice served as a columbarium. Holes the size of shoe boxes were hacked in the rock to house funerary urns. In silence, I watched Ana from a distance. She had picked a bouquet of wildflowers. She turned a key and opened the glass door of a niche in the rock. Two urns in it, a big one and a very, very tiny one that, from where I stood, looked like an eggcup. Ana lowered her head and kissed the wildflowers and draped them around the urns, the ashes of her husband and little daughter still inside. Dust to dust, ashes to ashes. Even from a distance, I could see that she was crying.

I thought about the silver trophies and the dolls and the baby toys on the bedroom shelf.

I was speechless, and so was Josep. He took off his black cap and twisted it in his gnarled hands.

"Josep? Is there anything else I should know?" I asked.

"Ever heard of Lydia the Madwoman? Lydia from Port Lligat?"

I seemed to skip from one surprise to the other.

Of course I had. In every one of the glossy Dalí books on my mahogany desk back in the President Building, Dalí praised her. He claimed that it was Lydia the Madwoman from Port Lligat, a stone's throw from Cadaqués, who gave him the key that unlocked the cupboards of his imagination and set surrealism free. Dalí always maintained that without Lydia, there might never have been surrealism. In every art book, Lydia is mentioned as the crackpot fisherwoman who sold her white-stuccoed, crumbling beach houses—*barracas* in Spanish—to Dalí: two shacks on the pebble beach, a mere two rooms, one shack a kitchen and a toilet, the other a bedroom and studio, twenty-one square meters of floor space under a collapsed roof. There was no electricity, no running water, no comfort whatsoever. Way back in 1930, Dalí bought both *barracas* for 250 pesetas—a couple of dollars, even at the time—and immediately started refurbishing the dwellings and buying adjoining properties and neighboring cottages. He planted cypresses and lavish olive trees with silvery leaves. Still, the living quarters were a mess. Dalí glued bread crusts to the walls and attached strings with old jacket buttons to the ceiling. The house and gardens were gradually extended until the ramshackle beach houses in Port Lligat became the confusing and labyrinthine Garden of Eden where Dalí had lived and worked for over fifty years. That's what art history books tell you, followed by a beautiful story of how Dalí painted *The Persistence of Memory,* his undisputed masterpiece, in the cramped bedroom annex studio with the skylight to the north:

It was the early 1930s. Gala was sitting next to Dalí, in the one easy chair in the house. She had read to him from the

German books and magazines he loved most, though he didn't understand a single word of the language. The poetic sounds coupled with the effortless flow of words and Gala's murmuring, almost whispering voice calmed him down to the point of total relaxation. Dalí used to say that Gala's voice sounded like four bells chiming in unison. Whenever she read to him, he called her Quatre Cloches, which is French for "Four Bells."

He looked up at the clock. Almost midnight.

Dalí was sitting at his easel, engaged in his secret fantasies, laboring over a tiny twenty-four-by-thirty-three-centimeter painting of the desolate Ampurdán landscape in brilliant colors while listening to an old and scratchy recording of Wagner's *Tristan and Isolde* on a windup gramophone. He never talked when he worked. When he got excited, he whistled.

"Shall I turn the music down?" Gala asked.

"*No! No!* Dalí likes it when W*áááá*gne*rrr* sounds like g*rrr*illed sa*rrr*dines," he replied.

That evening, they had eaten a delicious, very strong Camembert cheese for dinner.

The remains of the meal were still on the table. Leftover bread—ants were carrying bread crumbs away—some soft and drooping cheese, sliced tomatoes, an artisan glass of olive oil, and several dirty plates and cutlery.

Gala started yawning at five o'clock in the morning.

Dalí said to her, "Go to bed, my darling. You're falling over with sleep. Dalí will go on for an hour or so, until this painting is done with. What Dalí needs is a startling image to make this a *surrrealist* painting."

Gala went to sleep.

The landscape on the tiny canvas was deserted and forlorn, with a series of rocks that resembled mountaintops in a golden light. Dalí added the sleepy-eyed image of the great masturbator. It was an icon he had used before, but one icon still didn't make it a real *surrrealist* painting.

He sat at his easel, meditating.

Dalí was superstitious. He carried a splinter of wood from the Holy Cross in an old sock wrapped up in his pocket and touched it all the time, for good luck.

Suddenly, in a flash of genius, he hit on the idea of blending the wall clock and the Camembert cheese into one single image: a melting clock or—better still—a melting watch, dripping and drooping like the soft and overripe Camembert cheese on the table.

After all, isn't time amorphous, too?

Two hours later, the painting was finished.

It was now seven o'clock in the morning.

When Gala woke up, Dalí positioned her in front of his easel.

"Keep your eyes closed," he said, and counted. "Three, two, one. Now open your eyes. Look what Dalí has done. Isn't this a horrible painting?"

Gala was dumbfounded. "No one who has seen this painting once will ever be able to forget it for as long as he lives," she said.

"You! A*rrre*! A! Boooo-ti-fulll! A-ni-malll!" Dalí shouted.

He had a knack for surrealist titles. He named his new
miniature *The Persistence of Memory*. It was bought by the
Museum of Modern Art in New York for $350. In time, it
would become one of the art treasures of the century.

"That must have been shortly after Lydia sold her *barracas* to
Dalí," Josep said. "While Dalí almost overnight became world-
famous, Lydia was diagnosed with manic-depressive psychosis
and committed to an asylum for the insane here in Agullana
where she eventually starved herself to death."

"You mean to say that . . . that Lydia . . . who made all this
possible . . . who was at the forefront of surrealism . . . is
buried here? In this cemetery? In godforsaken Agullana?"

"Yes, Stán, she is."

"I can't believe it."

"It is true."

"The woman who set surrealism free?"

"Yes."

"Show me her grave, Josep."

I picked some flowers from a nearby rosebush and followed
Josep to the gravestone of Lydia the Madwoman. It had started
to rain. A hard, cold rain that froze my limbs. There I was, in a
stone-cold cemetery in the middle of nowhere, mourning three
people I had never known. I contemplated the inscription on
the simple rectangle slab, weather-beaten and slowly crumbling to dust after all these years.

HERE LIES LYDIA, THE NIGHTINGALE OF PORT LLIGAT, ANOTHER SAD VICTIM OF THE TRAMONTANA

Ana walked over and joined us, biting her lips and rubbing her eyes.

"Ana, what's tramontana?" I asked.

"Wind," Ana said. "The most perverse and relentless hurricane wind known to mankind."

"Tramontana is the devil's breath," Josep said. "It's just another word for going bonkers."

"People in the village of Cadaqués sometimes saw Dalí on top of his *barracas* at night, in the moonlight," Ana recalled, "in his nightgown, baton in hand like a musical conductor. As if he were Toscanini, he conducted the music of the wind."

"The tramontana sweeps across the Pyrenees with such force that I can lean against it and fall asleep standing up," Josep said. "I'll tell you, Stán, if you want to fathom Salvador Dalí and really understand the artist and the man, you'll first have to understand the havoc the tramontana wreaks on Ampurdán. Always remember that Dalí is truly Catalan. *Clar i català.* But he's also a fraud and a thief. In interviews, he maintains that Lydia the Madwoman gave him the original idea that was to become surrealism. In a revelation, no less. That's an absolute lie. The truth is that Dalí stole the idea of surrealism from a young artist painter in Cadaqués named Angel Planells, the son of the local baker, and then conspired to ruin this young man's life. Like he ruined your father's life, Ana."

She rolled her chestnut eyes. "That may be true, Josep, but without the tramontana, the genius of Dalí would never have flowered," Ana said.

Josep had the final word. "Without the tramontana, there would never have been surrealism at all," he said.

I shrugged. I didn't give it a second thought. I liked this gossip and chitchat, but I wasn't interested in surrealism professionally. I wasn't interested in art history professionally. I wasn't even interested in the tramontana. The bottom line was that, professionally, I was interested only in money.

"Are you married, Josep?" I asked.

"No," he said. "I never married. I'm sorry to say I don't know what *love* is." He grimaced. "But in life, it's never too late to learn."

Back in my executive office, all black and brown leather, shiny and spotless—I saw myself mirrored in the glossy surface on my desk—I pinned a large world map on the wall accompanied by tables of facts and paper flags indicating where my clients lived. The map was color-coded into different regions with pins in key cities. MMC intended to create a franchise, each with a Dalí gallery and office—a McDalí, we called them, like McDonald's—in major European and American cities and even in Japan. Until that plan came to fruition, my job took me to art fairs in Miami, Paris, London, New York, Madrid, Cologne, and Basel in Switzerland. I made my home in the Grand Hotel in Stockholm, George V in Paris, Cipriani in Venice, the old St. Moritz on the Park in

New York, and the Jimmy Stewart Suite in L.A.'s Beverly Wilshire Hotel. I even went to Cairo in search of a Dalí that I hoped to sell with a hefty profit.

To impress my clients, I had myself photographed in front of the famous bronze Dalí signature on the façade of the private Dalí museum in St. Petersburg, Florida. My clients were voracious. Nothing could stop their thirst for a better and more expensive art investment. Over and over, I repeated the catchphrase I knew by heart: *A British investment magazine has calculated that the art of Salvador Dalí has gone up in value 25.94 percent per year between 1970 and 1975. That's only for starters. When Dalí dies, his prices will skyrocket.*

At the time, no other investment could guarantee a 25.94 percent per year profit. I thought I was lucky. The dollar was at an all-time low. Gold, too, had become a lousy investment. In the real estate market, there was hardly any money to be made. Small investors lost their earnings. For me, as an art consultant and investment broker, Dalí was a gift from heaven. He had come at the right time. The artist was seventy-six years of age. In photographs in newspapers and magazines, he looked like a frail old frog. I hoped and prayed he would die soon.

Yet I couldn't sleep at night. When finally I fell asleep, I suffered terrible nightmares.

Every few hours I shot up, drenched in sweat.

In the morning, I had to take showers to wash the stench of anguish and guilt from my aching muscles. Yes, honestly, I felt guilty. I had the outer appearance of a winner, but deep inside

I felt like a loser. *Take the money and run.* I was taking the money—no, not taking it, *grabbing* it—but I wasn't running. I was raking in ever more opaque money, unofficial money, black money, *any* money. Cheating, deceiving, and swindling are exciting and a hugely enjoyable and rewarding business. It hadn't taken me long before I'd realized that MMC's investment diamonds were not clear and sparkling but mildly flawed, inexpensive cuts, and the prized real estate on offer as an investment were endless forests in the Canadian wilderness and cow-grazing fields in the flats of Texas instead of nice urban properties outside Dallas. The gems were virtually worthless, and so was the land. What about the Dalís I was selling as fast as lollipops? Perhaps they *were* lollipops: sweeteners to calm and satisfy MMC's ever-growing number of international clients. I was going through an inner crisis. Payback time would come; of that I was sure. When? Where? I couldn't know until I arrived, and even though it would be suicide, I tried to get there as fast as possible.

In Nice on the French Riviera, I met an angel. Not just any angel: the one I met had the longest tongue in the whole world and was so wicked, you can hardly imagine it. She was a heiress and had frizzy hair the color of cranberry juice. They say angels have no gender. Well, the one I met definitely was female. My angel was dressed in a long silk robe, all white and flowing, with white stockings, silver Chanel shoes, and white-laced gloves. She sprouted transparent butterfly wings on her back and had her eyes widened by white makeup and talcum powder dusted all over her face. Crystal earrings dangled from her earlobes. In one hand, she was holding a Bible.

I had seen this angel before: in a walk-on part as an extra in *Midnight Cowboy*, the 1969 Hollywood movie about two male hustlers, starring John Voight and Dustin Hoffman, and I recognized her immediately. The hair color, the shoes, the faraway look in her eyes, the talcum powder, even the wings. We shook hands. I'd never shaken hands with an angel before.

"Ultra?" I asked. "Ultra Violet?"

"*Oui?*"

She was so excited, at first I thought she was high as a kite. She slurred her speech. Her eyes were unfocused and darted from left to right. Then I realized she wasn't stoned at all. She was in a religious trance, which is perhaps worse than being stoned.

"You're French," I said, "You're an artist. You spent your childhood in the family castle. How come you ended up in Hollywood?"

"Andy Warhol did that," she said.

"Tell me."

"What is there to tell? Dalí and I were having tea at the St. Regis Hotel when a shy man in a silver wig paid his respects to Dalí. The man said to me, 'Gee . . . You're so beautiful. You should be in film. Can we do a movie together? You'll be my superstar.' 'A movie? When?' I asked him. 'Tomorrow,' Andy Warhol said. He'd pay me twenty-five dollars a day. I changed my name to Ultra Violet and in his limousine, Salvador Dalí drove me to East Forty-seventh Street in Manhattan, where Andy Warhol had his studio."

"You mean, you knew Andy Warhol . . . and Salvador Dalí, too?"

She didn't listen to me. She had a story to tell and would tell it in the way she wished. Once she'd started, she couldn't stop talking. "I was dressed in an exquisite Chanel suit, all gold and pink and blue, a black velvet bow in my hair," Ultra Violet said. "The building on East Forty-seventh Street was dilapidated, the fire escape rusting. The fourth-floor studio was known as The Factory. There was a party going on. A birthday party, I think it was. Pulsing disco patterns of dots and stars, brightly colored, rippled through the studio. Nico was there, the strikingly beautiful Viva, Valerie Solanas—she was a radical feminist who shot Andy a couple of years later, Jim Morrison, Verushka—who was a *Vogue* model in a mini-miniskirt, and some more flower-power children. A battered couch was so piled with bodies that it looked like a lifeboat. Someone had baked a chocolate cake. It looked marvelous, very elaborate, with chocolate swirls all over the top and sides. I ate a large piece. Delicious. Half an hour later, my face went numb, as if anesthetized. I touched my lips. They felt as if they weren't there. A lot of giggling went on, and suddenly I realized what had happened. The chocolate cake had been laced with marijuana. Now everybody was getting hysterical. To me, it looked as if a nonstop opera was being staged. A cowboy roller-skated into the studio. He had a transistor radio dangling between his legs, three inches below his crotch, and was dressed rodeo-rider style, a red scarf around his neck, leather vest and black leather boots, but no trousers and no underpants, his huge genitals exposed. They were sprayed gold and resembled golden golf balls. On the transistor, he was listening to a Maria Callas recital, turned up to overpowering decibels. On a screen between two pillars, Andy Warhol's 1963 thirty-five-minute black-and-white film *Blow Job* was projected. No sound track. Andy got so exited that his silver wig tilted to all sides."

". . . and Dalí? What did he do?"

Ultra Violet smiled as she spoke. Her voice was soft and sweet. "Dalí was masturbating—all his life, he was a compulsive masturbator—and of course, Warhol took Dalí's Polaroid photograph the moment he had an orgasm. At the same time, someone was shitting in the Factory elevator."

Oh, sure, I thought. "What did *you* do?"

"Nothing. I watched. I didn't enjoy it."

Ultra Violet saw doubt in my eyes.

"I had my own room—a former maid's room—at the St. Regis Hotel, next to Dalí's suite," she said. "At the time, I worked as a secretary in the French Embassy on Fifth Avenue. That was my day job. At night, I was Dalí's notary. I had to keep track of his ejaculations and record them in one of his father's old ledgers. Dalí's father was a notary, too, you know. One evening, I was summoned to Dalí's suite. A tall nude female fashion model was reclining on a couch draped with burgundy velvet. A giant lobster dipped in a bath of gold rested on the side of the model. Dalí raised her arm and sprinkled a handful of dried ants in her armpit. Two growling ocelots—tiger cats—were tied to the couch. Their teeth had been pulled out. While Dalí was drawing the model, the rapid pencil strokes sounded like whiplashes on the paper. *Tac-tac-tac.*

Dalí gave me a quick kiss on my lips and said, 'Now it's you*rrr* tu*rrr*n to d*rrr*aw.' I applied my modest skills and penciled legs and a torso. Dalí pulled the drawing from my hand and signed it with his bold, page-long signature. He asked me, 'Will you pose fo*rrr* Dalí?' With the precision of a clockmaker, he sketched my profile.

Then he slipped to his knees at my side, caressed my midriff with the live lobster, and said, '*Jouons à nous toucher LES LANGGGUESSS!*' Let's play tongue-touching. He put his tongue in my mouth. It tasted like jasmine. '*Mon amou*rrr,' Dalí said, overpronouncing every vowel, '*Bonjou*rrr!' He tickled my cheeks with the waxed points of his stiff, upturned mustache. I was boiling with passion. Nothing is normal about this man, I thought. '*Isabelle la catholique,*' he said, '*je t'ado*rrre!' I was trapped under the lobster claws. 'Sex is an illusion,' Dalí said. 'The most exciting thing is *not* having sex.'

The telephone rang. Dalí threw the lobster out of the open window, picked up the receiver, and said, '*Allo?*' The next day, Dalí and I flew to Cadaqués. I became his constant companion for five years. He ordered me to drink his urine to raise my genius level. All I got was pimples."

I'd heard enough. This is a crazy story, I thought.

"Bye-bye Ultra," I said. "See you later, alligator."

Ultra Violet spread her wings and flew off to the distant bloodred horizon.

At least, that's what she tried to do.

One day in autumn, a steady client of mine—the butcher in his blood-spattered apron and white rubber boots—summoned me to one of his outlets in a country village. He now owned a meat factory, too. Leaves were falling. It was raining. Of course it was raining. It's always raining in Europe. In his freezing workshop, he emptied a basket of offal into a chrome machine that looked like a giant dishwasher, added handfuls of salt, pepper, flour, and flavoring and a granulated substance that looked suspiciously like sawdust, and pushed a START button. The machine trembled and then started spurting and spitting out sausages in all sizes and formats. Like many of my clients, the butcher had begun to question the validity of his Dalí investments.

"When do you intend to resell?" he asked.

"Whenever Dalí dies."

"When will that be?"

"A year. Two at the most."

My own words scared the shit out of me. Of course some clients had second thoughts. *When Dalí dies, his prices will skyrocket,* I'd always maintained. But Dalí could live to be a hundred, couldn't he? I wasn't Dalí's doctor. How could I know?

"Please hurry up," I retorted. "I'm freezing. It's terribly cold in here." I was wearing a hygienic hairnet and one of my client's blood-spattered aprons over my hand-tailored suit.

"What are you waiting for?" the butcher asked.

"Your money, of course. The money in your Chinese vase."

"I haven't got any money left."

I had to change tactics. "Ever heard of J. Paul Getty?" I asked.

"The richest man in the world!" the butcher's son shouted from nearby, overhearing.

"Exactly. Rich beyond his wildest dreams. As the saying goes, Getty saw dollars whenever he thought of a painting. Wrong, Getty himself said, it's quite the opposite. Whenever I think of dollars, I see a painting." I paused. "A Dalí painting," I added playfully.

"Believe me, Stan, I'm no Getty!" the butcher exclaimed.

"I'm not a butcher. I love eating them, but I can't make sausages. But I'm a Dalí expert. You know that. I can make you rich beyond your wildest dreams, too. Remember: Cartier, Louis Vuitton, Ferrari, Rolex, they are product names. The most expensive products in the world. Dalí is an expensive product name, too. There's something else you should remember, my friend. Money that sleeps is wasted money. The more money you take out of your Chinese vase, the richer I'll make you."

Before I left, I had again emptied the Chinese vase.

Christie's in King Street in London, around the corner from the Queen Mother's residence, invited me to an evening sale of the Edward James collection. Born into extreme wealth and luxury—some say he was the bastard son of King Edward VII, while others maintain that his mother actually was the King's daughter—Edward James had inherited a vast American copper and railroad fortune at a very young age and turned his back on the rigid aristocratic circles of Edwardian England. He befriended, supported, and collaborated with fledgling artists of all stripes who would become household names in later years, including Salvador Dalí, Leonora Carrington, René Magritte, composer Kurt Weill, playwright Bertolt Brecht, ballet choreographer George Balanchine, Aldous Huxley, composer Igor Stravinsky, and photographer Man Ray among others. The eccentric English aristocrat supported them financially while building up a collection of paintings and art objects that subsequently came to be accepted as the finest collection of surrealist work in private hands. At the time of Christie's sale, Edward James was living the life of a hermit in the mountains of Mexico, in the remote village of Xilitla, amid waterfalls, tropical birds and butterflies, and wild orchids. Although he was only seventy-four years of age, he had turned his estate into a charitable foundation that supported emerging artists and craftspeople in the field of musical-instrument-making and tapestry weaving. As for his own welfare, he preferred to live and die in poverty.

The salesroom was packed. Christie's specialist auctioneer of impressionist and modern art took the hammer. There was a dense crowd standing at the back of the room. I was there too, with my sales paddle. A sales paddle is a numbered, wooden paddle, like a Ping-Pong paddle. In the international salesrooms at Sotheby's and Christie's, when you want to buy something, you hold it up so that the auctioneer can read your number, and when the lot is yours, the hammer goes down and the auctioneer says, "Sold to number fifty-one!"

One lot after another changed hands.

In less than fifty seconds, New York art dealer Alexander Iolas laid down over a million dollars for a few highly surrealist paintings Dalí had exchanged for a pair of badly fitting shoes and a meal in a fancy restaurant. He always bought shoes that were a size too small. Sore feet keep your mind alert, Dalí used to say. His 1937 *The Sleep* oil on canvas—a disturbing image of a slackened, lengthened face, eyes closed, supported by crutches in the dreamlike landscape of Ampurdán and the one undisputed museum piece in the sale—sold for a record £360,000 sterling plus the buyer's premium. The hammer price, which the auctioneer announces as the final bid, does not include the typical buyer's premium or seller's fee. A buyer's premium is a charge levied by the auction house and paid by the buyer in addition to the hammer price. It's half their profit and makes the auction house a lot of money. In return for the premium, no services whatever are provided for buyers. Any services the buyer needs are charged for separately. Nowadays, Christie's can charge up to an amazing 17.5 percent and Sotheby's a truly astonishing 19.5 percent in premiums, not including taxes. The auction house gets the same commission from the seller, which means salesrooms are making 35 to 40 percent of the sales price on every item that passes through their doors. When I was in business, the premium was set at a mere 10 percent plus taxes charged to the buyer and the seller.

I was nervous. My hands were clammy. Whenever I lifted my paddle, someone was outbidding me. I tried hard, and yet I couldn't buy a single Dalí from the Edward James collection, not with all the money in the butcher's Chinese vase.

In the end, every item was sold, for a grand total of $3.9 million, which was phenomenal at the time. One after another, the auction prices had shattered all previous Dalí records.

Dalí wasn't dead, but I thought I could breathe again, at least for a couple of years.

Once the sale was over, I had a chat with a specialist auctioneer.

"Congratulations," I said. "The world witnessed an historic evening."

"No doubt about that," he replied, and fondled his crimson tie. "It was also a turning point in the Dalí art market. From now on, it will be all downhill."

"Downhill? What do you mean?"

The auctioneer smiled. "There are no bargains in the art world," he said mysteriously. "A dealer offers you a bargain? It's stolen; it's a fake. Might be fake *and* stolen. You're right, this was the most important sale of major Dalí paintings ever. It was also the *last* big Dalí sale *ever* in a major auction house. From now on, as far as we're concerned, Dalí is finished."

The air went out of my lungs.

I was thinking of the 300,000 prints in Gilbert Hamon's Paris warehouse.

I was thinking of the handbag manufacturer splashing out a million dollars for an illustration on paper ripped out of a museum catalog.

I was thinking of MMC's financial advisers grabbing and pulling and squeezing our client's balls.

Staggering to the corner of St. James's and Piccadilly Street, I went into Russell & Bromley and deliberately bought myself a pair of new shoes at least a size too small in order to keep my mind alert.

If I wanted to survive in the art business, I had to change tactics. There was too much at stake. My parkland villa was at stake. My cars, my salary, my net commission, my company shares, my fancy suits, my gold Cartier watch, my debt, and most of all my reputation and my future. I knew that fresh investors' money would boost my morale—there will always be suckers making huge amounts of money, not knowing what to do with it—so I needed to devise a scheme that, I hoped, would allow me to survive and hang on to the good life. But first, I went back to Ana in Spain. She took me out in Barcelona. We climbed all ten thousand stone steps to the top of Antoni Gaudi's Sagrada Familia and drank *horchata de chufa*, a typically Spanish drink that looks like milk and tastes like almonds. I tried to eat raw sea urchins, Dalí's favorite snack food. They tasted like snot. A failed priest who had worked for a Paris fashion designer wanted to sell me a huge Dalí collage, a portrait of Chairman Mao in black-and-white over the face of Marilyn

Monroe, splattered with paint. His asking price: only twenty million pesetas or a mere $100,000, the price of a luxury flat in Barcelona at the time, but a bargain for a Dalí that size. Before I could reach for my wallet, I remembered what the London auctioneer had told me a few weeks previously. An art dealer offers you a bargain? Could be stolen or fake. Might be fake *and* stolen. Who knows? The failed priest wasn't even an art dealer. I didn't buy the Mao–Marilyn Monroe collage.

Like any ordinary tourist, I walked Barcelona's world-famous street, the vibrant and lively Las Ramblas with its Wax Museum, Liceu Theater—the local opera house—florists, souvenir shops, human sculptures, bird vendors, fortune-tellers, Erotica Hall, and La Boquería Market. I ordered a tasteless daiquiri at the Café Zurich where Hemingway used to savor his cocktails fifty years ago. Close to Plaça de Catalunya, on the right side at the beginning of Las Ramblas, there is a famous old fountain, nineteenth century they say, almost hidden between the trees and flower stalls and animal vendors. It is called the Canaletes Fountain. According to local legend, if you drink from it once in your life, you will always come back to Barcelona. I was greedy and drank so much water from the fountain that my belly almost exploded.

"Ana?" I said as we walked to a "tourist rip-off" art gallery that I knew sold dubious Dalí prints next door to the Picasso Museum.

"*Qué?*"

"Did you ever meet Dalí?"

She covered her mouth and rolled her eyes.

In the art gallery, my attention was immediately hijacked by a display of recent Dalí ink drawings. I noticed that the trademark Dalí signature in the right-hand corner of each drawing was always a slightly different scribble, as if each drawing had been signed by a different hand. A strong hand, very young and resolute, while Dalí was an old man. I wondered why an artist would confuse the public over something so valuable as his signature. Had anyone in the art world ever bothered to notice? The more I explored what I had found, the more confused and impressed I became.

"Amazing," I whispered.

"Stán, we have to get back to the airport," Ana interrupted. "Your plane . . ."

I didn't give up. "Look at that, Ana. Can you figure it out? Every signature is different," I said, and asked the gallery owner for the provenance of the drawings.

"I bought them right from the source."

"Directly from Dalí?"

"No. Dalí never sells anything. I bought them from Captain Moore."

"They are not dated. When were these drawings executed?"

"Mid-seventies? Something like that. Why do you ask? You're some kind of an expert?"

"Actually . . . Yes, I think I am."

"If you're an expert, as you say, you should know that Dalí's signature is the enigma of the art world," the gallery owner said. "Like Dalí himself, his signature is constantly changing and evolving."

I smiled. "Thank you," I said, and left.

The gallery owner stepped up to the door, locked it, and turned the sign to CLOSED.

The next day, back in my MMC office in the President Building, I studied a pile of Dalí art reference books, court records, international auction house and museum exhibition catalogs, magnifying glass in hand. I completed a chronological sequence of the evolution of Dalí's signature, the way a fakebuster in a forensic forgery investigation would handle it, carefully checking what I found out to be 666 different Dalí signatures. Exactly 666? I know, the number seems a little hard to believe, but the answer is, yes, exactly 666. If you talk about Dalí, you know that nothing is what it seems. Still, I couldn't believe it. In ancient history, 666 was thought to be the Number of the Beast. There was a time when people really thought that the year 666 would herald the advent of the Antichrist.

A smile spread across my face. Dalí never used the same signature twice, and he reveled in creating ever-new variations. Some signatures were in themselves real works of art. But . . . not two Dalí signatures were alike. Which is the *real* Dalí signature? I wondered. All of them? Or none of them? A photographer friend took close-up photographs and enlarged all 666 signatures, blowing them up to giant proportions. I locked myself up in my private bathroom, used clothes-pegs, hung the enlarged signatures on a washing line to dry, and compared them to a very early, absolutely authentic Dalí full signature as reproduced in the December 14, 1936, edition of *Time* magazine and the bronze Dalí signature on the façade of the privately owned Salvador Dalí

Museum in St. Petersburg, Florida. I chuckled when I saw the end result of my cut-and-paste job. Any graphologist would have a field day studying and cataloging all those hasty scribbles and scratches. Some later signatures had an underline; some had not. In almost every later signature, the S from Salvador and the D and the Í at the end were totally different. From 1978 on, most signatures were definitely shaky. They were not even close to the early, authentic Dalí full signature. Wouldn't it be a marvelous idea to collect these several hundreds of *genuine genuine* and *genuine fake* and *fake fake* signatures in the ultimate Dalí scrapbook? I thought. *Genuine genuine:* Dalí's own personal signature, no doubt about that. *Genuine fake:* could be Dalí's signature but is probably someone else's. *Fake fake:* definitely someone else's. What a sensation that would be! But *I* couldn't do it; it would kill my business and ruin my income.

The more confusion the better, Dalí has said on many occasions. Confusion frees creativity, he said. Perhaps he was right, I thought. Let bygones be bygones. Forget about everything that happened in the past. I took the photographs from the washing line, exercised my scissors on them, and then flushed the snippets down the toilet. Someone knocked on the door, and my MMC president entered. He grabbed me by the face as if he were the Godfather, kissed me on each cheek, and then presented me with a giant-size Rolodex containing the names, addresses, and financial information of thousands of extremely wealthy people all over Europe.

This is the sucker list, I thought.

"How are sales?"

"Dynamite, Mr. President."

He pumped his fist. "Sell more, Stan. Sell harder."

I had an idea. Cheese. That's where I had my roots. Making holes in Emmentaler cheeses. I asked my secretary to contact as many dairy farmers and cheese producers as possible and try to fix an appointment. She attacked the yellow pages and arranged for me to meet the owner of the most important cheese factory in the Grand Duchy of Luxembourg, a country smaller than its name. It is an independent sovereign state of rolling hills and is nicely tucked between Belgium, France, and Germany. Banking services and other financial exports account for the majority of its economic output.

The farmer was a brusque, cheesified man. "I'm busy. Don't bother me," he snapped.

"I won't."

"I know nothing about stocks and shares."

"Neither do I."

He looked up. Puzzled.

"Venture capital?" he asked.

"Nothing," I said.

He must have wondered what I was doing in that appendix of a country.

I noticed a bicycle for road racing in his courtyard.

"Who won the 1958 Tour de France?" I asked.

"My countryman, Charly Gaul, of course!" he yelled.

"Good! Who was second?"

"Well . . . hmmm . . . you see . . . I don't know."

"Vito Favero from Italy," I said. "An unknown. Third overall was Raphaël Geminiani."

To say the least, I had done my homework.

"Geminiani! Yes! A *strong* Frenchman!"

I could see the cheesemaker mellowing fast. Mellowing and melting.

"Do you know as much about *art* investments as you know about cycling?" he asked. "That's what you've come for, isn't it? To sell an investment and steal my money? Forget it. I didn't get where I am financially by pissing money away on bad investments."

"I know *nothing* about art investments," I replied.

"You don't?"

"No. I don't even know what art is."

"Neither do I."

"There's only one artist I know something about."

"My banker said I shouldn't listen to you."

"Good advice."

The cheese farmer chuckled. "Who the fuck are you trying to swindle me with?"

"No one. No one at all. I'm not trying to swindle you. I'm not selling you anything. To be honest, I have no sales experience." No juggling interest rates here, I thought. Time to pull a white rabbit or two from my hat.

"What are you doing here, then, if you're not selling anything?"

"I thought I'd bring you some money."

"Bring me money? You?"

"Yes."

"Why? Why should you?"

"You like cheese, don't you?"

"No, I don't. I never eat it."

Careful, I thought, watch out.

"You're an intelligent man, I can see that," I said, and shook my head. "You know all about Charly Gaul. But have you ever heard of the greatest surrealist painter who ever lived?"

"What's his name?"

I sighed. Every day, people were asking me who Salvador Dalí was. The *real* Salvador Dalí. Yes, I knew the facts. I read about Dalí. I studied his life, yet I still didn't know the *real* Dalí. Would anyone ever know? What could I tell the cheese farmer?

"Dalí," I said. "Salvador Dalí."

"Yeah, I've heard the name. That TV fool with his upturned mustache."

"Yes."

The cheese farmer nodded. "He's an old man."

"True," I said. "Full-fat Edam is old cheese, too. Crumbly cheese. The oldest and the best, experts say, aged at a minimum of ten months to preserve essential flavor. Nice round Edam cheese with its red rind and yellow-orange flesh, awarded Best Foreign Cheese by the American Cheese Society. Well, Salvador Dalí is *almost* a full-fat Edam. Mind you, *any* famous artist is an old cheese. Bonnard lived to be eighty, Braque and Duchamp eighty-one, Max Ernst and Matisse eighty-five, Monet eighty-six, Joan Miró ninety. Picasso died at ninety-three, and Chagall almost lived to be a hundred. The older, the better. Now take Gouda with its mild, creamy, and pure taste. Did you know that a famous Dutch competitor of yours has started exporting Gouda under the label of famous Dutch painters? Their cheese is a masterpiece of dairy art, their publicity department says. Nonsense, of course. But they get away with it. They've got a Rembrandt Gouda—rich and tangy in flavor—aged to perfection, like a four-hundred-year-old Rembrandt painting. A Mondrian Gouda is a nutty full-cream cheese, slightly sweet and filled with sun-dried tomatoes, green olives, Mediterranean seasonings, and a dash of garlic. Or take their Vincent van Gogh smoked Gouda with added flavor, a museum piece in itself."

The cheese manufacturer was staggered. His mouth fell wide open.

Some speech, I thought.

Grab, squeeze and—*snòk!*—pull.

"Be honest, any museum in the world loves a Rembrandt or a Mondrian and a Vincent van Gogh on its sacred walls," I said. "Bingo! Tourists will flock to it. But would *you* hang a Rembrandt Gouda and a Mondrian Emmentaler or a Vincent van Gogh Gruyère in your house?"

The cheese farmer smiled. "I don't know," he said briskly. "I never saw a Rembrandt in my life. I've never seen the inside of a museum."

"Would you agree that Salvador Dalí—indeed, the fool with the upturned mustache—is as famous as Rembrandt?"

"Yes, of course." No hesitating, not for a second. "I've read an article about Dalí some time ago."

"In *Panorama* magazine?"

"That interview, too."

"Would you like to *own* a Dalí painting?"

"Why should I?"

"Why not?"

"Give me one good reason."

"You've got walls, haven't you?"

"Of course I've got walls!"

"How many?"

"That's a silly question."

"No, it isn't. The more walls you've got, the more Dalí you can hang on those walls."

"I don't intend to hang my house full of Dalí."

"One would be enough?"

"Yes, perhaps. If financial return is okay."

"An *expensive* Dalí?"

"I only want the best."

I cocked my head. "You know," I said, "you'll be a very, very rich man soon."

He didn't understand.

I explained. "There will always be cows," I said. "There will always be milk. As long as there are cows and milk, there will be cheese. Gouda, Edam, Gruyère, German Butterkäse, ricotta, cheddar, Finish Tilsit, feta from Greece, Camembert, French and American Brie, blue Gorgonzola cheese, Boursin, you name it. But Dalí is dying. He is *almost* full-fat Edam, remember. He'll be dead soon. When he dies, his production line stops. The factory grounds to a halt. No more Dalís. No more supply. Demand will be as strong as ever, stronger even. Take my word, Dalí prices will go through the roof. Now you understand why I asked if you got walls at home?"

He nodded.

"Listen," I said. "No hard feelings. Forget what I said earlier, about bringing you some money. I didn't bring you any. I fooled you. Yes, I did. Who's interested in money? I know my advice is *better* than all the money in the world. But if you don't want it . . . Hey, I just noticed something."

"What is it?"

"You *smell* like cheese."

The cheese farmer got red with anger. He looked as if he were going to have a stroke any minute. There was a moment of uncomfortable silence.

"It's true, isn't it?" I said.

"Are you finished?"

"I'm sure people catch the smell of cheesy toe jam from a mile away," I said calmly, and sighed. I had told the cheese farmer everything he wanted to hear and everything he *didn't* want to hear. I was pleased with myself. Time to close, I thought. "You know what an expensive Dalí smells like?" I asked. "Like Charly Gaul winning the Tour de France. That's a once-in-a-lifetime achievement. You want an investment, call your stockbroker. Call your banker. You want to experience the happiness money is capable of buying? Talk to me. If I need cheese, I'll come to you. If you need a Dalí, you come to me. Is that a deal? Dalí is the future and the sky is the limit. You know what Keats said?"

"No."

"Ever heard of Keats?"

"No."

"A poet."

"Oh. What did he say?"

"*A thing of beauty is a joy forever.*"

"That's nice."

"It is, isn't it?"

The cheese farmer quieted down, lost in the moment. He thought it over. I felt as if I were in a state of shock, unsure of what I had just done, and repeated to myself what my MMC president had said to me only days before. *Always make the customer think he's getting laid when he's really getting fucked.* That was some advice.

"Have you got a Dalí for me?" the cheesified man asked.

"Not at the moment."

"Can you get me one?"

"Maybe . . . I can try."

"What's stopping you?"

"Supply and demand," I said.

"I want a *beautiful* Dalí."

"Fuck beauty."

"You are vulgar."

I cut him short. "No, I'm a realist. If you want something beautiful, hang your cash on the wall." Great one-liner. I got that one from my president, too.

"What would you advise me to do?"

I frowned. "Drawings, maybe. Hard to find, though."

"I can give you ten thousand."

"Ten thousand *what*? Luxembourg francs? That's peanuts, my friend."

"Dollars," he said, "American dollars."

I looked at my gold Cartier watch. Time to go.

"Wait! Wait! I'll make it fifty thousand!"

I sighed. "Fifty thousand hardly buys you a portfolio of signed prints on paper," I said.

"I don't want paper—I use paper to wipe my ass."

"Buy an oil," I said. "On canvas."

"What will it cost me?"

"I'll call you."

In the late 1930s, Elsa Schiaparelli was a household name in fashion, on a par with Dior and Chanel. She held a salon on the Place Vendôme. Salvador Dalí and his wife, Gala, lived in Paris, too. Elsa Schiaparelli asked the artist to publicize a new body cream and lip gloss and commissioned a torn-dress design. Dalí accepted and painted a dreamy Ampurdán landscape with an angel pouring oil over the breasts of a naked beauty admiring her face in a mirror. A donkey's head—a typical Dalí cliché—was lying in the sand. There was also a sprinkling of soft melting watches, lobsters, crawling ants, wooden crutches, and telephones. The pay was good. It was easy money. The surrealist landscape was reproduced as a background design in *Vogue*, and more commissions followed. The fashion world had found a new darling in Dalí.

He dashed off numerous illustrations on small canvases:

high-heeled shoes turned upside down so that they could double as a woman's hat, the inside of a bathtub covered in fur,
dress buttons made from chocolate, and a lobster mayonnaise
dress with real lobster and real mayonnaise. Shortly after I visited the cheese manufacturer in the Grand Duchy of Luxembourg, one of the commissioned 1930s paintings came up for
auction at Christie's in New York, a small, square oil on canvas
titled *Portrait of Elsa Schiaparelli*. It represented two huge female hands, fingertips together as if in prayer, with false, bright
red fingernails made of tiny mirrors. A *genuine genuine* Dalí,
no doubt about that, 100 percent pure, though there was no
certificate of any kind. According to the auction catalog, it had
never been reproduced and the provenance was unknown. I flew
to New York. There were no other bidders, and I bought *Portrait
of Elsa Schiaparelli* for the bottom price of forty-four thousand
dollars plus the buyer's premium and taxes. If ever there was a
bargain, that was it. Back in my office, I quadrupled the initial
selling price and—without any feeling of guilt or remorse—
added my own 25 percent commission. Gross profit: almost
$150,000. I called the cheese farmer and talked him into buying
the Dalí painting until I was blue in the face. He was hestitant,
and I wondered why. For all I knew, he'd thought Schiaparelli
was some kind of half-matured Gorgonzola.

I packed my Louis Vuitton travel bags and went on a shopping
spree. At a Christie's evening sale of impressionist and modern
art in London, I bought a charming Dalí on wood the size of a

matchbox for less than twenty-five thousand dollars. The image represented two baked beans necking and making love in
the Ampurdán dreamscape. Another tiny masterpiece. *Literally
tiny.* I tore and threw the invoice in a wastebasket, put the
matchbox in my trouser pocket, and walked through customs
twice. No need to pay taxes if you can avoid it. I'm not a gam-
bler, though. I don't play cards. I never bought a lottery ticket
in my life, yet I hit the jackpot once or twice.

Quite by accident, I strolled the grounds of a car trunk sale
and spotted a Dalí photocopy—not on paper, not even on painter's canvas, but on a kind of coarse tarpaulin. Worthless, of
course. A photocopy is a photocopy, no matter what. Only the
image looked good. Lots of yellow and brown cubist squares. I
knew the image; I had seen a similar tapestry in the Dalí Museum in Figueres, and the original canvas, property of the
Minami Art Museum in Tokyo, is color-reproduced in every
Dalí art book in the world. It was titled *Gala Contemplating the
Mediterranean Sea which at Twenty Meters turns into a Portrait of
Abraham Lincoln*—also known as *Lincoln in Dalívision*—and
represented a nude woman gazing out a window in the trompe
l'oeil or "trick the eye" or "fool the eye" technique the old mas-
ters invented four hundred years ago. Looking at it from a certain
distance, through half-closed eyes, the image of the nude woman
in the window transforms itself into an Abraham Lincoln portrait. When Dalí painted the original artwork, it was one of his
first optical and "hoaxing" illusions on canvas.

I bought the photocopy for almost nothing, wetted it with a
spray bottle of mineral water, and carefully rubbed a sliced,

peeled raw potato over its surface to clean off any dust and fly shit. From an artist's DIY supply shop, I got a 100 percent semigloss acrylic polymer emulsion—a kind of gel—and smeared a couple of layers on the tarpaulin, using my fingers and a brush, and rubbed the gel up and down the image of the woman in the window. I didn't need a hair dryer for instant re- sult. I left it overnight in order to dry and acquire the dull, typical appearance of museum dust. The next morning, I was the proud owner of a Dalí "oil on canvas" reproduction that was impossible to distinguish from the real deal except for its size—but who cares? The original canvas measures two-and-a-half-by-two me- ters. Mine was about the size of a handkerchief. After I had my *Lincoln in Dalívision* beautifully framed, its total cost came to roughly three hundred dollars. The ornate frame, hand-carved and decorated in gold leaf, cost me five times the price of the "original" artwork.

The owner of the Ostend Casino asked me if I could organize a Dalí exhibition of museum quality. I jumped in my car and drove to Ostend beach and the promenade pier on the Belgian coast. The casino decor was superbly attractive. Dice, playing cards, roulette wheels, poker chips—it was all there, as well as video slot games and jackpot systems. To make the three-month show an all-round success, I borrowed some "real" Dalí paintings from my client investors—*Don Quixote,* the copulating beans, the *Portrait of Elsa Shiaparelli*—and mingled them with Gilbert Hamon's so-called limited-edition prints, some Dalí bronze sculptures, and the attractive *Lincoln in Dalívision* ornately framed photocopy.

Especially for the opening night, I had manufactured a clever video montage of archive Dalí footage. The video was projected on a wide cinema screen and showed the inside of the artist's studio. With a bored expression, singer and model Amanda Lear was lying on her back on a red sofa, a live lobster crawling over her crotch. A gossip columnist in top hat was standing nearby, furiously scribbling on a yellow pad. Dalí held a mask to his face that was the mask of none other than Salvador Dalí. A telephone started ringing. Dalí grabbed the receiver. The receiver turned into a live lobster. Dalí wriggled his fingers in fright and dropped the lobster on the floor. When he looked at the floor, the lobster was gone. All around were just-completed and half-completed canvases with the most bizarre surreal images: exploding pine trees, an archbishop in drag, burning giraffes on spidery legs, a cloud of feathers, and surreal melting watches and clocks. A Dalí close-up now filled the screen.

SALVADOR DALÍ:
Dalí needs two thousand live ants, fourrr trrransvestites, a white Arrrabian stallion, thrrree hundrrred dead grrrasshoppers, fourrr dwarrrfs, fourrr giants, and the suit of arrrmorrr of Jeanne d'Arrrc, the Maid of Orrrleans.

AMANDA LEAR:
For a painting?

SALVADOR DALÍ:
Forrr a parrrty.

AMANDA LEAR:

The party will be a work of art?

SALVADOR DALÍ:

Yes! Dalí also needzzz pink champagne from Perrrelada, a live Afrrrican elephant, two fisherrrmen from Cadaqués in a white-and-blue marrrine uniforrrm, and a jarrr of Frrrench honey.

AMANDA LEAR:

Also for the party?

SALVADOR DALÍ:

No, for a paintinggg!

AMANDA LEAR:

They say someone wants to make a film of your life.

SALVADOR DALÍ:

Im-pos-si-ble. No scrrreen in the worrrld izzz larrrge enough for the geniuzzz of Dalí. They would have to prrroject it on ze moon and to porrrtray everrry second of Dalí's life. The film would have to be seventy yearzzz long.

GOSSIP COLUMNIST IN TOP HAT:

Why do you paint?

SALVADOR DALÍ:

To be showerrred with a diarrrhea of gold, money, and checks.

GOSSIP COLUMNIST IN TOP HAT:
Some people call you a madman.

SALVADOR DALÍ:
Do they? Haha! Compar*rre* our bank accounts.

GOSSIP COLUMNIST IN TOP HAT:
Which painting is your favorite?

SALVADOR DALÍ:
Ze one that sold for ze most money.

GOSSIP COLUMNIST IN TOP HAT:
For our readers who don't know: What is surrealism?

SALVADOR DALÍ:
Dalí is su*rrr*ealism!

GOSSIP COLUMNIST IN TOP HAT:
Are you famous?

SALVADOR DALÍ:
What is *fame*? Jesus Chr*rr*ist is the most famous man in ze whole wor*rr*ld and he wasn't awar*rr*ded the Nobel P*rrr*ize either.

GOSSIP COLUMNIST IN TOP HAT:
Who is the best surrealist painter apart from Dalí?

SALVADOR DALÍ:

Yves Tanguy because he can fa*rrrt* with such fo*rrrce* that he blows out a candle f*rrrom* mo*rrre* than two mete*rrrs* away, and Dalí unfo*rrr*tunately can't do that. Dalí is now w*rrr*iting-*ggg* his au-to-bi-o-g*rrra*-phie! In the A-me-*rrri*-can edition, they cen-so*rrr*ed my chapte*rrr* on fa*rrr*ting. You cannot fa*rrr*t in the U-ni-ted States of A-me-*rrri*-ca. Did you know that fa*rrr*ting is only allowed in Catholic countries?

AMANDA LEAR:
So what keeps you going?

SALVADOR DALÍ:
Dalí's Divine Mustache!

The scene dissolved into multiple panels of constantly changing images, like a multi-projector slide show. The panels showed Salvador Dalí's most famous creations, taken from his greatest paintings: melting watches, ants crawling out of an open hand, a woman's naked body with drawers opening out of it, as well as floating extraterrestrial cities lost in space. On a split screen, in black-and-white, we saw documentary footage from Dalí's life: playing a concert-size harp made with barbed-wire strings, riding atop an elephant, painting two surreal human figures engulfed in a swarm of flying fried eggs and running around his studio swatting flies with a fly swatter, holding up a certificate of authenticity and flipping it over, revealing a wild signature scrawled across the back.

Applause all around.

I remembered Orson Welles once saying, in his documentary *F for Fake*, that the art world is a huge confidence trick, to which "actor" Elmyr de Hory, perhaps the greatest art forger of all time, duly replied that the art world is a world of make-believe. From painting to painting, from fake to fake, the art forger turns a simple line drawing into gold. Orson Welles argued that not even John D. Rockefeller or J. Paul Getty were able to do that.

My car-trunk purchase was the star of the show.

"A bunch of squares," visitors to the exhibition said, and wrinkled their noses.

"Is this a joke?" someone asked.

"What's so funny about a nude Gala?"

"Close your eyes," I said. "Almost. Try to see as much as you can see through your eyelashes."

They did.

Gala's bottom turned into the lips of Abraham Lincoln.

Gala's hair and the back of her head changed into his eyes.

Ooooh! and *Aaaah!* and *Ooooch!*

"I can see it! I can see it!"

"Me, too!"

The naked Gala gazing out of a window had become the portrait of the sixteenth President of the United States.

"How much does it cost?" a well-known politician asked.

"Never ask a woman her age," I replied. "Why should you ask the price of Gala's bottom?"

Laughter all around. Applause and laughter.

"I might want to buy."

"This picture is reproduced in *every* Dalí art book in the whole wide world," I said, not moving an eyebrow. "Insurance value is two hundred and fifty thousand dollars. No check accepted. Cash only."

"It's pretty," the politician said, "but is it art?"

"The art world is a world of make-believe," I replied.

"Two hundred," he said.

"Two hundred *what*?"

"Two hundred *thousand*."

"I'm sorry. Dalí is not a clearance sale. If you're looking for a bargain, you should go to your local discount supermarket." I tapped the framed photocopy. "The minute Dalí departs this life and ascends into heaven, the price of this . . . painting . . . triples."

"Okay. Two fifty. Thousand," the politician said.

"Dollars?"

"Dollars."

"That's a deal."

He agreed to the asking price. The poor man acquired a virtually worthless car-trunk-sale photocopy on tarpaulin for a quarter of a million U.S. dollars, delivered to me the next day in a brown paper bag.

The bronze Dalí sculptures I exhibited in the casino exhibition had an interesting story, too. I got them on consignment from Pierre Schwartz, a soft-voiced art dealer who specialized in French impressionist paintings and used to run an art gallery in the Faubourg St.-Honoré in the fashionable Paris shopping district famous for its wealth of luxury boutiques. He was a skinny little guy, maybe fifty, with a long face and heavy black eyebrows. I first ran into Schwartz in New York, at an art fair held in the basement of a four-star hotel. In his shoe box–size booth, he displayed a mishmash of cheap melting wristwatches, Dalí tarot cards, silk scarves, ashtrays, mugs, soup plates, tea towels, and one or two bronze sculptures bearing the famous Dalí signature. One was an old surrealist elephant saddled with a melting lobster. It didn't look like a surrealist elephant; it looked like a dying donkey.

"Not my fault," Schwartz said.

"Of course not. *You* didn't make it, did you?"

"Well . . . ," he said.

The old trick. In an artist's supply store, he had bought a beautifully proportioned and fully adjustable wooden mannequin of a horse or an elephant or perhaps a donkey. Art school students had used it as a reference tool for learning the basics of animal drawing. Then came the next step. Schwartz drenched endless rolls of pharmacist's gauze and rolls of toilet paper in a liquid mixture of plaster and lime and carefully wrapped the gauze and toilet paper around the wooden skeleton. Dripping with plaster, it looked like a ghost from outer space.

At that time of the year, the artist was staying in the Hôtel Maurice in Paris, and Schwartz talked himself into his suite and managed to show his miserable elephant to Dalí.

"Would Señor Dalí authenticate this surrealist elephant against cash payment?" he asked.

"Never! Not for as long as I live! Get away! Go!" Dalí

shouted. He was furious. The antennas of his mustache quivered with indignation.

"How would you do it differently, Señor Dalí?"

Dalí made a fatal mistake. He grabbed the elephant and furiously began kneading it, his fingers burying deep in the wet and soft and dripping plaster. "Like this . . . and this . . . and this!" Dalí shouted.

Schwartz quickly snapped some Polaroid photographs.

His rage over, Dalí threw the surrealist elephant at the skinny art dealer and kicked him out of the hotel.

Pierre Schwartz looked at me and smiled. A naughty smile. "I had him," he said.

Grab, pull, and—*snók!*

Dalí is smart, everyone knows that, but that day, Pierre Schwartz was smarter. He had the wooden and plaster and toilet paper elephant cast in bronze, in a limited edition of 250. He plucked a signature from one of Dalí's most famous museum paintings and had the signature worked into the mold and cast in bronze, too.

"Two hundred and fifty surrealist elephants at ten thousand dollars wholesale each," Schwartz said. "Makes me two and a half million dollars."

There was nothing Dalí could do.

His fingerprints were in the wet plaster and into the mold and were thus transferred on each bronze cast, and if that wasn't enough, there were the set of Polaroid photographs to prove Dalí's involvement. Fingerprints and Polaroids. In uncertain times, they're the perfect certificate of authenticity.

Pierre Schwartz taught me some of the tricks of the trade. Next time we met, we had lunch at Harry's Bar in Venice. Mind you, Harry's Bar is no cheap place. Minestrone soup for starters was twenty dollars, scampi all'Armoricaine—in a tomato, herb, and wine sauce, nothing fancy—worked out at almost fifty dollars a plate. We drank the famous Bellini cocktail of one part white peach juice and three parts *prosecco* or Italian sparkling wine. The meal over, Schwartz noticed he had forgotten his wallet as well as cash money and credit cards. He apologized, so it was up to me to pay for the meal. What else could I do? Sometimes even renowned art dealers can behave cheaply.

"You want to make it big?" Schwartz asked.

"Not if it costs me a fortune."

"Won't cost you anything."

"Nothing?"

"No. Nothing at all."

"You're telling me I can make a fortune without a hefty down payment?"

"Yes, of course you can."

"How come?"

"We'll make a *new* Dalí. You and me together."

"You? Me? Together? A new Dalí?"

"We'll split fifty–fifty. Cost and profit. I've got the know-how, you've got the clients—that should do. We'll be partners."

Impossible to make a Dalí if you're not Dalí, I thought.

"Clients. Know-how. That's all?"

"Yes, that's all."

"Okay. I'm your man."

"Good. Give me one of your original Dalís."

"Oil on paper will do?"

"Sure."

"*Don Quixote*?" I asked.

"That's an idea."

"It's no longer mine. I sold it."

"Your client will get it back, don't worry."

Six weeks later, DHL brought me a large and very heavy parcel wrapped in cardboard with strings. The sender had its business address in the Swiss free port, or free trade zone, of Chiasso, near the Italian border. My heart was pounding. I tore the cardboard and almost fainted. The single parcel contained six hundred identical limited-edition Dalí prints on Arches and Japon paper, all of them pencil-signed and numbered. Also, each and every signature was identical to the next one. They looked like "electronic" signatures, as if someone had used a computer-steered pencil to put the mark on each sheet, six hundred times over. As for the quality of the prints—well, let's say the image was *Don Quixote* blown up to giant dimensions. It looked like a junk reproduction. Color was bleeding off one side. I didn't know what it was—a clone? a copy? a duplicate? a facsimile? a replica? a fake? a forgery? It wasn't a *real* lithograph, and thus a genuine work of art—that I knew for sure. Now this crap really pisses me off, I thought.

It seemed as if Pierre Schwartz would sell Dalí's bowel movements if he thought someone would by them. Well, someone would. Buy them, I mean. The very next day, Schwartz was on the telephone. From Paris? Venice? London? Chiasso? Who knows. We didn't have caller identification back then.

"Did you get the *Don Quixote* shipment?"

"What is it you've sent me?" I said, biting my anger.

"It's a Dalí print."

"The fuck it is."

"Dalí's signature is on it."

"Before or after you printed it? Don't bullshit me, will you? Where's my *Don Quixote*?" I asked angrily. "The original. It's no longer mine, I told you that."

He laughed. "It's mine now," he said.

"Yours? How come it's yours?"

Again he laughed. "Let's say that was part of the deal."

"No, it wasn't."

"I'm sorry, it is now."

Silence. I sighed.

"I can't sell your prints," I said. "They're not even remotely similar to the original."

"I don't see any difference. By the way, they're not mine. Not anymore. They're *your* prints now."

"You've given up on quality," I said, "you're interested only in quantity."

"Quality doesn't make you money," Schwartz said, "quantity does. You wanted to make it big, no? Make shiploads of money?"

"The prints look awful."

"Next time, I'll find a new printer."

"There won't be a next time."

Silence on the line.

"Did Dalí see these prints?" I asked.

"He hand-signed them."

"Don't bullshit me, Pierre."

"It doesn't matter. Keep printing; that's what Dalí says. Keep printing as long as you can maintain the numbers. Sell each print one thousand dollars wholesale. A Dalí is not a give-away."

Six hundred prints multiplied by a thousand dollars per print, that's no chickenfeed.

I sat down at my desk and thought for a moment and started spinning the giant Rolodex my president had given me. Names and client information were neatly typed on every card. I punched numbers into the phone. A woman's voice answered. I made an appointment. I put on my best suit and tie and took a few hundred prints of *Don Quixote* to the dentist I had called. There I was, sitting on a sofa in his reception area, waiting patiently with my portfolio on my knees. I waited for an hour. When the dentist finally could see me, I spread the prints on his desk and all over the floor.

"This is your chance of a lifetime. Dalí will be dead in less than five years," I said.

The dentist nodded. "What happens when he dies?"

"The value of this portfolio will go through the roof."

Again he nodded. "What happens if Dalí *doesn't* die in less than five years?" he asked.

"No problem. MMC buys back at double today's selling price. Guaranteed, on paper, signed and dated. That's a twenty percent profit per year. No classic investment makes you that kind of money in that short a time." Sucker, I thought. If you believe that, you'll believe anything.

"I'll take two hundred."

"Be my guest. Make it three."

"Do I get a discount?"

"Dalí is no clearance sale."

Waiting for an hour in a reception area to cash $300,000, that's good business. Back home, I counted out my take and stuffed the stacks of money in the freezer compartment in the kitchen.

Am I becoming a gangster? I wondered. Who else keeps money in the fridge?

I have to take what I can take, I thought. Take it and do it now. MMC isn't going to last forever. Dalí isn't going to last forever.

I needed a bigger fridge.

The MMC president—*my* president—was in charge of overall investments. That meant real estate and diamonds as well as works of art. Of these three, only fine art was pulling its weight. Real estate was a disaster. Once an unsuspecting team of private investors went on holiday to the Grand-Mère site in Canada where—so they had been told—a luxury holiday resort with skiing facilities had been built with their investment money. Grand-Mère sounds good; it's French for "grand-mother." Nice name for a holiday resort. They didn't find Grand-Mère. No one ever found it. It just didn't exist.

Diamonds weren't much better. They failed in all four C's: clarity, color, cut, and carat weight. The label "Cut in Antwerp" is an international quality label refering to the best diamond cut in the world, yet our stones on offer had imperfections or flaws, tiny spots of white and other colors, or cracks that caused them to split. Some had undergone laser treatment. In other words, none of the stones was any good as an investment diamond. Dallas real estate was an altogether different story. In those years, the *Dallas* television series was a worldwide hit. Larry Hagman as JR swindled, betrayed, conned, cheated, blackmailed, tried to break up marriages, and even instigated a coup in an oil-rich Asian country. We did our best, we dressed as JR—sharp suit, cowboy boots, Stetson—and had leased the Southfork Ranch as a show house, but try selling Dallas real estate with a reputation like JR, especially when the real estate isn't even yours.

What can I say about the works of art? I had gambled everything on Dalí. *If the artist dies, his value will skyrocket. Excessive demand and no more supply. The sky is the limit.* There was one problem, however. Dalí wouldn't die. Stubborn, stupid man. Of course investors started complaining. I could have foreseen it. They wanted a return on their money and they wanted it *now*. They phoned my office and I got cold feet, I avoided their calls. My secretary told them I was abroad, so they pestered my president. He slammed the phone down. Angry letters arrived from lawyers and solicitors all over the world. Some investors went to the police and filed a complaint. The gendarmes arrested me on a motorway in France. I

talked myself out of even bigger trouble. While visiting a Los
Angeles Art Fair, I was picked up by two FBI agents and grilled
for a couple of hours.

You won't believe this, but one night, his bedsheets soaked
in blood, my president woke up to find himself sleeping next
to the severed head of his favorite horse, one that had won
trophies in the MMC colors and was making him yet another
fortune. Someone had borrowed a frame from *The Godfather*.
The house of cards was falling down. Even in the middle of
the night, I got threatening phone calls from angry cus-
tomers.

"I bought three hundred Dalí prints from you. You guaranteed you'd buy them back at double the selling price! Where's
my money?" That was the dentist I'd conned into buying *Don
Quixote*.

"Be patient . . . Dalí is a sick man. It's worth hanging on . . .
It won't take long before he . . ."

"Before he . . . what?"

". . . before he dies."

"How do you know? Are you a doctor?"

"Don't you read the papers?" I said. "He's incontinent. He
wets his bed. He's in a wheelchair now."

"If he doesn't die soon, I will report you to the police."

I was defrauding them of their rightful profit, some clients
claimed. As if *I* had pocketed their money. Threats poured in.
MMC paid off the most dangerous ones. I was panicking, and
I hastily tried to resell some Dalí drawings and watercolors at
the international auction houses. They refused to accept the

Dalís I had acquired through Captain Moore. I couldn't understand. After all, it was *impossible* that they were fake, since the man who sold them was not only Dalí's business manager but also his private secretary. These Dalís, they had to be real. Dalí's *capitán del dinero* wouldn't fool Dalí's clients, would he? A few weeks later, both auction houses, in London and New York, politely declined even the Dalí oil paintings I had bought from them. The auctioneers said they were swamped with suspect Dalís and refused to accept *anyone's* Dalí for sale. Every day, I checked the obituaries in the papers hoping to find Dalí's name. I *needed* him to die. My own survival depended on his death.

The intimidating phone calls continued.

A caller threatened to cut off my balls.

Grab and squeeze—and *snòk!*

Only this time, the balls were mine.

I asked my president if we had a problem and if he had a solution to the problem.

"Cards on the table," he replied. "I'm a liar. I like to lie. I lie to other people. I'm gonna lie to you. Are we clear on this? Because I want to be honest with you, Stan, okay?"

"Okay."

"What I'm gonna tell you today, you won't ever repeat. Okay?"

"What are you gonna tell me?"

"Keep an open mind. Just go on as if nothing happened. There's money to be made on Dalí."

As if I didn't know that.

I sighed. "Have we got a problem?" I asked again.

"Problem? What problem?"

Walking along Madison Avenue, I noticed my *Don Quixote* print on display in a poster boutique, signed in pencil, numbered and framed, exactly as I'd been selling it for a thousand bucks. It sold for seventy-five dollars on Madison Avenue. Of course I panicked. Again. I ran to a skyscraper on the Avenue of the Americas. The entry plaza was complete with trees and plants and flanked by restaurants and cafés. I took the elevator high up to the top floor. Large, modern, with high ceilings and a wood-lined waiting area. Art books lined the office from wall to wall. There were floor-to-ceiling windows with a magnificent view over the city that was absolutely breathtaking. But I hadn't gone there to enjoy the view. I wanted reassurance. I also wanted to cover my ass. There were clients out there ready to shoot me.

Michael Ward Stout, a flamboyant and thick-set man in his mid-forties, welcomed me to his office. He was Salvador Dalí's American lawyer. He looked like film comedian Oliver Hardy from Stan and Ollie fame, genteel and boyish. We'd met before, on a plane once and in the arrivals hall of the El Prat Airport in Barcelona, where he was desperately trying to make a phone call, until Ana stepped in and helped him. He knew I had been buying and selling Dalí for years.

"I don't have a lot of time," he said. "I'm doing this as a favor to you, so if we could just—"

"You sure have a lot of books," I replied in mock wonder.

"Yeah, well, I'm an attorney."

"You read them all?"

He was charmed; I could see that. "Mostly."

"Looks like a public library."

"What are you getting at?"

"Prints. Dalí prints."

"What do you want to know?"

"I've got some. Well, my clients have. Six hundred in all. I'm worried."

Michael Ward Stout spread his hands on his desk and drummed his sausagelike fingers on the tabletop. He sighed and said he was absolutely powerless.

I sighed and drummed my fingers on the tabletop, too.

"Your prints, are they good ones?" the lawyer asked.

"That's exactly what I'd like to find out," I said.

Again he sighed. "It's a disaster, and it all started in the early sixties," the lawyer said.

As I understood it, Captain Moore had asked Dalí to give a surrealist twist to some old Goya etchings. In those days, everyone was cashing in on Dalí's name, as was Dalí himself. He agreed to the Goya etchings on condition that he be paid half a million dollars for the ten-minute job. Cash, up front. But Dalí became hesitant. He postponed the project. Delays are dangerous, as every businessman knows. Fearing Dalí might die before the Goya project was completed, Captain Moore gave Dalí a few hundred blank sheets of Arches and Japon paper to pencil-sign. In case of Dalí's untimely death, the Goya images could then be printed above Dalí's signature.

"Man, what a revelation that was!" Dalí's American lawyer said.

"I don't understand. A revelation for whom?"

"For Dalí. For Captain Moore. For Gala."

"Why a revelation?"

"Because Dalí needn't bother to create a new image. He made half a million—cash, up front—signing blank sheets of paper. Over the next fifteen years, he refused to sign lithographs or prints or etchings, only blank sheets in preparation for printing. The surrealist image was added later, as a post-image so to speak."

"Printed later, you mean?"

"Yes."

"How many blank sheets, in all?"

"No one knows," the lawyer said.

Again I pictured the Gilbert Hamon strongroom in Paris and broke into cold sweat. No excuses: I was taken in by a bunch of frauds.

"Hundreds of thousands, maybe millions?" I asked.

No reply.

"I'd say, *probably* millions," I said bitterly.

In the early days, every signature was slightly different, though. Dalí finally got to where he could sign a blank sheet of Arches or Japon every two seconds. In the mid-1970s, he stopped signing even these blank sheets, not because he wanted to—the pay was perfect—but because he *had* to.

"He was too ill," the lawyer said, "Dalí's hands were shaking, he couldn't hold a pencil anymore."

"Others signed in his place?"

No reply. Not even a nod.

I got angry. "I've got six hundred identical, badly executed copies of *Don Quixote*," I said. "I think they're mechanically signed. I passed them on to my investor clients for a thousand dollars wholesale per print. Now they sell seventy-five dollars retail here in New York. Framed. What am I going to do? How do I explain this to my clients?"

I had been naïve. Or plain stupid. I thought I owned the moral right to *Don Quixote,* since I had bought the original watercolor.

"I'm sorry, you don't," the lawyer said. "You're not the copyright holder. I know at least six or seven different *Don Quixote* editions, all signed and numbered, selling all over the world from seventy-five dollars to an all-time high of over four thousand dollars for the identical image. Monsieur Hamon in Paris even published his own limited edition on a small format. He was entitled to do so, because he bought a contract and paid for it. What do you want me to do?"

"You're Dalí's American lawyer," I said, "Show the world that you're a brave man and admit that Dalí prints are the equivalent of a full-scale locust plague."

They are the plague of the art world, I thought.

"It stinks," I said. "It's a pile of shit."

The lawyer shrugged. "Dalí is my client," he said. "It is my duty to defend him; that's what he pays me for. Believe me, I will be the first to admit that he has set something in motion that nobody can control. I know, I have been told that, surrounded by hundreds of sheets of blank paper, Dalí would feverishly sign each and every one, like a machine cranked up all the way, one sheet every two seconds at forty dollars per signature."

If he did it for an hour, Dalí was seventy-two thousand dollars the richer. Sometimes he signed with *both* hands at the same time. It was sad, but the only thing that seemed to interest Dalí and Gala was cash in hand, up front, as much as possible, and no questions asked. People have seen it happen, and they felt humiliated. What could Michael Ward Stout do? He was a lawyer, not some kind of biblical Moses.

"For years now, I've been trying to stop the tide, and I couldn't," he said. "It is my fear that newly made Dalí prints will be sold even in fifty years' time."

We looked one another in the eye.

I could see desperation, and resignation also.

"You're right, it stinks," he said. "But I don't think Dalí is the villain in all this."

"If not Dalí, who is?"

We talked about Captain Moore, who seemed to have secret warehouses all over France, Andorra, and Spain stocked with tens of thousands of blank sheets of lithographic paper, all bearing the familiar Dalí signature.

"A *genuine genuine* signature?" I asked.

The lawyer blushed. His face was red and sweaty. "I don't know," he said.

I felt beaten to a jelly. "This is a monstrous fraud," I said.

Was this the beginning? Or the end? Or the beginning of the end?

The previous year, American, European, and Japanese art dealers had printed and sold dubious Dalís to the amount of $1 billion wholesale. The Dalí name had become a license to print money.

"It's a spider's web encompassing the whole world," I said.

"I'm sorry to say that perhaps you're caught in the web," Dalí's American lawyer said.

"I am talking about the *Don Quixote* print," I said. "The design is an original 1940s surrealist work of art, illegally printed on 1960s Arches and Japon paper with a 1970s signature that is probably also a fake. It is advertised as a limited-edition hand-colored and numbered original, signed by the artist. In fact, as I understand it now, *Don Quixote* is none other than a cheap photomechanical reproduction worth perhaps five dollars or ten dollars at the most. A Xerox copy, basically. The artistic value of this material is zero. I've been taken for a ride. I bought mine from Pierre Schwartz. All six hundred of them."

"When was that?"

"A couple of months ago."

The lawyer sighed. "I don't know Pierre Schwartz. Never heard of him," he said.

"Dalí hand-signed the prints, he assured me."

"I can only tell you that exactly a year ago, on the fifteenth of February, 1980, Dalí fell ill and I am absolutely certain that he has signed nothing since. Not even a check or a bank draft."

"What can I do?"

I could shout. I could file a complaint.

"Why would you do anything? The police will probably

seize the print you've seen on Madison Avenue," the lawyer said. "The scandal will be all over the papers. Will that help Dalí? Will it help you?" I should clearly let sleeping dogs lie.

He was right, of course.

I was staying on the fourteenth floor—actually the thirteenth, *superstition!*—of the St. Moritz on the Park with a lovely view over Central Park. I dragged myself to my hotel and phoned Ana transatlantic, which wasn't easy at the time. It seemed as if the Spanish telephone system was still in its infancy.

"I've got something to tell you, Stán," Ana said.

"Do I already know about it?"

"No, you don't."

"Is it private? Is it about us?"

"It is. Very. You're listening?" she asked.

"Yes, Ana, I'm listening."

"You sure you're listening?"

"I am."

"You're sitting down?"

"No."

"Sit down."

"Okay. I'm sitting down."

"I think I . . . I'm pregnant."

"W—W—What did you say?"

"I'm pregnant, Stán."

"What? What did you say? Ana? There's a crack on the line."

"Lluis is on his way. Our son."

Bam! Knocked out.

I undressed and fell on my bed, crying silently. An hour or so later, I put the television on and phoned room service. While a cart was rolled into my room, a news flash on a local channel grabbed my attention. In the New Jersey warehouse of a respected art dealer, ten thousand obviously fake Chagall, Miró, Picasso, LeRoy Neiman—a popular American artist best known for his brilliantly colored images of sporting events—and Salvador Dalí prints were seized, confiscated, and incinerated. A police search of Captain Moore's home in Paris uncovered another ten thousand faked Dalí lithographs. Dumb and dazed like a sleepwalker, I opened the door and pushed the cart out, as far as I could. Behind my back, the door fell shut, and there I was, naked in the hotel corridor, in the middle or the day.

"Help! *Help!*" I shouted desperately, and again tears sprang from my eyes.

I had my first and only encounter with Andy Warhol in the old New York Coliseum Convention Center on Columbus Circle. He was there to sign a series of posters and screenprints such as *Guns, Dollar Sign,* and *Diamond Dust Shoes* and to announce a new print that would be published to commemorate the hundredth anniversary of the Brooklyn Bridge. Though it was still years before his death, the eyes in his bony face were already dead when I saw him. He was as thin as a fashion model. All the time he was chewing gum. His silver wig looked like a nylon broom turned upside down, glued sideways on his bald head and cut so badly that fluorescent strings were sticking out on every side. I didn't miss the opportunity and extended my hand. He looked at it without touching me. As if my hand were a dead fish. Andy Warhol never shook hands. I introduced myself.

"Gee . . . where are you from?" Andy asked.

"Belgium."

"Oh, Belgium. That's in Brussels, isn't it?"

"No, Andy, Brussels is the capital of Belgium."

"Gee . . . Belgium? Never heard of. Somewhere in Scandinavia, I guess."

He was so pale. He was a shy man, wearing jeans and a denim shirt. His shoes were unpolished. While he was talking, he restlessly signed whatever was held in front of him. Posters and screenprints and opening-night invitations or dollar bills and ties and handkerchiefs or the back of someone else's poster. When he bent over, I could see that it was not only FixAll but also a metallic snap embedded in the front part of his skull that held his wig in place.

"Andy, you know Dalí, don't you?" I asked.

"Gee . . . who told you?"

"Ultra Violet."

"Gee . . . yes! Ultra . . . she took me to one of Dalí's Sunday afternoon teas in the King Cole Bar."

"Where's that, Andy?"

"The St. Regis Hotel."

"That's where Dalí stayed when in New York, no?"

"Gee, yes . . . I guess."

"Dalí gave Sunday afternoon tea parties?"

"Oh yes! Right under the 1906 Maxfield Parrish mural. Parrish is one of my favorite artists, you know."

"No, I didn't know that."

'Well, it wasn't afternoon tea really. Dalí said the gathering was his Court of Miracles."

"That was every Sunday?"

"Gee . . . yes! Every Sunday from five P.M. to eight P.M. Happy hour, really. The guests indulged in pink champagne—Dalí had the champagne brought over from his native Ampurdán—but I don't drink alcohol."

"Can you describe Dalí to me, Andy. What did he look like, when he was here in New York?"

"Such a strange man." Warhol giggled and signed a crumpled dollar note someone handed to him. He sniffed his nose all the time, as if his sinus was blocked up. "Dalí wore a gold lamé jacket and blue suede shoes, like Elvis Presley. He was in the company of an elderly aristocratic Spanish lady and introduced her to me as . . . King Alfonso. There was a famous disco dancer, too, he was supposed to be King Alfonso's Crown Prince. Six P.M. sharp, Gala strode into the bar, arm in arm with an actor in a long-running Broadway musical."

"Did Gala say anything to you?"

"Oh . . . yes!"

"What did she say?"

"She introduced the actor. 'Andy,' she said, 'this is Jesus Christ Superstar*rr*.'"

"Did she speak English well?"

"Gee . . . awful. It sounded like Russian! Dalí gave her a

peck on the cheek while making a business proposition to me at the same time."

"What business proposition?"

"Dalí suggested we combine artistic forces and the two of us paint a triptych of three power-women who changed world history: Eva Braun, Clara Petacci, and Evita Perón."

Hitler married Eva Braun in the final days of the Third Reich, Clara Petacci was Mussolini's mistress, and Evita Perón became a legend after she married the Argentine dictator Juan Perón.

Andy Warhol giggled. " '*La* Petacci in the middle,' Dalí said, 'upside down and *muerta*, dead, the way she was hanging on the gallows next to Mussolini.' 'Oh gee . . . really,' I said, but Dalí was serious, I could see that. '*Sí! Sí! Sí!*' he shouted. 'Dalí will give you a *título: Super Whores of the XthXth Centurrry!*' "

"Dalí rolled his *r*'s, didn't he?"

"Gee . . . yes, he also didn't say 'twentieth century,' he said, 'XthXth.' Tenth tenth century. Well, his English wasn't good. Sounded like French to me."

"What happened then?"

Andy Warhol laughed with the sound of tinkling coins. "I asked Dalí what he was working on," he said.

"And?"

"Gee . . . he said he had painted Mao and Stalin portraits on Holy Host wafers so that you could eat and swallow them if . . . if you wanted to get rid of Mao or Stalin once and for all. I had my Polaroid with me and wanted to take Gala's photograph."

"Did you?"

" 'No photo Gala!' she screeched in Russian. They always seemed to screech and shout, Dalí and Gala."

"That was the end of the story?"

"Gee . . . I offered to exchange paintings, one of mine against one by Dalí, but Gala threw a fist at me. 'Neverrr! Neverrr!' she yelled. 'Warrrhol is photogrrrapherrr and Gala *hate* photos. Gala is neverrr photogrrraphed!' Anyway, they were just entertaining." His wig tilted. "Gee, Stan . . . Can I take *your* photograph?" Andy Warhol asked.

"Of me?"

"Uh . . . um . . . yes . . . sure. Why not?"

Clicking his Polaroid, Andy Warhol exclaimed, "Fab! Great!" His eyes were enormous and owl-like behind his glasses. Later I learned that he was nearly blind by this point.

Night had fallen when I got on the plane to Belgium—somewhere in Scandinavia, I guess, as Andy Warhol had said. Upon my return in my home country, angry investors were demonstrating in protest and shaking their fist at me at the MMC office in the President Building.

Punch-drunk and jet-lagged after a restless day of dozing and lying awake for hours, I got up, washed, shaved, went down for an extra-late breakfast, and walked straight into a group of ten or twelve uniformed policemen drinking coffee in my kitchen. Four more secret service agents holding shotguns were waiting for me in my luxury dining room. Adeline—my black housemaid from the Congo, I'm godfather to her only daughter—had let them in. They flashed gilded starlike badges pinned in their wallets. The agents wore stiff white shirts, dark suits, and black shoes, highly polished. I could smell their aftershave. They showed me a warrant for my arrest. On top of being jet-lagged, I suddenly had a splitting headache. The police handcuffed me and pushed me into the backseat of an unmarked patrol car.

I asked why I had been arrested.

The policeman driving the car shrugged. "Only the inspector knows, if he knows at all. It is our job to arrest you, and that's all we know. You could be a drug dealer, as far as we know. What have you got to sell? Six kilos of cocaine? Forty pounds of zero zero?"

"What is zero zero?"

"High-quality hashish, of course."

It was raining. Sirens screaming, the patrol cars sped through wet streets to the High Court of Justice—a nineteenth-century stone fortress—where I was bundled into a squalid interrogation room in the bowels of the courthouse. I was instructed to hand over my gold Cartier watch, my belt, shoelaces, my wallet with my passport and credit cards, and to empty my pockets. Steel handcuffs again. They were fastened to a boiling radiator. I couldn't help it; I was terrified and I was close to shitting my pants. The inspector leafed through my passport and furiously attacked the keyboard of an old semiautomatic Olivetti typewriter.

"What did you do before you worked as an art investment counselor?" he asked.

"Ever heard of *Panorama* magazine?" I replied. "I was their man in Hollywood."

". . . before that?"

"I made holes in cheese."

The inspector laughed his head off. "I see," he said, shaking uncontrollably, "you've always been selling hot air."

Two hours later, still handcuffed, I was led into the court-room.

Although they were a size too small and without laces, my shoes were too big for my feet.

"Is it true you sold nonexistent real estate in Dallas, Texas?" the examining magistrate asked.

"No, that's not true. That's a lie. I didn't. I never sold real estate."

"You sold no-good diamonds?"

"Again, no. I didn't."

The examining magistrate sighed. "I'll refresh your memory," he said. "Some of the diamonds your company sold, they turn out to be so-called blood or conflict diamonds. Illicitly mined stones from diamond mines in the Congo and Sierra Leone, smuggled into this country using fake invoices. The proceeds of their sale to your company may have been used to finance the arms trade and some of the most vicious tribal wars in Africa."

I honked with laughter, suddenly feeling relieved. "I had nothing whatsoever to do with any diamond or real estate sales," I said. "I can't be held responsible for everything MMC did, and I won't pay for its wrongdoing, I am an employee. An examining magistrate gets a salary at the end of the month, no? So do I."

"But you sold Dalí paintings, didn't you?"

"Yes."

"You admit to that?"

"Yes."

"*Fake* Dalí paintings?"

"I don't know about that. I bought them from Sotheby's and Christie's. International salesrooms. Or from Dalí's business manager. They were sold with an approved certificate of authenticity."

"MMC sold blood diamonds. The diamonds had certificates, too. I'll ask you again: Did you ever sell fake paintings?"

I shrugged. "Listen, Your Honor," I said, and the examining magistrate picked up his ears. "As far as I know, there are three kinds of Dalí paintings. The very best are what I would call *genuine genuine* Dalís. This is my own categorization, of course, *genuine genuine*, I don't vouch for any scientific accuracy. All *genuine genuine* Dalís—those paintings up to about 1940—are locked up forever and a day in the Museum of Modern Art in New York, in the London Tate Gallery or the Centre Pompidou in Paris. Some are in the Dalí Museum in Figueres and the Museo Nacional Reina Sofia in Spain. That's it. A typical Dalí painting in the early years was an admirable surrealist landscape of rocks and passing clouds, in wonderful shades of gray and lilac and earthly colors. The landscape was peopled with soft watches hanging over dead trees, like drooping Camembert cheese. His paintings were frozen nightmares. Every art expert in the world agrees that these *genuine genuine* Dalís are one hundred percent authentic, hand-painted by Dalí himself, no doubt whatsoever. On a second level, we have the *genuine fake* Dalís from the 1940s up to the late 1960s. I'll tell you something, Your Honor. While living in California in the 1940s, on the run from war in Europe, Dalí met Walt Disney. He visited Disney's cartoon studio and was truly amazed when he discovered that Walt Disney couldn't draw at all. His assistants did all the work. Dalí liked what he saw and created his own Disney-like Dalí factory. Therefore a *genuine fake* is a painting Dalí *might* have seen, or even touched, although in all probability it was entirely painted by studio assistants. Finally there's the overwhelming mass of *fake fake* Dalís, everything that has come on the market after 1972 and undoubtedly everything after February fifteenth, 1980, when Dalí fell ill. His New York lawyer is absolutely certain that the artist has signed nothing since, not even a check or a bank draft. You see, Your Honor? A *fake fake* Dalí is a painting, a drawing, a watercolor, a print, or a bronze sculpture Dalí himself probably doesn't even know exists. But is this *my* fault? Can *I* help it? I was only providing a financial service to high–net worth individuals, helping them recycle their cash capital. That's a hell of a job, since the number of high–net worth individuals worldwide is estimated at nine-point-five million."

"You knew all this, about *genuine genuine* and *genuine fake* and *fake fake* Dalís, when you sold your Dalí paintings to your investor clients?" the examining magistrate asked.

"I didn't *know*. I guessed. I had an inkling. I told you, Your

Honor, this *fake fake* business is my own classification. Perhaps it's a figment of my imagination."

"The signatures, were they genuine?"

I shrugged.

"A signature acts as a seal and a sign of authenticity and gives provenance to a document," the examining magistrate said.

"Try telling Dalí," I replied. "The man's got six hundred sixty-six different signatures."

"Why did you go on selling Dalís if you knew that much?"

Why?

What could I say? Money, of course. Hard cash in order to afford myself the lifestyle of the rich. My parkland villa with a black housemaid, two cars, winter vacations in Africa, my gold Cartier watch, five-star hotels, fancy shoes and suits made-to-measure, and other grandiose extravagances. Remember the hit song from *Cabaret*—the movie musical? *Money makes the world go around.* One day, I flew first class to New York, had a late lunch at Sardi's and an early dinner at Gallagher's Steak House and took the return evening flight back home.

"I admit, Your Honor, I am guilty of greed," I said. "If I sold fake Dalís, I sold them knowingly because I could turn them into good, honest money. But I can't be held responsible for the mass of Dalí fakes and forgeries flooding the art market. I'm not an artist. I can't sing, I can't dance, and I can't paint. I agree, there must be someone behind this. Some mad genius who is pulling the strings. Who? I don't know. Mafia, perhaps? Ku Klux Klan? Darth Vader? Who knows."

"You consider Dalí to be an *artist*?" the examining magistrate asked, and he threw me a mock smile. "Andy Warhol with his cans of Campbell's tomato soup, is he an artist? Picasso with a toilet pot upside down on his head? Are they *artists*? You must be joking. Rubens was an artist. That Italian fag who painted the *Mona Lisa,* what's his name again, he was an artist, too. I love the *Mona Lisa* smile. But—*Salvador Dalí*? Is he an artist? Where did you get that idea? He splashed pig's blood from a helicopter on a canvas. Instead of a paintbrush, he used a cauliflower. Dalí went to the Louvre to make a copy of a Vermeer painting and came back with a rhino horn painted on his canvas. That's not the work of an artist, if you ask me. That's the work of a jester. A clown."

No accounting for taste, I thought.

"Your Honor, have you ever heard of Duchamp?" I said. "Marcel Duchamp? The Frenchman? He was a forerunner of the surrealist movement. In 1917, Duchamp submitted a factory-made urinal to a fine art exhibition in New York under the title *Fountain.* The 1917 original got lost, whereupon Duchamp—in 1964, almost fifty years later—bought an identical copy of the same urinal in the same factory and signed it and dated it 1917. Today, the copy of the urinal is on display at the Centre Pompidou in Paris. It is valued at three-point-four million dollars. A urinal, Your Honor, is that art? What is art?"

The examining magistrate wasn't interested in my course of art history. "I've requested a detailed list of your American Express and Diners Club transactions," he said. "You're a high-flyer, aren't you? The best five-star hotels in London and Paris, lunch and dinner in the most expensive restaurants—El Bulli, Harry's Bar, you name them—and twice-monthly trips to Spain in business class. Who do you think has been paying for all this fancy stuff, in the end? Your clients, poor suckers. You're a crook, aren't you?"

His words landed like hammer blows on my head.

"No, Your Honor, I don't think I am," I said. "Perhaps I'm a charlatan. I'm an MMC employee first. I just want to talk about the facts. You can't refute the facts. Whatever I did, I did it for the good of the company."

The examining magistrate wouldn't buy it.

My parkland villa opposite the Middelheim Sculpture Park was confiscated. My furniture and my paintings, too. So were my cars, an Alfa Romeo and a sleek silver Citroën CX Prestige, the European car of choice for business executives and politicians. My known bank accounts were frozen. I was broke and bankrupt. I'd lost everything except my half-stuffed safe in a Spanish bank vault and my ingrained ability to think positive. Blood was dripping from my wrists. I wanted to get rid of the wretched handcuffs. My body ached and my head glowed, as if I had a temperature.

In a businesslike manner, the examining magistrate informed me that, for security reasons, he had to ask for my immediate and unconditional detention. I would be held in prison for a period of thirty-one days initially that could be extended thereafter. The maximum time period for which a person can be detained without trial was two full years. Blood drained from my body. My lips were cold. My limbs went numb. I was transferred from the courthouse to the city penitentiary and locked up in a police cell with one barred window. The stench of bleach and disinfectant was overwhelming and cut my breath. In those days, a prison cell was not a three-star hotel room, as it can be today. Gray concrete walls, no lavatory, no sink, no showers, no color television set, no fridge box, only a single 25-watt lightbulb, a metal bunk bed, a small wooden table, a wooden chair, a plastic shit pot, and a few books from the prison library. No blanket, no mattress, nothing. Steel, stone, and concrete.

I was a fox in a trap.

For the fox, the trap means death.

I felt empty and miserable. Perhaps I had to die before I could start living again. Such pain and anguish. I was thirty-nine years of age. Life had slipped through my fingers, like desert sand, and I had nothing to account for it. Behind every door I tried to open, another door remained tightly shut. I was desperate, truly desperate. My kidneys hurt and my brain sizzled. I had cut myself in so many pieces that even I found it impossible to puzzle it all together again.

The smell of homemade soup wafted through the prison corridors.

Suddenly I was hungry as hell. I banged the steel cell door. "Could I have a bowl of soup, please?" I shouted at the warden.

"What do you think this is? A Hilton Hotel?" he barked.

I slipped to the floor, my back against the hard, cold wall.

Alone in the dark, I listened to the unfamiliar night sounds.

Well past midnight. Time to take a long hard look at myself.

What was I guilty of? I had been loyal to my president. I adhered to MMC company policy. Is that a crime? Despite all the evidence to the contrary, I still didn't want to admit to myself that I had become a con man. A *nice* con man, well dressed, educated, and charming. A two-faced Jekyll-and-Hyde character, perhaps. I read the best books and saw the best films and dined in the best restaurants, but I also swindled and betrayed and conned and blackmailed my clients. Wait! Wait a moment! Where did *they* get *their* investment money from? The handbag manufacturer mass-produced dirt-cheap counterfeits with stitched fake labels and sold them in fancy boutiques as overpriced authentic designer Louis Vuitton and Chanel handbags. That's a crime. The butcher stuffed huge quantities of fat, flour, and sawdust into his so-called quality sausages. That's a crime, too. At least, the undertaker couldn't be blamed; he had the good Lord in Heaven on his side. But all the others? Always remember that every great fortune in the world is built on a life of crime, my president once told me. Are we all con men conning each other?

For me, prison was a rapid descent from heaven into hell, skipping purgatory, but it was also the quickest voyage to redemption ever. Perhaps for the first time in my life, I was forced to encounter my own limits as a human being. This was the price I had to pay for my avarice. Still, I was alive. Perhaps one day, I could start the difficult climb back to heaven, though time wasn't on my side. Was I getting old? I felt an ancient wreck, but thirty-nine is not *old*. Would I have enough buoyancy and willpower to start all over again? Who is the real villain in all this? I wondered. Was it Captain Moore? Monsieur Hamon? Pierre Schwartz? Was it me? The art world as a whole? Sotheby's? Christie's? Perhaps it was Dalí himself. None of my business, I thought. I'm fed up with art and artists and the art world. It's all make-believe. It's a masquerade. I want to regain my life and become anonymous. A shadow among shadows. Maybe I can go back to making holes in wheels of Emmentaler cheese and spend the rest of my days in the underground cold store.

Exactly two weeks after my arrest, I was released on a technicality. The examining magistrate—or a police officer, who knows?—had accidentally omitted a written interrogation from my legal file. That was a violation of my rights. An incomplete file is always an invalid file. I got my wallet back with my passport and credit cards and the small change out of my pockets, my gold Cartier watch, my shoelaces, and my leather belt. In no uncertain terms, I was instructed not to leave the country pending the upcoming trial. Prison gates opened, I pushed through the doors, dirty with grime, a free man again, though I'd lost the money in my bank accounts, my cars, my parkland villa, my Charles Eames and Le Corbusier furniture, even my dog and two cats. My fridge had been confiscated. I was as broke as could be. Couldn't even afford a train fare. I was ashamed of myself. I sneaked along the walls, like a thief in the night, and hid in McDonald's toilets. I didn't have a roof above my head and I didn't have a bed to sleep in. What was I going to do? I sneaked to my mother's house and knocked on the door. She didn't recognize me. We hadn't seen each other for fourteen years. I asked her if she could lend me some money. She declined. My lawyer said the examining magistrate had passed on my criminal file to Interpol. It had been sent out to the member countries—177 in all—who made up the international police organization. I was blacklisted. I could be arrested any time, any day, wherever in the world. If I wanted to board a plane, I had to produce my passport, and airport police would certainly lock me up. I couldn't stay in a foreign hotel unless I used someone else's name. Or a fake name. What could I do? My only possessions were the clothes I was wearing, a prison comb, a prison toothbrush, and three rolls of prison toilet paper. I needed money. I had to make a living. Was I going to be a small-time crook for the rest of my life? My lawyer had told me Ana had contacted him and offered to help. The streets were cold and wet with rain. I went into a hotel, and from the lobby, I called Ana in Spain.

I was over the moon when I heard her voice. "I'm out," I sighed.

"What are you going to do now?"

"I don't know. First, I need some money."

"You've got money. Here, in the bank. In your safe."

"Take it, it's yours."

"Why, Stán?"

"I can't come to Spain."

"Why not?"

"I'm not allowed to leave the country."

"How's the weather in Belgium?" Ana asked.

"Miserable," I said. "It's cold. It's raining."

"The sun is shining in Ampurdán," she said. "Nine o'clock at night and the sun is shining. It's been a hot day. Many more hot days to come. Sun is always shining in Spain, even at night."

"I'd like to sit in the sun. I'd like to enjoy the warmth of the sun. Prison was cold. Icy. I was numbed with cold."

"Remember that song Lluís Llach sang for us in the old Ampurdán Motel?" Ana asked.

"Sure. 'T'estimo.' *I Love You.* I'll never forget."

"T'estimo, Stán."

"I love you, too, Ana."

"Get over here *pronto*," she said. "Let's enjoy the sun. Together."

"I can't, Ana, I told you. I'm not allowed to leave the country."

"Find a way! Your son is kicking in my belly."

I asked my lawyer what I should do.

He nodded. "Get the hell out," he said.

Opposite the dark, imposing prison walls, there was a florist. I went in and bought fourteen red roses—one for each day of my detention—and asked a friend to drive me to Charles de Gaulle Airport near Paris, crossing the border along side roads and byroads, in an attempt to avoid border control at the motorway and close scrutiny of my passport. In Paris, I purchased an overnight bag, a pair of nail scissors, and a one-way ticket to Barcelona. I paid with American Express, then cut all my credit cards in half and threw the halves in a wastebasket, the nail scissors on top.

My plane crossed the Pyrenees and the Spanish border. Everything dark and still. Night fell. For me, though, the sun was already beginning to shine.

Suddenly I recalled a short dialogue I once read.

"Did you live a happy life?" the writer asked the Greek philosopher.

"It takes a lifetime to answer," Socrates replied.

I admit, I'd lived a happy life. But I was only halfway.

Part II

Avida Dollars

The red roses were for Ana, of course. We didn't get off to a good start once I arrived in Barcelona, though: she kept me waiting for more than two hours. Catalans are always late. That's what they call "Catalan jet lag"—everything is an hour or two behind the rest of the world. There I was, in Spain, pacing up and down Barcelona's El Prat Airport terminal, wondering whether she'd given up on me or not. I tried to phone her and let the phone ring a hundred times. No reply. I sat down at an all-night bar and had white wine, *patatas bravas,* and some tapas. The finger food tasted wonderful after two weeks of prison shit. I could see colorful posters everywhere. *Barcelona Més Que Mai.* "Barcelona More Than Ever." Was it a coincidence that Dalí's American lawyer was gesticulating in a nearby phone booth? Or was he spying on me? That's what happens when you get out of prison.

You become paranoid.

In all probability, he was only trying to set up an appointment with his client.

When Ana finally arrived, damp still from a late-night shower, the airport terminal was deserted. The lights had been dimmed, and huge robotlike machines were polishing the marble floors.

"Let's drive around," Ana suggested. "A little moonlight spin."

Excellent idea. I wasn't tired, just anxious, and I readily agreed.

We got off the motorway at Lloret de Mar and took the scenic Ampurdán inland route. I rolled the side window down and listened to crickets and the hoarse croaking of frogs and the melancholy cry of a night owl. While we passed it, church bells high up in Girona Cathedral chimed the midnight hour. A million stars above and a landscape of maddening beauty beneath, dusted with the crimson-tinged, fragrant smell of white jasmine, which is the voluptuous perfume of Spanish nights. In every village we passed, on the Ramblas, grizzled men sat on benches, in groups of two and three, smoking Ducados, made from the blackest Spanish tobacco.

Ana's yellow Ford Fiesta wobbled up and down the steep, narrow spiral road that clings to the side of the Black Mountain in between the villages of Rosas and Cadaqués. Here was the otherworldly lunar landscape of Cap de Creus National Park, with its rosemary hedges, vines, olive groves, gray slate, and bizarre volcanic rock formations. On a nearby hilltop above the sea, rising up from the transparent Mediterranean, I noticed candles flickering in a hacienda trimmed in the pink and purple of delicate, deeply colored bougainvillea, spilling over the whitewashed walls of the villa house, the swimming pool a patch of emerald lit by myriad underwater spotlights. The hacienda stood in isolation, all calmness and peace, a stark silhouette against a background of wonderfully dark green mountainside studded with wild olives and almond trees. The cloudless sky was just a shade darker than the hazy slice of the Mediterranean.

There was a sign at the roadside by the villa house. SE VENDE, it said, "FOR SALE." That much Spanish I knew. I got out of the car and walked up to the hacienda, tramping my way past sharp curves, through bushy undergrowth and thorny thistle and nettles. I thought about the tiny prison cell I'd left only days before and almost cried my heart out. There I was, on top of a mountain, inhaling the pure fresh night air that came wafting from the wild, unspoilt Pyrenees nearby. Out in the sea, I could see wind-beaten islands and the search beams of a lighthouse that lit the night twice every ten seconds. The landscape was idyllic, erotic, and miraculously beautiful. I was alive again.

"I'm gonna buy this house, Ana," I said.

"You see the village down there?" she replied. "That's Cadaqués where Salvador Dalí and Gala first met, in 1929, when Gala came here on vacation."

"I . . . I'm so happy," I said.

"What will you do for a living, Stán, if you stay in Spain?"

"I'll write a book and make love to you from dawn to dusk and through the night till morning."

"You won't have time to write your book."

In daylight, everything was different. Dead rats and families of croaking frogs and lizards floated in the four corners of the swimming pool. Seabirds were wheeling above. Where the Pyrenees met the sea, on the easternmost part of the Costa Brava, the rugged mountains with their sharp curves and idyllic coves looked inviting and menacing at the same time. The scrubby headland was pocked by bizarre sculptural rock formations. I wasn't bothered. In fact, I liked it like that. The place couldn't be further from my ordinary life. No FBI agent or undercover Interpol detective would ever find me on top of a dark, bush-covered mountain in this faraway corner of the world. The villa house was fully furnished and decorated in style, with Spanish antiques, flowery chintz-type bamboo sofas, a well-equipped kitchen, and an open fireplace. There were two bedrooms. I needed a roof above my head, and I'd found my roof. From my contacts in the village, I learned that Gabriel García Marquez had once lived in Cadaqués, as well as the widow of the man who wrote *The Little Prince*—the world's bestselling book— Antoine de Saint-Exupéry. Orson Welles and Ava Gardner lived in the village at other times. Could anyplace on earth be better than Cadaqués for a fugitive from justice? On the hill opposite my hacienda, I noticed the ruins of a castle with a bell tower. They were the last remains of the old medieval kingdom of Catalonia. This is paradise, I told myself. Even though it will soon be winter—the cold, cruel, and harsh Catalan winter— this will always be paradise. We'll be merry here. Don't worry about winter. After every winter comes another spring and a hot summer. A local estate agent handed me the key to the hacienda in return for half a bucket of the investors' money that I had stashed away in a Barcelona bank vault.

Sadly, the weather soon changed. The next couple of days turned out to be chilly with a clear blue sky. Nights were cold and dark and full of whispers. The gentle breeze was turning into a strong wind that was razor-sharp and tingled my face. In between valleys and past the rocky headland, over the top of the hills, I could see the ripple of the sea, whitecaps on the waves, and an old yellow fishing boat lying upside down on the crescent pebble bay. The blinding light of the white sun was so sharp, it hurt my eyes.

My new house hadn't been lived in for some time and needed work done. It was humid inside. I cleaned the rooms, rearranged the furniture, and replaced light fittings, bought new toilet seats and cups and saucers and threw away dirty cutlery, stained linen sheets, and moth-eaten blankets and floor tapestries. I also installed a brand-new kitchen. Day and night, I poked the open fire. The house wasn't really a villa; it had more the feel of a small Spanish-style hacienda, with a gallery of bow-arches under the roof that gave patches of shadow and a turret with winding stairs I intended to turn into a library.

Interior walls were decorated with colorful Arabian scenes from *One Thousand and One Nights* including "Ali Baba and the Forty Thieves" and "The Seven Voyages of Sinbad the Sailor" in gilt frames. My hacienda was perched on top of the mountain. The next house was down at the foot, where the deep-blue sea licked and caressed the bay that engulfed the magical and mysterious Ampurdán landscape. In between myself and the house at the foot, there was nothing but shrubs, coves, thorny undergrowth, nettles, thistle, and the trunk of a dead olive tree that looked like a crutch. At night, down in the village of Cadaqués, neon signs of bars and restaurants could be read, bright as the lights in a pinball machine. Car headlights chased one another along the coastal roads, and the silhouettes of passing fishing boats were recognizable in every detail.

While I collected dead wood around the house, Ana went shopping in the narrow medieval streets of Cadaqués. She came back with bread, butter, cornflakes, toasted rice cereal, milk, and ground coffee—lots of milk and even more coffee—and a car trunk full of bottled water. She'd also brought sunglasses and a single bottle of pink champagne—well, *cava* actually, *cava* is Catalan for "cellar"—from the nearby Perelada winery.

"Are you hoarding up?" I asked.

Ana merely smiled.

Suddenly the sun sank behind the mountains, its purple rays crawling over the landscape, while huge dark clouds drifted over the valley, covering the slopes in shadow. It looked as if the horizon were a blazing, burning fire.

Day for night is the name of a movie technique in which a crew films with a blue filter in early morning or late afternoon. As a result, the film appears to have been shot at night. Here it was in front of my eyes, day for night, *la nuit américaine,* without even a film crew on hand. The fierce wind rattled the wooden shutters. The sky was piled high with clouds, and the crisp air had a sulfuric smell.

A flash and then a *bang! bang!* and all overhead lights dimmed and went out.

"*Madre de Diós!* The tramontana!" Ana said, and crossed herself.

"What's the matter?" I asked.

"Northern wind," she whispered. "The devil is angry. He's blowing his breath at us."

She started barricading the house, putting chairs and cupboards against the doors on the inside and inserting metal poles in front of the windows—they reminded me of prison bars—and nailing the shutters firmly in place.

I didn't understand.

"For God's sake, Ana, what are you doing?" I asked.

"The tramontana will drive us insane," Ana said. "Tramontana is just another word for going bonkers. Josep said that, didn't he?"

"Which tramontana?"

"The one that's coming."

"When?"

"Who knows? Tonight? Tomorrow morning. The wind is picking up. Dark clouds move in."

I sighed. Yes, I clearly remembered what Josep and Ana told me in Agullana. When he was a boy, Dalí went up on the roof as soon as the tramontana started blowing. He was seen conducting the wind, in his nightgown, baton in hand, like a conductor whipping and cheering his orchestra. Is Dalí mad? Josep had asked. If he is, it is because of the tramontana, like Lydia the Madwoman from Port Lligat who was also a sad victim of the tramontana.

I heard a monotonous rumble in the far distance, a pounding, as if the belly of the mountain were grumbling. The sky turned to a mix of black and bloodred stripes, the colors of the devil, and the rumbling and grumbling lasted several hours. Dead birds dropped out of the sky. It got frightfully cold. We poked the fire and bundled ourselves into one of the flowery sofas for an agonizing night. At sunrise, the wind lifted the garden furniture off the ground and blew it over the roof. The strong, cold, downslope wind reached force 8 on the Beaufort scale, bringing about a gale warning. I looked through chinks and cracks in the barricaded windows and saw cars zigzagging and veering on the mountain road and plunging in the canyon. The sea at the foot of the mountain lashed into a fury. The tramontana wind raised waves up to three meters in the anchorage, with considerable spray, and foamed the rock reefs in the little bays and open creeks and underwater tunnels.

I thought it had started raining. A cold, powdery drizzle.

"No, not rain," Ana said. "That's sea dust."

It was just the prelude to the most violent storm I've ever witnessed.

Wave crests started to roll over.

Finally, after two days and three nights—the longest days and nights of my life—the relentlessly pounding and howling wind died down. Again the wrinkled hills turned back into a miraculously beautiful, almost cubist landscape. More dead rats and live lizards were obstructing the swimming pool, plus a gathering of driftwood and tumbleweed. My garden furniture was smashed to pieces. So was the steel transmission tower of anticommunist Radio Free Europe over on the next mountaintop. We had endured sleepless nights and withstood the days on a diet of cornflakes and stale bread and gallons of milk and coffee and urgently needed to stock the larder. We're lucky, I thought, Cadaqués is famous for its salted anchovies. Let's stock anchovies next time.

Ana took the sparkling wine from the fridge. Brut Rosado. There had been power failures for hours, and the bottle wasn't cold. She said she wanted to congratulate me, since I had endured my first tramontana. That's why she bought the bottle, I thought. To celebrate. I was wrong.

"Dress up, Stán," she said.

I had only my prison clothes.

"Dress up? Why? Because we're going to have champagne?"

"No, *we're* not drinking."

"What are we going to do?"

"We're paying a visit to our neighbor. That's what new arrivals do in Ampurdán; they offer their credentials."

"Which credentials? I was in prison, Ana. I'm in hiding."

"He won't mind."

"Who?"

"Our neighbor."

In the day's failing light, we struggled through the dense undergrowth of thistle and nettles, on a winding path littered with broken flint and dead birds. We stumbled along for twenty minutes, all the way down to the tiny fishing village of Port Lligat around the bend in the bay, north of Cadaqués, past an eerie cemetery. The sun was setting behind the mountains. It was rapidly getting dark, and we hadn't brought a flashlight.

The landscape opened up onto a bleak coastline, waves quietly lapping on the shore. Fishing boats were jumbled on the beach. A chamber orchestra was piping a *sardana* on a tenora, a tible, and a flabiol, as those typical Catalan clarinets are called. Three white swans drifted lazily on the water. Each swan had a burning candle on its back. There was only one house, so to speak. It certainly wasn't a traditional house, more like an assemblage of tiny white-stuccoed chalk-and-plaster fishermen's cabins or cottages, each room hardly three by four yards and built on top of the other, like a beehive, and merged into a labyrinthine structure. In the half dark, I could distinguish the faint contours of a dunghill next to the cottages. It looked like a sculpture with outstretched arms and legs. An overgrown cypress tree was sticking out of the hull of an old and stranded rowboat nearby. A rusty bicycle without tires was chained to a tree. The house was topped with two giant white egg-shaped boulders on the uppermost roof and surrounded by gnarled olive trees. It seemed the most extravagant house I had ever seen.

Ana rang the bell. After about three minutes, a little old wrinkled housemaid with a cane, dressed in black woolly tights on her swollen legs, opened the low, narrow entrance door and flung her arms in the air.

"Ana?" she cried. "*Qué tal?*"

They hugged and kissed, like old friends.

"Stán?" Ana said, and rolled her chestnut eyes. "This is Señora Paquita."

Señora Paquita's hair was dyed the color of coal. She looked like a reel of black cotton.

We were standing in a corridor of red church tiles. It wasn't a corridor really, not long and narrow but very low and almost square, with an old windup telephone on a round table and the skin of a tiger—a *fake* skin—on the floor and dried flowers and potpourri in a corner next to an antique cupboard. The room was elegant and tasteful. There were no paintings on the wall, only a dusty crossbow and some framed black-and-white photographs. There were more dried flowers and potpourri and a stuffed owl on top of the antique cupboard, next to a stuffed white polar bear, life-size and moth-eaten, and a rack of silver walking canes. Seven steps covered with colored straw matting were leading to an open door upstairs that gave out into a kitchen. Next door was the dining room, but there was no door. I could see domestic furniture: a long low table in dark hardwood and a low wooden bench. There were unlit candles on either side of the table. In the dining room, the floor was covered with dark brown sisal mats woven into a pattern of rectangles. There was a poster pinned on the wall above the table. It depicted an elegant bullfighter in a gold-colored suit of lights. EXTRAORDINARIA CORRIDA DE TOROS EN HOMENAJE A SALVADOR DALÍ, read the heading beneath the bullfighter on the giant poster. In a flash, I recognized the poster as the same one I had seen in Ana's house in Agullana. The rooms we were standing in were low and incredibly tiny, with steps and stairs and alcoves, and the original design—two shacks on the pebble beach, a mere two rooms, one shack a kitchen and a toilet, the other a bedroom and studio, twenty-one square meters of floor space under a collapsed roof—could still be seen in the overall layout.

"Señora Paquita is Dalí's housekeeper," Ana said. "Her husband is Arturo Caminada. He was a hairdresser, long ago. The only hairdresser in Cadaqués. Her husband works for Dalí."

"Everyone in Cadaqués works for Señor Dalí. All his life, my husband has been Señor Dalí's jack of all trades," Señora Paquita whispered. "His chauffeur, his handyman . . . his manservant."

"Yes, Mama told me," Ana said.

"How is your mother, Ana?"

"Good. Very healthy. Cross fingers, Señora Paquita. She lives in Barcelona now."

". . . and your father?"

"My father died, some years ago. Cancer, you know."

It was cold in the house. Señora Paquita told Ana the heating wasn't working. The boiler had broken down, and there were no funds for repairs.

Salvador Dalí was sitting in a wheelchair on top of the seven steps covered with colored straw, half into the kitchen, as if he'd been expecting us, in a white flowing nightrobe that covered his legs and the chair's wheels. It looked as if he wasn't sitting in a wheelchair but rather on a kind of throne, his feet resting on a low footstool. He wore white socks and sandals. Old medals and ribbons were stitched to his robe. His famous waxed mustache was gray now, almost white, drooping and misshapen. He was balding. What was left of the hair on his head was gray, too, dirty or greasy, with straggling ends up to his shoulders. His stomach was swollen, as if he were pregnant. His left hand, large and limp, rested on his swollen stomach, while his right arm shook from shoulder to wrist. His lower lip dangled, and his once-bulging fish eyes were matte and milky, like frosted glass. They stared straight ahead.

I was shell-shocked. I could hardly breathe. Less than a week ago, I was in a Belgian prison, charged with selling *fake fake* Dalís and stealing my client's money. Now here I was, in his own house in Spain, face-to-face with Salvador Dalí himself, my only neighbor for miles around. I had my house on the hilltop, he lived in the only house at the foot of the hill, and there was nothing in between but vines, olive groves, volcanic rock, and gray slate.

I couldn't believe it. Salvador Dalí was my only neighbor.

I looked around. There was no bread glued to the walls. Old jacket buttons were no longer attached to the ceiling.

"M—M—Maestro . . . ," I heard myself stammering. "Maestro."

Like a fog, the sour smell of his unwashed body drifted through the house.

Ana mounted the seven steps and put the Perelada Brut Rosado in his lap.

Dalí didn't take her hand. He didn't kiss it theatrically. He did nothing of the sort. He didn't do anything at all. He just sat there.

"Thank you, Ana," Señora Paquita said. "You remembered. How good of you." She smiled and said to me, in Catalan, while Ana translated: "Years ago, pink *cava* from the castle of Perelada was his favorite drink. But Señor Dalí doesn't drink anymore. He doesn't eat either. His health is deteriorating rapidly. Poor old man. Since Gala moved out of the house, and died, Señor Dalí has lost his will to live. Sometimes he sleeps all day; at other times he crawls the floor like a giant snail." Again she smiled, remembering something. "Two summers ago, we walked to the beach," she said. "Isidro Bea and Young Dalí were pushing Dalí's wheelchair. Six fishermen walked by, carrying a coffin on their shoulders. Dalí comforted the grieving widow and her family; he then turned to us and said, 'I'm lucky, I won't die today because someone else has died already.' "

I'd never heard a more surrealist one-liner before.

Dalí gave no sign of life while Señora Paquita told this story.

He looked like a replica of himself in a wax museum. As if he had died already.

Who is Isidro Bea? I wondered.

Who is Young Dalí?

"Dalí's mustache . . ." I asked, "What happened to Dalí's famous mustache?"

Suddenly his eyes moved and he began to speak. You could see that he suffered and tried to concentrate. Señora Paquita put her ear to his mouth, almost touching his lips. She patted his limp hand. The only sound I could hear was some tired gurgling in the back of his throat. It sounded like water boiling over. Salvador Dalí was very tired; I could see that. He had to be left alone.

Slowly Ana and I walked back toward the door. Ana turned and blew him a kiss. There was not a flicker of emotion on Dalí's stone face. Spittle was dripping from his mouth. His lips moved. Dalí spoke slowly. No, he didn't speak. He gargled, in Catalan.

"What does he say?" Ana asked Señora Paquita.

"He says his name is Salvador Dalí and *that* is the worst of all illnesses!"

Dalí gargled again.

Señora Paquita rolled her eyes. "Señor Dalí is in a delirium," she said in Catalan.

"Did you get that?" I asked Ana.

"*Sí!*"

"What did he say, then?"

"It's all gibberish."

Slumped in his wheelchair, suddenly the most famous painter alive started howling like a wild animal, moaning and groaning, and his old hands that looked like claws scratched at the air. I noticed that his long fingernails were dirty, sharp, and as menacing as knives.

Señora Paquita had tears in her eyes. Ana, too. In a corner, I noticed a wooden kitchen chair with driftwood and starfish glued to the legs. A convex mirror in the dining room reflected the whole scene. There were bottles of white Martini and Spanish brandy on a shelf. A cricket was chirping in a tiny cage.

"I'm sorry, Señor Dalí is tired, it's time for you to go," Señora Paquita whispered.

"You remind me of my grandmother, Paquita," Ana said as we took our leave.

We silently climbed the hazardous path to our hilltop. In the faint moonshine, the Mediterranean had the silvery color of dancing mackerel. The knife-sharp stone and hard rock underneath had left my shoes in tatters. I wasn't equipped for climbing mountains; I was used to walking the streets of New York and London and Paris. Hell, I even didn't have a spare suit or a tie anymore, only a pair of Spanish jeans, counterfeit presumably, some T-shirts and Lacoste polos in bright colors. Yet my head was buzzing with excitement. If I had lived on the mountaintop fifty years earlier, not Salvador Dalí but Lydia the Madwoman would have been my only neighbor. Proud cypresses filled the sky and scented the night air. In the far distance, the bell tower tolled the midnight hour. The seaside and mountain landscape were a strange wilderness of wind-sculpted rocks and broken gravestones sunk halfway into the rocky ground, all looking remarkably like a Dalí masterwork.

Days later, hailstones and strong winds again lashed the Mediterranean into a fury. To the north, the mountaintops of the Pyrenees were dusted with snow. Clouds were drifting by fast. The thin mountain air cut like a blade. *Another* tramontana on the way.

As if to add to the difficulties, I received a letter from the examining magistrate informing me that in my home country, I had been convicted for fraud, in absentia, and sentenced to two years in prison. An extradition request was filed through Interpol. My brain sizzled. I was dizzy, as if I'd been drinking too much, and wanted to get out. I needed some distraction. Ana noticed my thoughtful gaze in the bedroom mirror. She had bought a bottle of pink Perelada Brut Rosado sparkling wine for Dalí, and I told her I wanted to explore Perelada. Ana warned me that Perelada is not a town, not even a village. It's just a vineyard, that is to say, a *castillo* surrounded by lush gardens. Still, I insisted, and she promised to get me in on one of their famous surrealist nights in the castle's bodega. Wind howled and thunder rumbled and a black screen of overlapping clouds positioned itself in between the Pyrenees and the churning sea, like a wall of steel. The bottom of my pool was covered with dead rats, inches of yellow beach sand, and broken shells. The bell high up in the ruins of the bell tower tolled all through the night.

See that hill, glowing in the sun? See those pink houses? That is Perelada, Salvador Dalí wrote in his diary on June 15, 1920. He was sixteen years of age. The outside of the gorgeous fourteenth-century Perelada castle—a walled enclosure that was once a Carmelite convent in the rolling Ampurdán hills—was painted all-pink, like the famous Spanish Chupa Chup lollipops that are sold in sweetshops the world over. According to legend, the lush Perelada gardens were designed by a French architect who also worked on the Palais de Versailles garden and forest. Though it had rocks and streams, too, and a vast collection of outdoor sculpture, Perelada was more modest than the Versailles grounds. I know now that every town, every village in Spain has its own peculiar smell. Here, even the pink night sky and millions of glittering stars truly smelled like *cava,* the local *champán* from grenache grapes harvested in the vineyards where the tail end of the Pyrenees plunges into the Mediterranean. Ana had managed to get an invitation for a surrealist evening show in the *taberna* of the Perelada castle where an all-night dinner party with music and dance would be held in honor of Salvador Dalí. I didn't know whom or what to expect. That night, Amanda Lear was the star of the show.

As is customary in Spain, where no one ever dines—or even lunches—on his own, Ana had invited some friends, Hernán Cortés—not the conquistador of the Americas—and his wife, as well as two rally-racing brothers who were to compete in the famous off-road desert race known as the Paris–Dakar Rally. Except for me, everyone in the *taberna* was chain-smoking and talking as loudly as possible. Late-night dinner guests littered the bar, eating tapas as if there were no tomorrow. They all had bad haircuts. Lots of counts, margraves, viscounts, and capitalist Texas yokels on holiday, with more oil money than brains. A professional string quartet played chamber music.

The local *cava* was off-dry, fruity, and fresh, with a pale shrimp color. I don't normally drink that much. After a few drops, I could see stars, a rainbow, and fireworks, and I thought I was happy.

"Do we celebrate?" Hernán asked.

"Yes," I said curtly.

"What shall we drink to?"

"My life in prison," I said.

Under the table, Ana stamped my foot. She sensed something was wrong. "*Cariño*, are you okay, sweetheart?" she asked.

I forced a smile.

I'm a fugitive, I thought. Two years in prison. That's over seven hundred days and nights. What am I doing here, drinking champagne, enjoying myself?

"You seem pensive," Hernán said.

"I'm fine."

The stench of bitter Spanish tobacco filled my nostrils and ruined my lungs.

Then, like an explosion, a mustachioed figure burst into the *taberna,* his bright red Catalan cap or *barretina* raised, his fish eyes rolling, a Salvador Dalí impersonator or body double or look-alike who was none other than Amanda Lear in person. She was twenty thousand volts of energy. Looking smart and sexy in a white shirt and evening jacket with tails, the disco queen of Europe and icon of the gay nightclub circuit jumped on a medieval wooden table, surrounded by fans lusting after her. I knew she was a media phenomenon—she was on the cover of *Marie France* and *Elle* magazine—and I could see and sense that she was a survivor. The years seemed to have slipped by her, like water on the feathers of a duck. In the late sixties and early seventies, when her circle of friends included David Bowie, Marianne Faithfull, Brian Jones and Keith Richards of the Rolling Stones fame, she had been Salvador Dalí's "official" muse and close companion, but to be honest, though she was still striking, less than ten years later, Amanda Lear was a fading star.

A team of assistants carried the world's longest baguette into the tavern and then began to break off pieces of bread and distribute them among the late-night dinner guests.

"Greetings, my disciples!" Amanda Lear said in a husky, guttural baritone. Her perfume was an old American fragrance called Jungle Gardenia, ideal for casual wear. "It is I, Salvador, which means the 'savior' in Spanish. Indeed, Salvador is your Redeemer. Welcome to his Last Supper! Salvador! Salvador! Salvador! I could repeat the name tirelessly. You will eat this bread which is Dalí's body and drink this soup which is Dalí's blood!"

Waiters placed a giant bowl of fish soup in the middle of the table.

Amanda Lear walked the table and dropped a sponge in the

soup and then, surprisingly, she stuck her hand with her long red fingernails in the bowl, took the dripping sponge out of it and squeezed a serving of fish soup on my and everyone else's plate.

Ana and I watched in amazement.

"Drink! Dalí's! Blood!" Amanda Lear roared.

She didn't roll her *rrr*'s, as Dalí did.

At least ten waiters in a long row brought in covered plates, and in unison, they whisked away the silver domes. On each plate rested an individual can of sardines in olive oil, already opened, and each of the tiny fish was dyed red.

Dinner was served in eight courses. Each course was dyed a different color. Cured ham was a poisonous green. Like the sardines, broccoli was red. Salad was pink, and a vanilla custard dessert of *crema catalana* was a watery blue. Flutes were refilled with local champagne that turned from pink to purple and finally to black.

Ana's eyes were sparkling. "I wonder what color the check will be," she said.

"Hey . . . shut the fuck up!" a Texas yokel said.

There were imitation surrealist objects all over the tavern. Paintings, drawings, prints, sculpture, jewelry. The artworks— not copies, just Dalí imitations—were Amanda Lear's own imitations. A large unframed painting, covered with a dropcloth, sat on an easel. She jumped up from the table to unveil the painting. It looked like a Dalí portrait on canvas, a detail only, part of his nose, half of his famous mustache and his left eye, wide open.

"Brilliant!" Amanda Lear shouted. "This painting reflects all the different meanings you can attach to the word *painting*. Forget the dictionary. The dictionary needs to be completely redone, and I am in the process of redoing it because there isn't one definition about art you can rely on. I diluted my paint with the sweat of a thousand honeybees and the poison of a thousand wasps. Have a good look at this painting and sleep with confidence." Without blinking an eye, she gave her own fake mustache Dalí's trademark twist and disappeared behind the curtain while racks of raw cow carcasses on wheelbarrows were wheeled into the tavern.

"Amanda Lear is a transsexual," an American at our table said. "She's man-turned-woman."

"How do you know? She's gorgeous!"

"Gorgeous transsexuals. That's how Dalí liked them."

I thought about it. It's true that Dalí always claimed he had the nagging suspicion that Amanda was a boy. He even hinted at a sex operation, carried out in Casablanca. But Amanda later denied this and said it was all just a publicity stunt.

Later that night, Amanda Lear was billed to perform in the casino adjacent to the castle. She came on stage, all long legs, black leather, and whip. In a deep, masculine voice, she belched her seventies hits.

"Amazing . . . she's just amazing," Ana said.

The American tourist was dressed like a cowboy. John Wayne in *The Alamo*. He was smoking a large Cuban cigar. "You know what God said to Adam after he ate the apple?" he asked with a Texan drawl.

"No."

"God said, 'I told you not to trust that bitch. '"

Everyone laughed drunkenly.

I said I didn't understand.

"Oh, excuse me," his wife said seductively. "Eve *begged* Adam to bite the apple."

I still didn't understand.

"Who owns the paintings and sculptures over there, on the far wall?" the Texan asked.

"Why do you want to know?" I said.

"My wife loves paintings. She used to spend her money on her wardrobe. When the clothes stopped fitting, she turned to art."

"I want something smart to hang on my walls," the Texan's wife said.

I shrugged and said, "Don't you see? They're all Salvador Dalí. What you see is a once-in-a-lifetime show from private European collections." I had to be careful. Could I still use or abuse the J. Paul Getty name, as I had done so often before? Perhaps not. Perhaps be smart and use someone else who is rich beyond anyone else's wildest dreams. "Christina Onassis was here a couple of days ago. That's all I can tell you," I said with a sad smile.

"Come on, partner. I can keep a secret."

I sighed. "Well, she . . . she . . ."

"She bought everything? Isn't that right?"

"I'm afraid so, yes."

"Cash?"

"No. She made an offer, technically speaking."

The cowboy was getting drunk. "We didn't ride all this way to go home with a case of duty-free bourbon," he said vehemently. "Christina Onassis made an offer? That's okay with me; I'll make mine. It's as simple as that."

"I don't know. This is highly unethical," I said. "An offer is an offer . . . and besides, I had no idea art was so popular in Texas."

"New money loves old art," the Texan's wife said.

I nodded patiently. "You know," I said, "in addition to the aesthetic pleasure, there's an investment opportunity attached to Dalí's work."

"Like what?"

"Dalí isn't going to live forever."

"Big deal," the Texan said. "I ain't gonna live forever. Who lives forever?"

"What I mean is . . . when Dalí dies, the market value of his work will increase substantially."

I could have sold him the Perelada castle, if I had wanted to.

Most of all, it pleased me that I hadn't unlearned the old tricks. Yes, I could still pull them, if I wanted to. Perhaps one day . . .

Champagne bottles popped.

"Stán, what do *you* think of Amanda's paintings?" one of the racing brothers asked, sleepy-eyed.

"I like them better than the green ham or the dyed sardines."

"Was Amanda Lear *really* Dalí's lover?" asked Ana.

I shrugged. "I doubt it," I said. "Something must have flipped in Dalí's head. A man who has *normal* sexual relations with a man or a woman—*any* woman—doesn't make that kind of artwork."

"True," Ana said, "but perhaps Amanda Lear isn't just any man or woman."

After a while, Hernán suggested we leave. "If you like, Stán, you and Ana can stay overnight at our place. We have a guest room. Breakfast coffee is for free."

"I don't even know where you live."

"In Figueres," his wife replied. "Opposite Dalí's museum. When you wake up in the morning and draw the curtains, you can touch the thousands of sculptured loaves of bread on its outer walls that are topped with giant eggs. From our guest room, just like that."

There was no escaping Salvador Dalí.

"Thank you, Hernán. Some other time maybe."

"This was an eventful evening," Ana said as we walked to the exit.

There were a few flurries of snow in the air. Where had *those* come from? It was dark and cold. A fierce wind was blowing hard yet again. I could almost imagine Dalí on his rooftop, wearing his full-length white flowing nightshirt, conducting the music of the wind. There were tears in my eyes. Sad tears because of the memories lost, good or bad, but also tears of joy and happiness. I was over the moon, but perhaps all happiness is only temporary.

In the weeks that followed my first tramontana, between the bleached-out rocks, under the big sky and elongated clouds, I felt lost and lonely. I didn't know where to go or what to do. I missed Paris and London and New York. I missed the Cipriani and the George V and the St. Moritz on the Park. I longed for the adventurous life I'd lived all those years. I missed the beautiful people with their elegant shoes and the hubbub in Sotheby's and Christie's salesrooms. I missed the sales paddles. I missed my daily paper and the Sunday papers. I missed the smell of international coffeehouses and tearooms. Above all, I missed the surge of adrenaline in my blood whenever I was cheating or deceiving or swindling investors, and I missed the thrill—or call it delirium—of counting out their hard-earned or ill-gotten money and transferring it to my own pocket. I also felt remorse. Yes, I did feel remorse. I truly did. Whenever I looked in the mirror, I still recognized the charming, mischievous, and destructive traits of the swindler in my face. As long as those traits were there, I wasn't cured and as long as I wasn't cured, I was guilty as hell.

I was trying to become a better man, but the simple truth is that I also missed the kick of danger and adventure. I felt boxed in. I was in hiding, and the mountain was becoming my prison. Although I had a giant dish antenna installed, so that I could watch CNN and the French channels on television and have some contact with the outside world, I was scratching out the days and weeks on my imaginary prison wall. To keep myself busy, I vacuumed the bedrooms for the tenth time, rinsed and flushed the toilets twice daily with bleach, washed the kitchen floor twice a day, scaled the bathroom tiles with an old toothbrush, and peeled potatoes in between, for I had a problem there: every Spanish housewife is an excellent cook—except Ana.

She was sitting on our bed, painting her toenails.

Julio Iglesias on the radio, in a smash duet with Diana Ross.

"Help! Stop the world!" I shouted. "I want to get off!"

It didn't happen.

"You've come a long way, baby," Ana said.

"Because of you."

The pregnancy was showing. I was proud of Ana. She looked radiant.

"Will you marry me?" she asked.

"I'd love to, Ana, but I can't—you know I can't. Not now. I'm still a fugitive."

Lost in thought, I walked down through the amorphous olive groves to the edge of the water.

That old wreck of a man I'd met, slumped in his wheelchair, was he indeed the mad genius of modern art? Was he the wizard who turned whatever he touched into gold? Who designed shirts, ties, cognac bottles, calendars, ashtrays, stamps, bathing suits, oyster knives, tapestries, tableware, and sculptures while the world showered him with dollars? Who filled eggs with ink and broke them over a canvas? For me, that was hard to believe. The Frenchman André Breton had once been Dalí's staunchest surrealist supporter. When his old friend became world famous, he designed a clever wordplay. Mixing and scrambling the twelve letters of Dalí's name and surname and rearranging the letters in a different order, he came up with *Avida Dollars,* an anagram of *salvador dalí* and a damned good one, since *avida dollars* translates from Spanish as "dollar mad." That shadow in his wheelchair, who gave no sign of life, spittle dripping from his mouth, his feet on a low footstool, was he the same Avida Dollars who once raked in banknotes from all over the world and made more money than the President of the United States?

The sea licked the rocks like an aquamarine tongue.

I walked around Cadaqués and went into a tourist shop that sold posters and postcards and spent some time idly rummaging the poster rack. Al Pacino in *Scarface,* Marlon Brando's Colonel Kurtz in *Apocalypse Now,* Marilyn Monroe, of course, in black-and-white, her dress whipping up from the breeze as a subway train rushed below Lexington Avenue, Ben Kingsley as *Gandhi* and literally hundreds of David Hamilton and Salvador Dalí posters in all sizes and formats. I leafed through the Dalí posters.

"You interested in Dalí?" the only salesperson in the shop asked in a falsetto voice. He was pudgy and round-faced with a pleasant smile.

"I might be."

He was wearing a T-shirt with Dalí's famous *Discovery of America by Christopher Columbus* printed on the front, the explorer stepping out of the ocean, pulling a boat on shore, while a beautiful almost naked boy seen sideways is holding a large cross. In the background, the same boy is seen from behind, naked now, his soft bottom exposed. Only a year ago, I stood in admiration before the large oil on canvas in the private Dalí museum in St. Petersburg, Florida. Then the salesperson showed me a photograph of a cherubic ten-year-old sitting next to Dalí and Gala at the large hardwood table in Dalí's dining room.

The table was laid out with empty sea urchin shells. The boy in the photograph was the same boy as the one holding the cross on his T-shirt depicting *Discovery of America by Christopher Columbus*.

"Where did you get that T-shirt?" I asked.

He smiled. "I shouldn't wear this," he said. "I really shouldn't."

"Why not?"

"Dalí is not a nice person at all. He is cruel. He is selfish. He's a fascist."

"How do you know?"

The salesperson laughed, and his belly wobbled like a jelly. "I was Dalí's sex toy," he said, and pointed his manicured finger at the naked boy in the Dalí painting on his T-shirt. "See him? That boy, that's me. I was twelve, at the time. I didn't hold a cross when I was sitting for the painting; I was holding a broomstick."

"You? Dalí's sex toy? What did Gala have to say about that?"

He laughed. It was a mischievous laugh. "Gala helped Dalí," he said. "She fine-tuned his masturbation technique."

"When was that?"

"I lived in Dalí's house for—how long?—ten years?" the salesperson said. "My elder sister worked for Dalí. Maybe you've heard of her. She was Dalí's housekeeper before Señora Paquita came on the scene."

"I met Señora Paquita. I also met an art dealer who sells Dalí as well as impressionist paintings from the previous century," I said. "You know him?"

The salesperson fluttered his hands behind the counter.

"The *Paris* art dealer?" he asked, and laughed. "Gala treated art dealers the way she treated my sister and the other servants. She forced them to clean the house, down on their knees in their polished shoes and tailored suits."

That's what *I've* been doing for the past couple of weeks, I thought.

"What's your name?" the salesperson asked.

"Stan," I said, "I'm Stan. Or Esteban, or Stanley, if you like. Stán, I think they say over here."

"Are you Spanish?"

"I'm Belgian, actually."

"You look Spanish, though. Are you a tourist, Stán? Are you on holiday?"

"Do I look like a tourist? I don't see any tourists here, in winter. Are there?"

"No. They haven't arrived yet."

"See? I'm not a tourist."

"What are you doing here, if you're not a tourist?"

Suddenly everything came out. "I'm on the run, like Dr. Richard Kimble in that 1960s TV series. I'm a fugitive," I said.

He cleared his throat. "A fugitive from what? From justice?"

"Yes."

"How come?"

I had to shift the blame. "Sotheby's and Christie's didn't want to sell my clients' Dalí investments," I said.

"I'm not surprised. *Every* Dalí is a fake. Dalí faked his own paintings. All he ever wanted was to rake in carloads of money. Gala was even worse."

I'd heard that before. I still didn't believe it. I was still of two minds. We're not talking some unknown Sunday painter; we're talking the universally famous Salvador Dalí, right? Dalí a fraud? A money machine? No way.

"You live around here?" the salesperson asked.

"I slept and woke up with the ghost of Salvador Dalí for close to ten years, night and day. I sold his paintings. As an investment. He was my friend, without ever meeting him. He was my brother-in-arms. Dalí made me a lot of money. Now I live a stone's throw from his doorstep—met him once, it was a disaster—and the friend is turning into a foe. You know the Spanish-style hacienda on top of the Black Mountain?"

"I've heard about it. An Arabian prince used to live there, didn't he?"

I chuckled. "Don't know about that. It's where I live now. I bought the property."

"Siesta time," said the salesperson abruptly, and began to shut up his shop. "Want to join me?"

"Where to?"

"We'll have lunch at the Bar Boia."

We walked down to the pebble beach. He walked as if he were walking on eggs.

"You lived in Dalí's house," I said. "You shared his bed. I'm trying to find out who Dalí is. The *real* Dalí. You must tell me."

"It wasn't great fun, sharing a house with Dalí," the salesperson said. "Day after day, everything that could go wrong went wrong. Gala administered suitcases full of pills to Dalí. Maybe she was poisoning him! In the early 1970s, they suffered their first financial crisis. It was really getting stone cold, must have been January or February, and there was no money to buy heating fuel. While we were freezing in their house, Gala and Dalí left for Paris and New York, where they lived the life of millionaires. Here in Cadaqués, the servants were not paid for months. Gala claimed she had completely run out of money, though she was always carrying huge wads of foreign currency in her old-fashioned Chanel handbags. One morning in the mid-seventies, my sister opened a suitcase under Gala's bed. It contained thousands of dollars in 1936 one-dollar bills. A desk drawer was stuffed with unopened envelopes containing un-cashed bank drafts."

"I heard similar stories," I said.

"Who told you?"

"Captain Moore. I met him in Paris."

"He's a liar. What did he tell you?"

"That Dalí's transactions are always—*always*—in cash."

"That's not true. What about the bank drafts?"

"Well, *I* paid Captain Moore in cash. Swiss francs, if I re-member well."

"I'm sure Dalí never saw a nickel of it."

"Captain Moore told me that, as Dalí's paintings grew in size, they also grew in price. In the sixties, suitcases of cash were needed to buy a Dalí painting. One day, the manager of the Hôtel Meurice in Paris complained that for over twenty years, Dalí's possessions—cardboard boxes, a *montón* of suit-cases, leather Chanel and Givenchy handbags and an amazing area of shoe boxes—had taken up the hotel's only decent storeroom in the cellar. Dalí was asked to clear the room, and Captain Moore took the task upon himself and went down to the cellar. When he opened the storeroom, it was indeed piled from top to bottom with Gala's cardboard boxes and suitcases and leather handbags and shoe boxes. Each box, every suitcase, and every handbag was stuffed with hard cash, in used banknotes from every country in the world. Millions and millions had been stored away in a Paris cellar for a quarter of a century. At least half the foreign banknotes were prewar currency and were no longer valid."

"This is what Captain Moore told you?"

"Yes."

"It's true, I heard that story before," the salesperson said. "Must have been around the time Young Dalí made his first appearance."

"Who is this Young Dalí?"

"You don't know him? Amazing! You know Isidro Bea?"

"No. Don't know him. I've heard his name, though. Who is he?"

"Dalí's number-one assistant," the salesperson said. "His right-hand man. Suddenly he was there and took over the running of the secret studio. I'll tell you a little secret. I wasn't sitting for Dalí on his famous *Discovery of America by Christopher Columbus.* I was sitting for Isidro Bea."

"Dalí has more than one assistant?"

The salesperson burst into laughter. "More than one? He's got five! Six! Unknown to the outside world, Isidro Bea has been the *real* Dalí for almost thirty years," he said.

Was I on to something? Could I believe this?

If this is true, I thought, forget about *genuine genuine* or *genuine fake* Dalís on the art market. If this is true, the world is flooded with *fake fake* Dalís.

Bar Boia in Cadaqués—a *boia* is a buoy—is a *chiringuito,* a wooden shack on the pebble beach, ideal for passing a couple of lazy hours at siesta time. There were outdoor tables and chairs. The interior of the bar was decorated with straw baskets overflowing with fishing nets.

Half a dozen locals—all men—were standing at the bar, their Catalan gossip competing with the clink of cups and spoons and the constant gurgle of the coffee machine. Some were reading the *La Vanguardia* newspaper from Barcelona. The men drank *café solo* and *café con leche* and *cortado,* a short coffee, very strong, with a splash of hot milk.

"A *carajillo*?" the salesperson asked.

That's a strong black coffee laced with a dash of sweet Spanish brandy.

"A *cortado* please, and a doughnut."

The nauseating smell of the colorful diesel fishing boats anchored in the bay, in between the rocks and coves, mingled inside the Bar Boia with the salt of the sea and the sugar-scented wave of cream-filled beignets and biscuits soaked in rum.

The surface of the sea was flat as a mirror. There was barely a breath of wind. The sun had come out in all its glory, and the rocks in the far distance looked like oddly shaped stalagmites in the wild and rugged landscape of whitewashed houses and deep blue canyons as far as one could see.

"You mentioned Dr. Richard Kimble," the salesperson said. "Don't know him. Who's he?"

"A fugitive from justice, in an old television series. He escaped the police. I sometimes feel that . . . ," I said, and before I could finish my sentence, my heart stopped.

There she was, Ultra Violet, my guardian angel with the longest tongue in the whole world, under a yellow sunshade. She was sipping very strong coffee, and her butterfly wings were flapping away.

Do angels drink coffee? Yes, they do. I've seen it with my own eyes.

"Hi, Ultra," I said, twice. "Hi, Ultra."

She wore white-framed sunglasses. She looked up and told me she would have a Spanish omelet with onions and boiled potatoes.

"No, Ultra, I'm not the waiter," I said. "I'm Stan. The art dealer from Belgium. Well, *former* art dealer. Remember? We met in Nice."

"Oh, yes. Stan! How are you?"

"Stán is a doctor," the salesperson said. "Like Dr. Richard Kimble. He tries to stay ahead of the police."

I was surprised. "You know Ultra?" I asked.

They laughed hilariously.

"Stán is very interested in Dalí," the salesperson said.

"Who isn't? Are you interested in Gala, too? You look good. You could have been one of her lovers."

"Gala was always busy with loverboys," the salesperson told me. "The younger, the better."

Ultra Violet laughed. "So was Dalí," she said. "He could be a pain in the ass, and yet he was great fun."

"You think so?" The salesperson rubbed his head. "I was ten or twelve years old, and he used to send me back to the village bakery every morning, a one-hour walk back and forth over the mountain path, simply because he thought his baguette was not long enough."

Nice story, I thought.

"Did you know, Ultra, that Dalí often wore a bulletproof jacket?" the salesperson asked. "Gandhi is shot, Dalí said. Kennedy, too, and Martin Luther King. Now Dalí is next. He really believed he was a target for a terrorist attack. Dalí was a sick man, if you ask me."

"Yes. You're right. Sick here," Ulta Violet said, and touched her temple.

As I listened to their stories, I still wondered who Young Dalí was, and who was Isidro Bea?

"Dalí was into autoeroticism. I slept in his bed, and he never touched my genitals," the salesperson said. "He only stared at me and ruffled my hair."

Was that an inside joke? He was as bald as bald could be.

"I was ten when I shared his bed," he said. "The world over, museums exhibit great masterpieces. But somehow or other, I wonder if their visual pleasure counterbalances the emotional pain the artist has caused his fellow men."

"That's a riddle," I said. "I don't understand."

"Well . . . ," he sighed. "Gala gave my sister a dog's life. She spoke no Spanish at all, and her Catalan was hardly sufficient to instruct the house staff. Cleaning up Dalí's mess all day long, ironing, cooking, doing the washing up . . . For Dalí, servants were a nuisance, and Gala was even worse. A skull in rags, my sister called her, though Gala often made *me* laugh. One day, she dressed up a straw cat in Dalí's old underpants."

"Dalí loved fried eggs," Ultra Violet said. "Three, every day at lunchtime except on Sunday. They often quarreled. Gala got on Dalí's nerves. He was upset and flung the fried eggs against the wall. Sometimes they got stuck on the ceiling for weeks before they fell off."

The salesperson laughed. "When all the eggs in the house were smashed and none were left, Dalí and Gala ate caviar and blini—Russian pancakes—or sea urchins and sometimes lobster," he said.

"That's not what you want to tell me, my friend," I said. He held something back. I sensed another story behind his gossip.

He hesitated. "N-No," he said.

"Tell me. Get it out of your system."

Another sigh. "I'm prejudiced," he said. "I know I am. Maybe I blame Dalí for something that is not his fault after all. No one will ever know."

"What is it?"

"Gala and Dalí slept in separate beds. They had a matrimonial bed, very ornate, but that was only for show. She knew what he did but didn't want to see . . . didn't want to *know* . . . I had to show Dalí my pecker. He was an old man; he was fifty-five. I was ten, twelve. Mind you, Dalí wasn't really a pedophile. He just needed me and other boys my age to stare at so that he could let his trousers down and masturbate."

"That was Dalí, all right. He was like a machine. Whenever he spotted a boy with an angelic face and a youthful feminine body, his pants went down and he started jerking off. Sometimes Dalí was jerking off facing me *and* a mirror." He smiled. "Dalí had a problem, though. His penis was so small, he sometimes couldn't find the wretched thing. To be totally honest, he was *always* and *everywhere* a pain in the ass, that man."

"Your sister knew?"

The salesperson lowered his head and said, "Yes . . . my sister knew." His voice was almost inaudible. "I love my sister. She's a saint. She's *my* saint. The problem is, there was only one employer in the village, and that was Salvador Dalí. He owned everything, even the local garage and the only hotel. Everyone in Cadaqués was dependent on his goodwill. Without Dalí's money, there was no food on the table. But there was no goodwill in Dalí. My sister would have been reduced to begging if she had objected. So she let it pass. . . ." There were tears in his eyes. He looked at me.

"What are you staring at?" I asked.

The salesperson shook his head. "You should have a haircut," he said to me.

"I do that myself. Cut my hair, I mean."

"Always?"

"When I still had money to burn, I flew from Brussels to

New York for a wash and a trim at Vidal Sassoon on Fifth Avenue. I must have been a bit of a pain in the ass, too, back then."

He laughed. "I can see that," he said.

"*Tu sais,* Stan . . . did you know that our friend here was trained to be a hairdresser?" Ultra Violet said.

"But . . . he's a salesperson. He works in a tourist shop. That's where we met."

"I was fourteen," the salesperson said, "Dalí considered me too old to be his sex toy. He said he wanted to give me something in return for everything I'd given him and introduced me to a hairdresser and beauty salon in Barcelona. Dalí paid my tuition fees."

"Which salon was that?"

"Llongueras."

"I don't know him. Why Llongueras?"

"Simple. Llongueras is Dalí's hairdresser. His barber, too."

"Is he still Dalí's barber today?"

"Who else would do it?"

"Where's the nearest Llongueras salon?"

"In Barcelona, I guess."

"Let's go. I'll get my car."

I had bought a brand-new bright red and powerful Alfa Romeo GTV6, a fast sports car, depleting my savings in the Spanish bank vault even more. We drove from Cadaqués to Barcelona and went straight to the Llongueras master salon on Paseo de Gracia. I settled in the brown hydraulic barber's chair. There were more stylists around than players on a soccer field. Llongueras took one look at my hair and sniffed his nose.

"No haircut for me," I said.

"Hot towel shave?"

I nodded. I needed to gain time before I asked him about Dalí. Luckily I hadn't shaved that morning. Gently, he wrapped a hot towel over my face, to soften the skin.

"Is Salvador Dalí still your most famous customer?" I asked.

"No," he said, and kept my cheeks moist with hot shaving oil.

"Who is?"

"Huh-hummm . . ."

"Gala perhaps? Was she a customer of yours, too?"

"*Sí!*"

"Who else?"

"Our King, Juan Carlos," Llongueras said.

I tried to whistle in admiration. I couldn't. Lather all over my face.

"Tell me about Dalí," I said.

Llongueras took his time "In 1961, I phoned Dalí," he said. "Out of the blue. That was easy, his number was in the Girona telephone directory. I asked him to attend the grand opening of my first Barcelona salon as a guest of honor. We had arranged for a mural, a beautiful plaster bas-relief at the back of the salon, to be the star attraction of the opening. It was a wall sculpture portrayed as a picture and represented a ballet of singing mermaids. Seven o'clock sharp, Dalí got out of his car, a black 1950s Cadillac that is now in the courtyard of the Dalí Museum, and started washing his hair in the sink, under the cold tap. Then he asked for a hammer, his hair still dripping wet. The next minute, he smashed my beautiful ballet of singing mermaids to pieces. I was furious, but the next day, the grand opening of my salon was front-page news, thanks to Dalí performing his stunt. Talk about free publicity. Weeks afterward, Dalí came back, holding hands with a shy young man, and asked me to teach and train the boy to become a hairdresser."

"That boy was me," the salesperson interrupted proudly.

The razor made its first pass.

"In the mid-sixties, Dalí stopped combing his hair," Llongueras said. "He would phone me in the middle of the night and order me to come to Port Lligat at once. Two and a half hours later, when I arrived at his house, exhausted because of the difficult mountain drive, he would ask me to comb and fashion his hair and put rollers in. A typical Dalí *tontería*, of course. Plain silly. Over the next twenty years, I repeatedly flew to his hotel in Paris and New York to cut and comb his hair. Dalí prefers it long, shoulder-length. Not because that's what he likes best; it's pure vanity. Long hair is a good cover-up for his big jug ears. Whenever I give him a haircut, every six months or so, Dalí says, 'One centimete*rrr*, no mo*rrre!*'

"He once told me he would make a painting that would outshine every masterpiece Velásquez ever accomplished. For atmosphere, and because he wanted to be in the mood, he ordered a Velásquez wig. I fitted the wig, and Dalí exclaimed, '*Muy bien . . . sí . . . ahora soy Velásquezzz!*' Great . . . now I am Velásquez. He loved pink rollers in his hair. Whenever I put the rollers in, he smiled and said, 'Now I feel like a New Yo*rrr*k housewife in a supe*rrr*ma*rrr*ket!' Of course, he never paid me for my services. *Ni* *una sola peseta.* Gala didn't pay me either. She was distant and haughty, and while she grew older, she suffered severe hair loss and got hysterical. She wanted to claw my eyes out because losing her hair was my fault. Over the years, I made at least a hundred hair extensions for Gala. Did she ever say thank you? She never thanked anyone."

The last best towel of the shave—the coup de grâce—was plucked from a tub of ice water and slapped in my face. It was so damn cold, I almost pissed my pants.

"Did you meet Dalí?" Llongueras asked.

"Once, weeks ago," I said.

"How is he?"

"Old. Dying . . . and that famous mustache . . ."

Llongueras shook with laughter, I could see it in the mirror.

"W-What happened to his famous Dalí mustache?" I asked.

"A legend," Llongueras said. "Dalí never had a famous mustache. He used hair extensions. I know, because *I* made several mustaches for Dalí. One day, he gave a press conference. On impulse, he told the assembled journalists that he would cut off his mustache then and there, on the spot, *and true to his word, he did.* Stupid, of course. Immediately he regretted his decision and asked me to fabricate a fake mustache. After I enjoyed a cold Coca-Cola, I took the two drinking straws from the bottle and glued dark hair from another customer all around and told him to slide the drinking straws over the top ends of what was left of his original mustache. Weeks after, in view of everyone, he repeated his performance and ceremoniously cut the drinking straws in half. Dalí liked this *act* so much that he ordered me to fabricate some more mustache extensions, which he always kept with him, in a silver box. Whenever a photographer came around, he wetted the tips of his mustache with wine or sugar water and honey and slid the hairy drinking straws over the top ends. Dalí is fake from top to bottom. He fooled everyone—even the Beatles!—and got away with it."

"The Beatles? How come he fooled the Beatles?"

"George Harrison paid five thousand dollars for a single hair from Dalí's mustache that was a hair extension."

When we headed back to Cadaqués, the salesperson was silent.

Suddenly he said, "Salvador Dalí really is an ardent fascist. Did you know that?"

"You're joking?"

"There is a rumor that he was arrested in California."

"In California? When was that?"

"During the Second World War."

"Arrested? Why?"

"They thought he was a German spy."

"Dalí? A *Nazi* spy?"

"*Sí.*"

"Leave that to me. I'll find out."

I wrote to Washington, D.C., and requested Salvador Dalí's FBI file under the Freedom of Information Act. My reasoning was

that if a foreigner was arrested on American soil, the FBI had to
be involved. I was disappointed. It turned out to be a thin file
with lots of blacked-out sentences and fifty-one pages withheld
in their entirety. Whole paragraphs were deleted on what remained. All in all, the file consisted of a mere six pages. Yet what
survived was adequate proof that an unnamed FBI agent arrested Salvador Dalí and his wife, Gala, in the summer of 1942
on suspicion of being Nazi spies related to Operation Pastorius,
codenamed after Franz Pastorius, the first German immigrant
to America in 1683. The objective of Operation Pastorius was to
land two teams of Nazi saboteurs, one near Amagansett on the
New England coast and the other just south of Jacksonville,
Florida. The agents' mission: to destroy a factory in Philadel-
phia used by the aircraft industry. The report in Dalí's FBI file
originated from Salt Lake City, Utah. It read as follows:

FILE NO. 100-3938. CHARACTER OF CASE: INTERNAL SECU-
RITY. Report made by [████████████████████] SYNOPSIS OF
FACTS: Suspects reported as being three German saboteurs.
[████████████████] Investigation reflects SALVADOR DALÍ,
a well-known Spanish painter engaged in portrait painting in
New York City. [████████████████████████████████
████████████████████████] At Winnemucca, Ne-
vada, the writer searched the Cadillac automobile, bearing California license IL6460, while the occupants of said car were
sleeping in the Humboldt Hotel and found nothing of impor-
tance therein. Everything contained in said car had to do with
paintings. There were paint brushes, paint oils, finished canvas

oil paintings, etc. One canvas/oil painting was addressed to Mr. Salvador Dalí, Marquis de Cueves.[██████████████████] The automobile driven by Dalí was a 1941 Cadillac Sedan purchased on 11 JULY 1941 and had Motor No. 8362223.

[████████████]

██

██

██]

Interrogation of Dalí reflected as follows: He is a native of Figueres, Girona, Spain and was born 11 May 1904. He is registered with the Spanish Consulate in New York City, No. 654. He exhibited Alien Registration No. 2694040 and his Social Security Number is 564-26-9921. From personal observation and interview, the following description was obtained:

Age: 38 yrs.
Height: 5' 8"
Weight: 135 lbs.
Eyes: Hazel
Hair: Black
Mustache: Black
Complexion: Dark
Color: White
Speech: Cannot speak English

[██

██

██]

Investigation reflected that the Dalís [████] were in no way connected with the German saboteurs [██████] and were apparently on a legitimate business or pleasure trip; further investigation was not conducted, and this case is being closed upon the authority of the Special Agent in Charge. Authorized copies of this report were dispatched to J. Edgar Hoover's FBI headquarters in Washington as well as to the FBI bureaus in New York City, San Diego and Salt Lake City.

We had a problem. *I* had a problem. My passport had expired. I could see the bottom of my safe. If we wanted to hang on to our lifestyle, we would soon be needing extra money. Ana still had her house in Agullana. She wanted to rent it out, and we drove to Pontóns, a dusty village a couple of miles south of Figueres, to see Ramón Guardiola, her lawyer. He had retired from daily practice but was on hand for free advice. Guardiola was a neat man with a thin gangster mustache and lots of pomade in his wavy hair that looked slick and shiny. Thick horn-rimmed glasses rested on his nose like a saddle on a horse. We were let in through the garage. In the half dark I noticed a black SEAT—the old Spanish version of an Italian Fiat—that would be a catch for any classic car museum, rusting away under layers of dust and sand. My attention was drawn to an impressive series of Dalí posters plastered on the wall and the inside of the garage door.

Catalans aren't soft-spoken. They are guttural. They don't

just talk; they bark. While Ana and her lawyer were barking business, I had a closer look at the colorful posters. They were signed and dated. They had images of butterflies on them and cutouts of older Dalí paintings with dots and splashes of black Chinese ink printed all over. I knew the posters; I had seen them before. They represented famous French tourist regions and were commissioned by the Société National des Chemins de Fer, the French national railway system. The *Normandie* poster was beautified with a cutout photograph of the Mount Saint-Michael tidal island while the *Paris* poster obviously had an image of the Eiffel Tower. The signatures looked like variations on Dalí's typical handwriting, and yet I had the strange feeling I wasn't seeing what I should have been seeing. Something was wrong with the posters and I didn't know *what* was wrong.

"Señor Guardiola, where did you get these posters?" I asked.

The lawyer lowered his head, as if ashamed to tell. Then he sighed and said, "When I was mayor of Figueres, I was the driving force behind the Dalí Museum and became its first-ever director. You won't know that, but gratitude is not a word in Dalí's vocabulary. Appreciation, thankfulness, he doesn't know the meaning of these words. I instigated his museum, and he never even *thanked* me, and of course, he never gave me a present. Dalí *never* gives presents. One day, I spotted an enormous pile of muddy and water-soaked Dalí posters in an abandoned wing of the museum. 'What should we do with these?' I asked Dalí. 'They'*rrre* you*rrrs*!' he roared with a grand gesture. I phoned the sanitation department and ordered them to remove that mountain of rotting paper at once. As an afterthought, I removed a few posters from the pile and affixed them in my garage. You like them? You can have one."

I caressed the butterflies.

I rubbed the tips of my fingers over the dots and splashes of Chinese ink.

I examined the cutouts.

Ana said good-bye to Ramón Guardiola. He threw the garage door wide open.

Shafts of bright sunlight streamed in.

Again I caressed the butterflies. Good heavens, I could peel them off! I rubbed my fingers over the dots and splashes. The ink had become brittle and started pulverizing. I examined the printed cutouts. They weren't printed. They were *real* cutouts, old natural history and art book and atlas illustrations, glued into the dots and splashes.

"Señor Guardiola, I've got a surprise for you," I said. "Your posters, I'd like to have one, but if I were you, I'd hang on to them. They're not posters at all. They are original Dalí designs for a Société National des Chemins de Fer promotional poster campaign. These are *genuine genuine* water paints with *genuine genuine* cutouts. Handmade, not printed. You should lock them in your safe. Sell them. How many have you got here? Let me see, *Roussillon, Auvergne, Alpes, Normandie, Alsace,* and *Paris,* that makes six. Your garage is worth a fortune, Señor Guardiola. Two fortunes, actually. Your old SEAT and six *genuine genuine* Dalí water paints."

"*Madre de Dios!*" the lawyer exclaimed. "The old fool surprises me! Dalí gave me a present after all!"

Ana's son Teri—he was now almost eleven years old—had come to stay with us. We lived a life of domestic bliss. Ana gave birth to her second son, and I became a first-time father at the ripe old age of almost forty. Ana was thirty-four. We kept the promise we had made at the Ampurdán Motel and named our baby boy Lluís. *T'estimo, i em sé feliç.* He looked like me, I thought, and I looked like him. Same green eyes, *my* eyes. Father and son. Perhaps this was only a daydream, and I would be in for a rough awakening when he grew older. I promise that I'll do my best, I said to myself, but I don't know if I can be a good father. I'm still a fugitive. Perhaps I'll always be a fugitive. Perhaps the police or Interpol is on my trail right now. The warrant for my arrest was still out, and there was too much emotional pain—bad conscience and the nagging torment of guilt and the suffering of remorse—I'd never ever be able to shake off.

I kissed Ana and our baby tenderly. Time heals all wounds, they say. Months passed. I got used to living in one of the roughest and at the same time most idyllic corners of the world. I had started taking lengthy notes of my conversations about Dalí, on the backs of still-unpaid invoices, electricity bills, empty bread bags, the blank spaces on a travel agent's leaflets, and endless rolls of unused toilet paper. For every Dalí story, there was a better one just around the corner.

Spring and summer came and went. I walked down to the Bar Boia almost every day. Often the salesperson from the tourist shop was there. So was Ultra Violet, in her white flowing dress, white makeup, false eyelashes, and talcum powder carefully dusted all over her face. The angel dress was made of an old parachute. Her butterfly wings were daubed with blue paint. I noticed that on some days her front teeth were painted silver. While we sat outside, in the mild sea breeze, she complained she had had countless lovers, and yet the two greatest loves of her life, Salvador Dalí and Andy Warhol, had been cold and frigid and avoided every physical contact. Never had they even touched her in all those years. They had the opportunity, though: Ultra Violet played multiple roles in their films, often in the nude, and although she was past a certain age, she was still a beautiful woman. Indeed, she looked a lot like Vivien Leigh in the 1939 *Gone with the Wind*.

She sipped on a glass of Vichy Catalan, the salty local mineral water.

I asked for a *cortado*, please, *corto de café*, steamy hot milk and just a drop of coffee. *Amargo*, bitter, no sugar.

"Where do you live now, Ultra?" I asked.

"Oh, I've got my penthouse apartment in New York . . . and my family house in Nice, of course."

The truth was, I wanted to talk about Dalí, not about real estate. Despite my domestic tranquillity, my only neighbor at the foot of the mountain still occupied my thoughts.

"Ultra, will you now recount your days and nights with Dalí, please?" I said.

"Dalí and I . . . we were one of the most photographed couples in New York," she said, and flashed a radiant smile.

"But . . . *a couple?*" I tried to steer her back into reality. "You know what that means, sexually, don't you, *a couple*—man and wife?"

Quite unexpectedly, in a trance almost, Ultra Violet started recounting the most amazing story I'd ever heard. It gulped out of that frail, angelic body, and I didn't interrupt her, not even once, fearful as I was of stemming the flow of her narrative. The story began shortly after Dalí's daily siesta in the St. Regis Hotel in New York. He was staying in his splendid hotel suite, the kind reserved for heads of state, oversize, plush, with high windows and draped mirrors. Dalí was in great shape, flitting around, attending to several things at once. His skin was tanned, and his vivid hazel eyes were glowing with pleasure. The tips of his mustache, luxuriously waxed and always erect, were glistening in the light of a hundred candles in the crystal chandelier. There were masses of flowers in the suite. In the chandelier, Dalí had inserted stones from Port Lligat and freshly laid eggs sent to him daily from Cadaqués. He felt adventurous and gave his entourage his usual laundry list of bizarre requests: a tramp who spoke perfect Russian, the most beautiful androgynous and angelic starlets and catwalk fashion models in New York, girls with ballerina legs, a lady with a preference for standing on her head, a couple of tall professional homosexuals, bald hermaphrodites, an albino with a hunchback, and someone so fat that you couldn't see his eyes.

Ultra said that Dalí was wearing a black cowboy shirt. His bare feet were clad in Catalan espadrilles with black ribbons tied around his ankles. He walked to the windows, opened the curtains, and let the sun flood in. "We are going to have a par-rrty," Dalí said. "Invite *two* Nobel Prrrize winnerrrs, prrrefer-rrably Crickkkke and Watson. They know the secrrret of *DNA*." Swiftly, he conjured up a Magic Marker and drew a double DNA helix on the wallpaper and signed it. "Crickkkke and Wat-son a*rrre* geniuses," he said. He took a live lobster out of his pocket. The lobster was dipped in a bath of gold. "Thei*rrr* dis-cove*rrry* is superior to the invention of *firrre*, the *wheel,* and the wr*rr*itten alphabet. They will go down in histo*rrry,* just as Dalí will."

The two Nobel Prize winners came in—curious to meet the most famous living artist in the world—and Dalí ordered a puree of string beans. 'Eat thi*zzz!*' he commanded, 's*trrring* bean*zzz* nou*rrr*ish you*rrr* d*eeeoxyrrr*ibonucleic acid! Eat! Eat fast! You a*rrre* too thin! I need giants! I need fat me*nnn!* Dwar-rrfs and monsterrrs!' Crick and Watson were understandably puzzled. Suddenly they remembered they had a plane to catch and made a hasty escape. Perhaps Nobel Prize winners don't eat string beans, Ultra Violet thought.

From New York backstreets, Dalí's entourage had picked up the ugliest men around: midgets, deformed dwarfs, crippled Vietnam veterans, hopeless drunks, freaks and carnival per-formers, bums, bag ladies, subway beggars, twins, transvestites, bald basketball players, and hippies with long hair. Circumcised men were out: Dalí didn't approve of circumcision. A Greek sculpture isn't circumcised either, he used to say. Gallantly, he led them into his suite and issued his instructions, like a warlord. The starlets and catwalk superstars had to crawl on the floor, on all fours, balancing a spirit level on their backs, with lighted sparklers sticking out of their asses. While a catwalk model was undressing—she later married a famous movie actor—Dalí bit her toenails and licked her toes. The most beautiful New York toy boys lowered their trousers and sat with their bare bottoms on blocks of wet clay, while Dalí signed and framed the imprints of those gorgeous asses. In the middle of the room, a white stallion drank champagne from a silver bucket. For snacks, trays of animal eyeballs—cow, sheep, goat—were carried around on a platter.

Dalí had invented a name for his afternoon tea parties. He called them his sex circus or his ballet of passion. Apart from the cowboy shirt and Catalan espadrilles, he was dressed as Santa Claus with a clown's red nose, waving about a tiny flag—the Stars and Stripes. Snorting cocaine, the dwarfs and drunks and Vietnam veterans were copulating with the catwalk superstars. Whenever someone had an orgasm, Dalí was delighted and shouted: *"Brrravooo! C'est magnifique"* in French, stretching out each vowel, while the girls screamed: "I'm doing this for the Divine! Only for the Divine Dalí!" though Dalí himself wasn't fucking anybody. His eyes closed, he was farting and masturbating frantically.

The sex circus was a colorful chaos. Gala listened in devotion while the Russian tramp recited Tolstoy in Russian. Then she jabbed him with her shoe, and they had sex. Imagine, she was in her seventies! On any normal day, Gala screwed multiple men, and her lovers were reportedly the most expensive lays in the history of sex, since she paid her studs with small but *genuine genuine* Dalí paintings. Ultra recounted that Gala had inserted a black Mickey Mouse velvet bow tie in her wig. She looked horrible. After years of plastic surgery, she had become a surrealist painting herself. "Gala needs *morrre* money!" she shouted. *Jab-jab-jab* with her shoe, and sex again. A harlequin with a powdered face pedaled a unicycle around the room. He overturned a tray of cows' eyes, and the eyeballs spilled onto the floor and rolled away in every direction. Lobster telephones seemed to be ringing throughout the suite. A snake woman lit a cigarette. She bent her body in incredible ways and moved the cigarette to her vagina. Steadying her muscles, she smoked the cigarette with her vagina, cigarette smoke swirling from her anus. "Brrravo!" Dalí shouted. "Brrravisimo!" Some of the people that performed humiliating sex for Dalí in those days have become really famous since. He even asked Marilyn Monroe to join his sex circus, but she declined.

That day, Ultra Violet told me what a strange and unpredictable man Dalí could be. His penis he called his limousine. In reality, it wasn't a limousine at all. Apparently, it was as small as a Fiat 500. His fly he called his garage. The tall and balding Dado Ruspoli came out of the bathroom. He was an Italian nobleman with a big Roman nose and the largest cock in erection in the whole of Europe. Twenty-seven centimeters, imagine! Dalí's sex circus was planned down to the last detail.

He told Ultra: "You *arrre* my notarrry! Wrrrite everrrything down. Everrry orrrrgasm, everrry fuck must be *rrrecorrrded* for posterrrity!"

In a ledger, she wrote down Dado's name and cashed a registration fee. Then the Italian nobleman fucked the catwalk model in her ass. Dalí insisted on verifying personally if penetration was total because he couldn't be fooled, of course, and as he stuck his nose in between Dado's enormous cock and the girl's ass, Salvador Dalí unzipped his garage and took his Fiat 500 out and began jacking off, gargling and gasping for breath. His eyes rolled and rolled. After two minutes, Dalí screamed, his body shuddered, and a frothy speck of sperm slipped from what he called his limousine, like milk boiling over. That was the end of the show. The air was thick with cigarette smoke. Before leaving the hotel, every participant received a framed certificate hand-signed by Dalí himself.

What a story! A gem. Couldn't be surpassed. But—was it all true?

"It doesn't matter," the salesperson said. "Never solve the riddle, Dalí has said on many occasions."

Perhaps he was right.

"Is Dalí truly a genius?" I asked. "Or did the whole world play a part in this elaborate set-up with misleading jokes?"

"That's the point, isn't it?" Ultra Violet said.

It was getting dark. The dying sun painted the sea and the mountains in the fiercest hues and shades of red.

Ultra Violet was exhausted. "Dalí gave me the best advice a man can give to a woman," she said slowly.

"What advice did he give you, Ultra?"

"Whatever you do, he said, do something that attracts attention. Be a murderer, set fire to a hotel, talk dirty. Whatever. But *do* something. Can I have that Spanish omelet now?" she asked me.

That's an idea, I thought. Perhaps I can become a waiter. I wanted to do something, anything, and get going again.

Problem was, I had run out of money. No more Chinese vases, no more pots of gold.

Over the years on my mountain, I became an intimate of Dalí's inner circle of friends and collaborators. We drank *café con leche* and *cortado* every afternoon at siesta time and often wined and dined all through the evening. One hot, sunny day at the end of a languorous summer, we were watching trained swimmers who were snorkeling in the little archipelagos and islets and scuba divers exploring the depths and shallows in the open water. Every hour at the hour, a glass-bottomed boat blew its whistle and took tourists from the narrow, stony beach out at sea and around the islands. The longer we sat outside, the more friends and acquaintances joined us. Marc Lacroix among others, Dalí's official court photographer for years. He was a thickset Frenchman from Nice with a wild bouffant hairdo and voluminous eyebrows, and walked in with Ultra Violet, who also had her house in Nice. Even when there was nothing to laugh about, Marc Lacroix would be shaking with mirth. With his help, Dalí had developed the new technique of stereoscopic three-dimensional paintings based on optical effects, like *Lincoln in Dalívision*. As always, the salesperson was there, too. He never missed a beat.

On that day, Ramón Guardiola was present as well as some fellow Catalans who spent the long, lazy summer in Cadaqués, where they had a summer house: the veteran art critic Rafael Santos Torroella, balding Arturo Caminada—Señora Paquita's husband and Dalí's jack of all trades—and the sour Catalan filmmaker Antoni Ribas, who was now preparing a Dalí biopic starring Lorenzo—son of Anthony Quinn—as Salvador Dalí. Rafael Santos Torroella wrote several books on Salvador Dalí and helped rejuvenate the avant-garde art scene in Spain after Franco's Civil War. Amanda Lear was there, too. She had come on a pilgrimage to Dalí's old haunts. With her husky voice and endlessly long legs, she was sexy to listen to and stunning to look at.

A new arrival was Xavier Cugat, the former Rumba King and mambo and cha-cha-cha band leader, who had been one of my childhood musical heroes in the early fifties and was now a frail old man. He was once a well-known womanizer and had at one time married the blond bombshell Abbe Lane and later on María del Rosario Pilar Martínez Molina Baeza de Rasten, better known in show business as Charo, the singer, who played herself—with Cugat—in Elvis Presley's *That's the Way It Is*. The couple was the first to have their nuptials in Caesars Palace in Las Vegas. Xavier Cugat had been born in nearby Girona and had returned to his native Ampurdán after his first stroke. Though officially bankrupt, he still lived the life of a fifties movie star in a private suite at the Barcelona Ritz Hotel. He was affectionately known as "Cugie" and sat holding a chihuahua dog and clutching a pipe, though he didn't smoke.

Though thrilled by the chance to meet a childhood idol, I was even more delighted to finally be introduced to Young Dalí, who was exactly my age. He immediately invited me to the grand opening of his first solo show. Beyond the shore, the softly wrinkling Mediterranean reflected a leaden sun. The water was crystal clear and cold as ice. Young Dalí. Where did the nickname come from, I wondered.

Captain Moore arrived at the Bar Boia on a sputtering Mobylette that had seen better days. Sharp creases in his trouser legs. Even in the stifling summer heat, his blue blazer was immaculate. Button-down shirt, no tie but a foulard scarf instead. He had recently opened his own private Dalí museum in Cadaqués, in the closed-down village cinema that doubled as a hotel. I was amazed. Dalí's erstwhile business manager had become a frail, thin, and very old man since I'd first met him a couple of years earlier in Paris.

Stray cats sneaked between the wobbly tables and under the chairs.

"Too many cats around," Captain Moore said. "Tonight, local fishermen will club them to death and use the dead carcasses as bait on their fishing trips."

We welcomed Captain Moore to our table.

We shook hands. He slapped me on the back. He remembered me from before. Captain Moore wasn't wearing shoes.

No beach sandals either. Instead of shoes or beach sandals, he wore black velvet slippers with a gold coat of arms brocaded on the toes.

When he started working for Dalí in 1962, the artist was a famous but by no means a rich man. This would soon change. When Dalí parted with his *capitán del dinero* twenty years later, after an acrimonious dispute—about money, of course—they were each reported to be worth $32 million and counting.

Captain Moore was a great storyteller. I also found him a show-off. As soon as he sat down, he boasted that he had shaken hands with Churchill and Roosevelt and was on a first-name basis with Orson Welles and Grace Kelly.

"Weather around here is gorgeous," Marc Lacroix said out of the blue, perhaps to change the subject.

"I agree. Why in hell did a native son like Dalí choose to live in New York part of the year?" veteran art critic Rafael Santos Torroella asked.

For Captain Moore, that was a sign he was about to embark on one of his narratives.

"Because Gala was Russian by birth," he said. "She needed the cold. She loved New York in winter. I remember, on one of our trips to America, they had an appointment with the Duke of Windsor—the former British king—and his wife, Wallis Simpson, the duchess. If you're an artist and you intend to sell your paintings expensively, Dalí said, it's a clever thing to know famous people."

Had I heard that before?

"Dalí had to sell expensively because Gala always needed

money," Captain Moore said. "As a welcome present for Gala, the duchess brought some superb Russian caviar for lunch. The best, really. The caviar was served. '*Such* nice caviar, isn't it, Gala?' the duchess asked. Deadpan, Gala replied: 'Wonderful. Tastes like chicken shit!' She didn't laugh, though. She already had three face-lifts too many and was incapable even of smiling. Not that she had any intention of doing so.

"Dalí wanted to go out and take a taxi. He never had money in his pockets and needed some taxi money, so Gala gave him a hundred-dollar banknote. On arrival, the taximeter showed one dollar. A single dollar. Dalí handed the taxi driver his hundred-dollar banknote and telephoned Gala that he had no money left for the return journey. 'You were supposed to pay the taxi driver, not buy his taxi!' she shouted, and slammed the phone down. Gala was fuming."

"I've always wondered—though I've never asked—why did Dalí and you go different ways, Captain?" Amanda Lear asked.

"Isn't it obvious?" Rafael Santos Torroella said. "Dalí needed a new business manager who took only five instead of a ten percent commission on all sales, so Gala found a photographer from Girona. He spoke Catalan. He was younger and better looking than the Captain."

Captain Moore ignored the art critic. He smiled half-heartedly. "No, no, that's not true," he said, and shrugged. "When I left Salvador Dalí, he was a rich man. I was the first to introduce money-spinners in the art world such as Dalí prints and graphics, Dalí sculptures, Dalí perfume, and even gold Dalí jewels. I arranged commercial Dalí sales exhibitions in New York, Berlin,

Munich, Vienna, Paris, Rome, and Japan, a country flush with new money. Must have been those portable cassette players everyone's listening to. Accusations in the international media about falsifications led to a legal dispute between Dalí and me. It is true that Dalí started a Niagara of prints on paper, but—what's wrong with that? He had great fun and made lots of money. In 1974, I commissioned seventy-eight Dalí illustrations for tarot cards to be reproduced in an edition of two hundred fifty photo-mechanical prints. New York publisher Lyle Stuart won the publishing contract . . . in a poker game with Gala, for a ridiculous eight American cents. Then Gala lost even more. Instead of two hundred fifty tarot prints, Dalí had to sign seventeen thousand and five hundred blank sheets of paper to pay for Gala's gambling debt."

We were babbling happily in a mix of English and French and mostly Spanish with some Catalan thrown in.

"I modeled for Dalí. I'm on one of those tarot cards," Amanda Lear said.

"Which one?" Xavier Cugat asked.

"The card known as Temperance," Amanda Lear said. Whenever she spoke, she flung her long blond hair from one side to the other.

"Salvador Dalí is the Toyota of the art world," Ultra Violet said.

Captain Moore looked annoyed. He didn't like to be interrupted. "Demand for tarot prints went through the roof," he said. "The sky was the limit. As a result, Dalí lost count and signed an additional three thousand sheets, bringing the total to twenty thousand and five hundred instead of two hundred fifty. I made a fortune for Dalí. Personally, I was pulling in five million dollars a year. We were moving a shitload of Dalí merchandize, even Dalí jigsaw puzzles and Dalí condoms. All sold in more than sixty countries around the world. We were getting fat and happy milking the cash cow. Now they say Dalí is heavily in debt. In all probability, he'll die a destitute man. You tell me, who's the winner here and who's the loser?"

The milk's turned sour, I thought.

"Could it be true, Captain, that Dalí or his assistants signed hundreds of thousands of *fake fake* Dalís, as they say?" I asked.

Captain Moore vehemently denied this. "Never. They were not fake. They were unpaid for. One day in a police station, we were shown a series of supposedly fake Dalís," he recalled. "I asked Gala's expert opinion. 'The paintings are genuine, the signatures are genuine, but yes, they're still fake Dalís,' she whispered in my ear. 'How can they be fake when the paintings and the signatures are good?' I asked. 'Because Dalí hasn't been paid,' Gala replied."

It wasn't the revelation I had expected, but still, I was stunned. Could this be true?

Marc Lacroix was laughing hilariously. "One thing is for sure. Starting in the sixties, demand for Dalís—everything from paintings to prints to scarves to ashtrays, as long as there was a Dalí signature on it—went through the roof. Obviously Dalí couldn't keep up. Paintings had to be . . . improvised . . . invented . . . thrown together," he said, and recounted how huge

blank, unpainted canvases were strewn on the floor in Dalí's secret studio in Port Lligat. Naked women were smeared with differently colored acrylic paint and rolled over the canvases that
Dalí was signing furiously.

"I'm sure none of the paint-smeared girls touched him,"
Young Dalí said.

The French photographer laughed. "Dalí didn't like to be
touched," he said.

"Neither did Andy Warhol," Ultra Violet said.

Exactly what she'd told me in a previous conversation.

"Dalí often said to me: the most exciting thing about sex is
not having sex," Amanda Lear reported.

"You were in *Midnight Cowboy,* weren't you, Ultra?" Captain Moore asked.

"Wow! Have you met Dustin Hoffman on set?" said Young
Dalí.

"Yes."

"Wow! How is he?"

"Just like you and me."

"You *are* famous, Ultra."

"I *was.* For fifteen minutes," Ultra Violet said, deadpan.

Everyone laughed while Amanda Lear blinked her false eyelashes.

"*I* was on the set of *The Third Man,*" Captain Moore said.

His ego was as thick as his wallet.

". . . while *I* worked with Fred Astaire and gave Rita Hay-
worth one of her first singing jobs," Xavier Cugat quietly said.

Around us the windowsills were bursting with flowers. The sweet fragrance of mimosa and the cooking smells of paella *mixta* with chicken and squid wafted through the air. In the bay, in the ice-cold water, tourists were bouncing in the gentle waves. In the far distance, a lone fisherman looking for crab and mussels was climbing the Es Cucurucu cliff to the east of the bay.

"I was often a privileged guest at Dalí's house," Marc Lacroix recounted. "Some years ago, we were sitting in the lush garden. Someone rang the doorbell. There he was, the flamboyant Llongueras, the most famous hairdresser in the whole of Spain and the rest of the world. He had an appointment with Dalí. Of course, Dalí had forgotten completely. Gala was busy with a new young lover. It was a hot day, like today. The most beautiful stark-naked girls and at least twenty naked men were languishing around the phallus-shaped swimming pool in the shade of cypresses and olive trees. Great cocks and great tits. The men had a fly glued to their cheek. Every now and again, one of them had a hard-on and fucked one of the girls while Dalí watched and held up his gold-knobbed cane in a pontifical gesture and gave his instructions. 'Deeperrr! Deeperrr!' he shouted. Guests were not allowed to use a bathroom. A James Bond starlet was peeing next to the swimming pool.

"Llongueras came into the garden. In his suitcase, he had all the paraphernalia he needed to fashion Dalí's hair, not only a comb and a brush: even trimming Dalí's mustache was a world-class event that took hours. Tourists paid in advance to see it happen. Dalí sat on a big chair, a kind of throne. He spotted Llongueras and shouted: 'You'*rrre* right on time! Pick out the fuck you like most. A man? A woman? Two men? Two women? Thr*rree*? They'*rrre* all your*rrs*!' Unfortunately, Llongueras was in the company of his own wife, and it was no secret that Dalí wasn't her biggest fan. He said she looked like a Spanish Joan Collins, and of course that was spot on. Llongueras couldn't believe what he heard. His face went red. Loudly, so that everybody around could hear him, Dalí shouted, 'Do not wo*rrry*, my fr*rriend*, especially fo*rrr* you*rrr* wife, Dalí has got a choice of fi*rrrst*-class penis p*rrrosthetic* aids and dildos for vaginal and anal pe-ne-t*rrration*! Or*rrgasm* guaranteed, Dalí uses them himse*lfff*!'"

"Every day with Dalí was another day in the madhouse," Captain Moore said.

"Honestly, I found all of this quite ridiculous," Amanda Lear said. "Why did an artist of his stature surround himself with imbeciles?"

"Only two rooms in Dalí's house have doors that are always locked," Captain Moore said. "The secret studio and the pigeon coop in the garden with a giant white egg on its roof. The pigeon coop is also secret, since it is Dalí's private sex boudoir where he keeps his amazing collection of hard-core porn stuff and sex toys: snuff movies, videos, *Playboy* and *Hustler* and male magazines, penis extensions, dildos, vibrators . . . He has dildos for anal penetration in all shapes and sizes and as long as he was in relatively good health, he used them on himself on a daily basis. To give his dildos a more personal and *humane* touch, Dalí meticulously painted the portrait of a historical world leader on the head of each: the pope, President Kennedy, Charles de Gaulle, Mao Tse-tung, Fidel Castro, and even Mother Teresa—who was a man, according to Dalí. His 'fine art penises,' he called them. The largest dildo of all, a black latex one, featured the portrait of Adolf Hitler. When he had locked himself in his secret sex boudoir for a couple of hours, he slowly shuffled out afterwards, clutching his bottom, his legs wide apart and his face twisted in pain. 'Maestro, what happened?' I asked. Dalí grimaced. 'It's all Hitler's fault!' he groaned."

"Hey! Didn't he slur his *r*'s?" I asked.

"Not after what he did to himself, ha ha ha!"

Xavier Cugat said to Captain Moore, "You once told me, Captain, that over the years, you paid more hush money to starlets and professional hustlers willing to be fucked or gangbanged in Dalí's sex circus or passion ballet than you were invoiced for Dalí and Gala's lengthy stays at the Ritz Hotel in Barcelona, the Hôtel Meurice in Paris, and the New York St. Regis, all three combined."

"In the 1960s, one *day* in New York would cost us fifty thousand dollars," Captain Moore said, and shook his head in amazement. "His hotel bills could run up to half a million dollars a month. Can you believe it? When he had a sex party in New York, he wanted live lobsters for decoration. Butlers walked through the St. Regis suite pouring out bushels of lobsters that crawled off in every direction. The guys at the Fulton Fish Market loved me. I used to buy four or five hundred live lobsters at a time. I was locked up in Dalí's madhouse for next to twenty years. In Rome, he gave a two-hour conference in Latin though he doesn't speak a word of the language. He made it all up, on the spot. In Venice, he transformed himself into a nine-meter-tall giant on stilts. He requested the Vatican to film him in the Sistine Chapel nailed to the floor, in the same way Christ was nailed to the cross. Try to deal with that. Still, the man was a genius. Did you know Dalí wrote the script of Buñuel's *Un chien andalou* in a couple of minutes on the cardboard lid of a shoe box, while he was eating tapas in the Astoria Bar in Figueres?"

The more I listened to them, the more I was under the impression that they were all bending the truth. Bending it too far, maybe. I believed them, but by now, I also knew there was a hidden tale behind every over-the-top story. It led me to the conclusion that perhaps Dalí and some people in his circle were no more than a superior gang of playful crooks who had for years been trying to fool and deceive not only the art world or the financial world but the world as a whole. They'd made it; they'd fooled mankind in spectacular fashion. Working for MMC, selling Dalís as if there were no tomorrow, I had skidded the edge of the gang and reaped my profits. But I'd have to pay a price for it. While everyone else was just relaxing and having fun, again the possibility of years in prison weighed on me. If I'd had to go to prison, at least I wanted to know *why*, and I intended to get to the bottom of this. I started to press for the right answers.

"Captain, how many blank sheets of paper would you say Dalí signed?" I asked.

"In his lifetime?"

"Yes."

He shrugged. "How many leaves are there on a tree?" he said, and grinned.

"Three hundred thousand," Ramón Guardiola said.

"On all the trees in a forest?" asked Captain Moore.

I explained my life story to my new "friends" around the rickety Bar Boia beach tables. I told them I worked via Geneva and Antwerp for a disgraced financier and playboy—my president—selling Dalí paintings as an art investment to mostly European businessmen. Or rather, *genuine fake* and *fake fake* Dalí paintings. Yet they all came with a certificate of authenticity, I said, hand-signed by . . . Captain Moore . . . or by Dalí himself.

"Could it be that Dalí's life of debauchery—and *your* life as a cover-up, Captain—was a smoke screen that concealed the fact that much of his artistic legacy is nothing more than a fraud?" I asked with a coy smile on my face, trying not to seem too serious.

Because of the oppressive heat, Captain Moore was sweating profusely.

We were all sweating.

That moment, Captain Moore began sweating even more.

I turned to the salesperson. "You must know, you lived in his house. Did *you* ever see Dalí faking or counterfeiting his own masterpieces?" I asked.

Stunned silence. Had I perhaps told too much of the truth?

I snapped my fingers. The waiter came over.

"Have you got Perelada Brut Reserve, please?" I asked.

"Pink *cava*? *Por supuesto, señor.*"

"Can we have a bottle, *por favor*? *Muy frío.* Ice cold. Thank you."

"*De nada.*"

Captain Moore seemed resigned, once he had the drink in hand. My questions didn't seem quite so awkward anymore. Everyone seemed to relax.

"*Salut!*"

"Cheers!"

"*A votre santé!*"

We clinked glasses and took a sip.

"I made Dalí a multimillionaire," Captain Moore said. "People wanted Dalí's signature? We gave the world six hundred and seventy-nine different Dalí signatures."

"Exactly six hundred and seventy-nine? I counted six hundred and sixty-six."

"You missed thirteen," Captain Moore said. "Don't take six hundred sixty-six or six hundred seventy-nine as fact, though, more like a way of saying that we produced *countless* signatures. Dalí has as many signatures as there are Dalí artworks on the market, that is to say: tens of thousands, perhaps hundreds of thousands."

I grunted. "What a mess!" I said.

"Dalí *was* a cliché of himself as an artist," Young Dalí suddenly said.

All heads turned in his direction.

"Maybe Dalí wasn't the Muhammad Ali of modern art after all," said Rafael Santos Torroella, always the art critic. "Dalí himself said so on several occasions. He said he considered himself a mediocre artist, luckily for him his contemporaries were far worse. Take Picasso. He reminded Dalí of an outboard motor that has run out of control. Picasso paints with the speed of a machine gun, Dalí once said to me, a single painting of mine is far better than a thousand Picassos. In Dalí's view, Turner was the worst painter in the history of art. A Turner painting reminded him of fingers stained with nicotine. Compared to Vermeer or Velásquez however, who were the true giants in his eyes, Dalí felt a complete failure."

"A failure or not, Dalí is famous," Ultra Violet said. "But what is fame?"

"He certainly had more energy than Picasso," Captain Moore said. "But while for Picasso painting was a matter of life and death—if Picasso couldn't paint, he wouldn't live—for Salvador Dalí the art world was a means to an end: amass a vast fortune and become truly famous—Ultra is right—and pave the way for an even greater fortune. Dalí was a cultural exhibitionist, plain and simple, and an inveterate money-grabber, and Gala was even worse. In 1969, Kirk Douglas arrived in Cadaqués to star in *The Light at the Edge of the World,* a movie about pirates taking over a lighthouse on a rocky island, based on a Jules Verne novel. He was invited to Dalí's house for lunch and left his jacket on the back of a chair. Gala took the wallet out and removed the money."

Ultra Violet wondered if Dalí was a Peeping Tom who indulged in self-sex.

"You're referring to his sex circus? No way I could stop this," Captain Moore said. "Dalí needed it as he needed oxygen. Watching people perform a sex act was for Dalí what a toy is for a child. He was happy only when he could witness anal fornication. If he couldn't satisfy his voyeuristic impulses, he wasn't able to work. His creativity simply dried up—I often had to hold his hand and guide him when he was drawing—and with no artworks to sell, there would be no funds to finance his sex parties. It was . . . How do you call this? . . . It was a catch-22 situation. He couldn't do a paint job without a sex party, but while attending a sex party, he didn't do a paint job."

"Dalí was never in the art business," Amanda Lear said. "He was in *show* business."

"He knew he was perverted," the Catalan film director Antoni Ribas said. "That's why he was seeking psychiatric help. His first psychoanalyst was Jacques Lacan, who analyzed him in a taxicab. When Lacan died, he went to see Dr. Pierre Roumeguère in Paris. Dalí's life is a life of psychoanalysis."

"Psychiatric help? Dalí? You've got to be kidding," Xavier Cugat said.

"In my opinion, there were not one but *two* lunatics in Dalí's madhouse," the salesperson said, "Dalí *and* Gala. Dalí was a pervert who masturbated fanatically, and Gala was a nymphomaniac. Her sexual desire was excessive and abnormal. She looked like . . . like Faye Dunaway on speed. Almost ninety years of age, she paid her young lovers thousands of dollars to get fucked twice a day, and when she ran out of money, she paid for sex with a free Dalí painting. Isn't it true, Arturo? Correct me if I'm wrong."

Arturo Caminada—Dalí's jack of all trades—chuckled. "Dalí instructed me to take Gala out on the boat for lobster fishing and fuck her senseless," he said.

"Did you?"

"Of course!"

"That's not love," Amanda Lear said. "That's surrealism."

"When Dalí dies, no doubt his beach house in Port Lligat will be turned into a museum," I said. "Will visitors be told that the swimming pool actually has the shape of an erect penis, testicles and all? I doubt it. Will they be allowed into Dalí's sex boudoir in the pigeon coop and see and touch his dildos?"

"Some days Dalí used to brag about how he and Gala would take temporary custody of orphaned children so they could lock the children in a darkened room," Arturo Caminada said with a pained expression on his face. "Honestly, I don't know if this is true. Perhaps it was his idea of Catalan humor."

"In New York, he tied a loaf of bread to his head and took his pet tiger cats out for a pee," Captain Moore said.

"Dalí is a child himself. I've seen him wearing a crown made of sausages!" the art critic said.

Ultra Violet smiled. "He said Jesus Christ had smelly feet."

"Take your words back, Ultra," Rafael Santos Torroella said, shaking with laughter. "Dalí is a friend of mine, and Jesus Christ, too. I won't let them down."

"I don't know about Jesus Christ, but Dalí *had* no friends," Captain Moore said. "He had a royal household of ass-lickers, and I was part of that household."

"Dalí is an ass-licker himself!" the salesperson said.

"You remember when he made that pianolike instrument out of stray cats?" Ramón Guardiola asked. "If he pushed a key, a weight dropped on the cat's tail, forcing the cat to scream."

"I told Stan about the catwalk model. Dalí loved to lick her feet and suck her toes. She was his pet," Ultra Violet said, "but the minute she got a call from her agent with a twenty-thousand-dollar offer for a major part in a Hollywood big-budget film, she turned into Miss Hollywood Charm and dropped him like a stone. Dalí gave her a farewell present, though, as an apology for sucking her toes: a live iguana with imitation pearls around its tail. He gave Mia Farrow a present, too. When she started dating Frank Sinatra, Dalí was appalled. 'The wor*rrr*st sing*errr* in histo*rrry*!' he said. Dalí thought he was the ideal matchmaker and asked her to marry Elvis Presley instead. Of course, Dalí considered himself the Elvis Presley of surrealism. As a marriage present, Dalí sent Mia Farrow and Frank Sinatra a painted fish bowl with a live rat—the rat, that was Mia—who devoured a lizard."

"Who's the lizard?" the salesperson asked.

"Elvis Presley!" I said.

Xavier Cugat laughed. "No, Frank Sinatra," he said.

"For years, Dalí had promised the domestic staff a TV," Arturo Caminada said. "We expected color and got an old secondhand

portable black-and-white television set. Dalí didn't want to pay
for color. There's enough color in the house, he said. Of course,
Dalí had his own private color TV set."

"First time I met Dalí," Amanda Lear said, "he looked rather
ridiculous with his bulging eyes and his upturned waxed
mustache that was dyed pitch-black. He was in the company of
a couple of pederasts with the most laughable names: Louis
XIV, Saint Sebastian, Jesus Christ, Fillet of Plaice, Dado-Hard-
On, Nancy the Coal Miner . . . Nancy had the most beautiful
bottom I'd ever seen. Dalí introduced me to his court. 'A*lll* my
gi*rrr*ls a*rrr*e lesbians and my boy*zzz* a*rrr*e homosexuals,' he
said. 'Dalí clicks his *fingerrrs* and they copulate on command.'
He gave them drugs on occasion. We lunched on tinned sardines. After lunch, Dalí asked me to sit for him, fully dressed. I
only had to take off my panties. I was standing high up on a
glass table while Dalí was sitting under the table with his pencils and sketchbook, peeping under my skirt. He obviously
wanted to see for himself if the rumor was true that I'd had *cojones* and been a boy. Finally, he started drawing. 'Stand still,
Amanda, don't move,' he said, 'it won't take long. Don't look at
me.' I didn't hear any scratching of pencil on paper, and I
looked down, of course. Instead of making a work of art, Dalí
was frantically masturbating. Suddenly he had his orgasm and
yelled: 'Picasso is *Arrrt* capital *A*—Dalí is Dalí capita*lll D*!' I
loved listening to him when he was cracking jokes. A client vis-
its a prostitute in a bordello, he told me. The man is almost
naked, with bloody wounds on his hands and feet and a crown
of thorns in his long hair. The client leaves the bordello an hour

or so later. A friend asks the prostitute: 'Who is he?' and the prostitute says: 'I don't know, but his fucking is divine.' Dalí said it was the best joke he'd ever heard.

"One morning, Isidro Bea—Dalí's number-one assistant—was taken to hospital. Dalí panicked. He had a painting to finish, it was commissioned and paid for, and he asked me if I could replace Bea in the secret studio. On a blank canvas, I painted a large rock. Dalí looked at the rock and exclaimed: 'The porrrtrait of my fatherrr!' In those days, David Bowie was my boyfriend. Whenever I was with him in London, Dalí gave me a wake-up call. Bowie grabbed the phone and said, in a near-perfect Dalí imitation: 'Maestrrro Dalíí, good morrrning!' Of course, Dalí didn't like Bowie. He said he liked Alice Cooper more. As for myself, I desperately wanted to become a female David Bowie and almost succeeded. When I was top of the bill here in Spain and playedbacked a recorded hit song on Spanish television, Dalí angrily turned off the television. Next time I met him, he said: 'You've got the voice of a drunk!' I wanted to get married and introduced my future husband to Gala. 'Your fiancé looks like a baby seal,' Gala said. What an insult! I left Cadaqués and never saw Dalí or Gala ever again."

"Olé Olé!" Marc Lacroix shouted.

"I worked for Dalí without a salary, only for a commission of ten percent on all subsidiary sales such as prints, graphics, sculptures, perfume, jewelry, ashtrays, ties . . . ," Captain Moore said. "All through the sixties and mid-seventies, demand for these kinds of Dalís was at an all-time high. Sales exceeded thirty-five million dollars per fiscal year, oil paintings not included. Dalí loved money, lots of money, and so did I. Every morning, seven days a week, he wanted to see a big fat check on his breakfast tray. As long as I was his business manager, things were under control. But as Dalí grew old, he ran out of surrealist ideas. The source had dried up. His hands were shaking so badly, he couldn't even sign his own name, and often sat at a table with sunken eyes, in a stupor.

"I left Dalí. A new management came in and decided to sell Dalí's thumbprint instead of his signature. Because he couldn't hold a pencil anymore, the new secretary pushed Dalí's thumb into an ink pad and had it embossed. From then on, the Dalí Museum in Figueres issued photomechanic Dalí reproduction lithographs with both his *printed* signature and an embossed thumbprint. What the hell is this? I thought the first time I saw one of these so-called works of art. What are they doing? Then the following happened in the mid-1970s."

This is what Captain Moore recounted. An art gallery in Barcelona celebrated new artists and their work. Beautiful people were sipping *cava* and red wine. In a corner, Dalí's new secretary was brooding over a drink. He wore a loaded gun in a shoulder holster, like any Chicago gangster. Gala came over, smoking a cigarette in a holder two feet long, like a leading lady in a 1940s Hollywood movie, dressed in white ankle socks and black shoes and a faded Chanel dress at least thirty years old. Her head was shrunken. She was combed and rouged as if she had been fixed by a taxidermist, and she walked with a stoop.

NEW SECRETARY:
Gala, can we leave?

GALA:
We've just got here. You haven't looked at the show.

SECRETARY:
It's not *my* show.

GALA:
So? There are some fabulous new artists here. Do you see the man over there?

SECRETARY:
Who is he?

GALA:
His name is Manuel Pujol Baladas.

SECRETARY:
What a pretentious name.

GALA:
I agree. He is the new artist of the year. Works for the Walt Disney Studio in Barcelona. Don't you see he's mastered the Dalí style down to the last detail? All his life, Dalí was a money machine. The old machine is worn out and has to be replaced. We need a new machine. I think Manuel Pujol

Baladas could be our new machine. We'll rename him Young Dalí.

SECRETARY:
This was just decided?

GALA:
He doesn't know. I haven't told him yet.

SECRETARY:
Don't bullshit the guy.

GALA:
I won't. Why should I?

Young Dalí sighed. "Yes, that's how it happened," he said. "I was well known as Manuel Pujol Baladas. I was a successful commercial artist. Gala renamed me Young Dalí. One thing I know for sure. The moment the old Dalí passes away, I'll be arrested and locked up in prison. I know too much. I know Dalí's little secrets. Dalí's new management wants me out of the way. His secretary is armed, you know."

"By the late 1960s, Parkinson's disease had begun to hamper Dalí's work. He sufered paranoia, too. Before he put a spoon or fork in his mouth, I had to taste his soup and paella," Arturo Caminada said. "He feared that his new secretary was hell-bent on poisoning him. Dalí lives the life of an old fossil in his own house . . . he is terrified of what is about to happen."

The waiter brought two more bottles of pink *cava* in ice buckets that resembled top hats turned upside down. We raised our glasses and toasted.

"To Dalí," Antoni Ribas said.

"To Salvador," the salesperson said.

"To Salvador Dalí," Captain Moore said.

"The Divine," Ultra Violet said.

"The Redeemer," Amanda Lear said.

"To a great artist," Marc Lacroix said.

"*Was* a great artist," Young Dalí said.

Great *con* artist, I thought, and raised my glass to my president and all the suckers in the world who had ever been robbed of their rightful money in an ingenious scam.

"The truth is, Dalí hasn't touched a paintbrush in ten years," Captain Moore said. "He liked to doodle and turn his doodles into prints and lithographs. Easy come, easy go. Bronze sculptures were too time consuming. While having beakfast, he kneaded soft, warm bread into figurines that were cast in gold. Yet we needed big sales, because Dalí and Gala were hemorrhaging money. At forty-one, he was the richest artist in the world. He didn't make any real art for thirty years, but at seventy-one, he still lived the life of a maharaja. The financial bleeding had to be stopped."

"That's where I came in," said Young Dalí.

I vacantly stared out at the Mediterranean at my feet.

Amanda Lear half smiled.

"Gala liked my paintings," Young Dalí said. "She wanted to help me. 'I'll promote you the way I promoted Dalí when he was a struggling artist,' she told me, and asked me to come to Port Lligat. I had to bring some watercolors. I showed Gala my watercolors, and again, she was impressed. 'You're good, but you're not commercial enough,' she said to me. 'You're as talented as Vincent van Gogh and Modigliani. Always remember what happened to them. Van Gogh and Modigliani died in poverty. A good painting is like a crossword puzzle. Don't solve the riddle. A great painting has to remain a great enigma.' I thanked Gala for her advice. 'Do me a favor, go home and make me some beautiful watercolors in the old surrealist style of Dalí,' Gala finally said. I said no. I declined her offer. I wanted to hang on to my own style. Gala was furious. Late in 1975—"

"I've heard enough," Captain Moore said. He gulped his drink and trotted off, in short military steps.

"What happened late in 1975?" I asked.

Captain Moore sputtered out of sight on his worn-out Mobylette.

"Gala phoned me," Young Dalí recounted. "She was crying. 'We're desperate, you have to help Dalí,' she said. 'You're a good artist. Make some surrealist artworks in the famous Dalí style of the forties. I'll pay you handsomely, and the world will be at your feet.' What could I say? I was a struggling artist, thirty years of age, married, with a mortgage to pay and a second child on the way. We could use the money. Besides, a watercolor wouldn't take me more than a couple of hours, a Dalí painting on canvas two to three days at the most. I went out and bought a few Dalí art books, to get an idea of his forties surrealist style. Two weeks after Gala had phoned me, I drove to Dalí's house in

Port Lligat and emptied my car trunk. Gala examined each painting carefully, and Dalí studied them under a magnifying glass, as if they were his own original paintings. They were overjoyed with what they saw and paid me ten to fifteen thousand pesetas in cash for a medium-size watercolor and a hundred thousand pesetas for a small oil on canvas. A hundred thousand pesetas was approximately four hundred dollars at the time. My Dalís were original ideas and creations. I didn't copy an earlier Dalí, and none was signed. Dalí was now too ill with Parkinson's disease, he couldn't write his own name anymore—he popped vitamins and medication as if they were M&M's—so another studio assistant applied the signatures."

"So those are the famous *fake fake* Dalís," I said with a sigh. "They're yours."

"Yes, they're mine."

"Do you consider yourself a forger?" I asked.

"I made surrealist paintings to order. I never sold any myself."

"You know 'Secret Love,' that fifties Doris Day song?" Xavier Cugat asked. "*The secret's no secret anymore*. Well, the secret is out now, out in the open."

"First time I ever heard this. If you ask me, not Young Dalí but Gala is the one who should go to prison," Rafael Santos Torroella, the veteran art critic, said. "I never liked her anyway."

"Both. Gala and Dalí," the Catalan filmmaker said.

"Gala is dead and in the world of art, Dalí is God," Ultra Violet said. "Can anyone of you imagine God behind bars?"

Young Dalí pursed his lips. "It was such an elaborate scam," he said. "Gala and Dalí and the new secretary flooded the art market with *fake fake* Dalís. I got four hundred dollars for a surrealist Dalí. Without blinking an eye, the new management sold them to museums and private collectors all over the world for up to two hundred thousand dollars, in many cases with a certificate of authenticity from the Centre Pompidou in Paris on top. My surrealist paintings are on permanent exhibit in top museums all over the world, though they bear Dalí's signature. Whenever Gala found a buyer who was stupid enough to part with his well-earned cash, Dalí was photographed holding the *fake fake* painting and admiring it. Of course, you can't see his shaking hands on a Polaroid."

I felt proud. I was pleased with myself. Even in a routine conversation among friends, they had started using my own *genuine genuine* and *fake fake* categorization that I had invented myself.

"How many Dalí oils did you paint?" the art critic asked.

"Five hundred, between 1975 and 1982," Young Dalí said.

"How many watercolors on paper?" I asked.

"Two thousand? Three thousand?"

"You lost count?"

"Yes."

"A wild guess," I said. "How many fake Dalís are there in the world?"

"*Fake fake,* as you call them?"

"Yes."

"Half of all Dalí's are *fake fake.*"

"Half?"

"Easily. Even leading auction houses at one time sold my *fake fake* Dalí watercolors."

"Add to that the *genuine fake* Dalís. You mean to say that *three quarters* of all Dalís now on the market anywhere in the world are *dubious* Dalís?"

"That's a rough estimate."

Amanda Lear gulped. "This reminds me of something that happened when I was Salvador Dalí's muse and he was my art teacher," she said. "Dalí allowed me to use his pencils and his brushes. At the end of each day, Isidro Bea cleaned our brushes with turpentine. One morning, Dalí asked me to copy a Leonardo da Vinci angel from an art book. He took my finished drawing away from me, signed it, and gave it to Gala. Unbeknownst to me, Gala sold my da Vinci copy to Gina Lollobrigida, the Italian film star. It was a *genuine genuine* Amanda Lear and a *fake fake* Dalí with a *genuine genuine* Dalí signature."

"That makes it a *genuine fake* Amanda Lear," Ramón Guardiola said.

". . . or a *genuine fake* Dalí?" Young Dalí asked, and smiled.

"Ramón, you founded the Dalí Museum in Figueres," Xavier Cugat said, stroking his chihuahua dog and sucking on his empty pipe. "After what you've heard today, are you still sure all Dalís in the museum are *genuine genuine* Dalís?"

"I'm a small-town lawyer," Ramón Guardiola said. "Ask Young Dalí. *I* can't see if a work of art is genuine or not."

Again, all heads turned to Young Dalí.

"Twenty-five percent is *genuine genuine,* twenty-five percent is *genuine fake,* the rest is *fake fake,*" he said.

Wasn't that a great showstopper?

To round off the day, we had *churros,* a kind of doughnut deep-fried in olive oil and dusted with sugar. Xavier Cugat ordered a chocolate drink and dipped his doughnut in the hot and sticky chocolate.

I was edgy. Who will pay the bill for the pink *cava* and the doughnuts? I wondered.

Amanda Lear had tears in her eyes. "When Gala died, I tried hard to console Dalí," she sighed. "I did my best. I paid for a huge wreath and assured Dalí of my affection. 'My little Dalí, don't be sad . . .,' I said to him on the telephone. He interrupted me. 'The*rr*re i*zzz* no little Dalí anymo*rrr*e,' he croaked. 'It i*zzz* ove*rr*. Eve*rrr*ything i*zzz* ove*rr*. . . .' I've not seen him since, and I haven't heard from him."

Soon afterward, late at night, the wailing of a siren followed by the flickering blue light of an ambulance cutting the curbs woke me up. I jumped out of bed and went to the door and ran out to the edge of my mountaintop. The ambulance came to a stop in the bay at the foot of the mountain. Dalí's house was fully illuminated. Lights on everywhere, even in the pigeon coop. I heard shouting and banging of doors. A ringing telephone in the stillness of the night. The phone wasn't answered. I'd never before in my life seen that many stars glued to the blackboard. Not a cloud in sight. A million *chicadas* were chirping frenetically. The ambulance started the long, daunting climb uphill and became invisible in the untamed countryside behind the mountain peaks. Its flickering light colored the sky above in psychedelic colors. A few moments later, all was still, all was quiet. Dalí is gone, I thought. He won't come back. It's all over.

Part III

Señor Dalí

*A*ccording to an early-morning news report on the radio, Dalí was suffering from a severe bout of Russian flu. He talked of nothing other than his own death. Maybe this was indeed the end. It certainly was the end of an era. As I listened to the news in bed, someone banged on my door. Police, I thought. Day and night, I was in fear that Interpol would come and drag me away in handcuffs. Sleepy-eyed, I got out of bed and drew the curtains. Embers were dying in the fireplace. I remembered what my president had told me on our very first meeting in the luxurious surroundings of the Century Center Hotel. *If you can fool a man once, you can fool him always. Some suckers are born to be taken for a ride. Sucker them. Take them for a ride, give them what they deserve.* In a split second, it all came back: the anxiety, the nightmares, but also the excitement and the adrenaline rush. My heart was pounding when I opened the front door.

It wasn't Interpol. It wasn't another tramontana either. It was worse.

Catherine was at the front door, brandishing a gun. The beauty queen. The *ice* queen. The fake designer handbag queen. Her makeup was running with tears. She's gonna shoot me, I thought. Or shoot herself. One way or other, I'll have blood on my hands.

"Hi, Catherine," I said, "you're okay?"

Just when I thought I couldn't get more fucked . . .

"I found you," she said. "Now you'll pay me."

"Pay for what?"

"My *Last Supper,* of course. My Dalí masterpiece."

"Haven't you got it yet?"

"No."

"You're not threatening me, are you?" I asked.

"A million dollars," she said. "That's what we paid you." Catherine made a quick calculation. "You promised to double its value in five years. That's a twenty percent profit per year. We signed an agreement. A contract. You owe me two million plus. Dollars. Cash. I want it now or you'll never walk again."

"Put your gun away, Catherine," I said. "Let's talk."

"I don't want to talk. I want money."

"I haven't got any money. Not now, not here."

"You want me to go to the police?"

"You see this?" I said, and spread my arms. "Nature. A mountaintop. The middle of nowhere. There's not a bank to be seen for miles around. Where do you want me to get your money? Besides, it's too early in the day. Even if we could find a bank, it wouldn't be open until nine. Cadaqués is a fishing village of a few hundred inhabitants. The one bank there most certainly won't have a couple of million on the shelf. A million pesetas perhaps, but that's peanuts. Be reasonable and come in, Catherine. We were friends, remember? I'll make you some coffee."

Catherine came in and sat down. She put the gun in her handbag—Hermès—and blew her nose.

"Nice house you've got," she said.

"You know who my neighbor is, don't you, Catherine?" I asked. "My *only* neighbor for miles around?"

"No. Who is he?"

"Salvador Dalí."

"Don't talk to me about Dalí."

"What do you want to talk about?"

"Money."

"Dalí *is* money."

Catherine looked up. "Where is my painting?"

I smiled and clapped my hands. "You know what, Catherine? You're too pushy. You paid a million. Now you want *two* million. Or perhaps you want your painting. Too pushy and too ambitious. You can't have it all." I held the smile a little longer. "Do you remember what I told you, all those years ago? When Dalí dies, I said, your investment will skyrocket. All right, that was my sales pitch. Five years on, Dalí is even more of a brand name—Cartier Louis Vuitton Gucci *Dalí* Ferrari

Hermès. He's a rock star. Whatever Dalí touches, it turns to gold. I'll show you something. Come over at the window. See the white house down there, in the distance? With the giant eggs on top? That's Salvador Dalí's house. I told you, Dalí is my neighbor. My *only* neighbor. I didn't lie to you. Isn't that a miracle? I used to be an art investment broker selling Dalí. That was my first lesson in life: Dalí sells. *Only* Dalí. Now we breathe the same mountain air. I don't live in a castle like you do, but I feel like a king because I share a mountain with the most famous artist of the century. Isn't that wonderful? Dalí is incredible. He's a money machine. I've seen the value of his watercolors soaring lately. Really escalating. Can you imagine? Today, twelve small Dalí watercolors on paper are worth more than one big Dalí masterpiece on canvas. Why? Because twelve watercolors you can sell twelve times over."

"I'm glad you're here, Catherine. I'm also deeply sad," I said, and sighed. "Dalí is in pain. He's in agony. A couple of nights ago, he was taken to hospital. I watched the ambulance meandering up and down the mountain pass. Dalí is about to die—a week, a month, a year at the most—and you're asking me for two million dollars." I shook my head. "How can you do that, Catherine? Be reasonable. Think twice. You should have asked me for not one, not two, but three or four million. That's exactly what your *Last Supper* will be worth the minute Dalí ascends into heaven and the sad news of his passing away is splashed all over *The New York Times* and causes an international media frenzy." I looked at my watch. Yes, I still had my gold Cartier. "Let's go down to the bank in Cadaqués," I said. "See if we can arrange a bank transfer. We'll have coffee at the Bar Boia on the beach. Their *café con leche* is delicious."

It was so easy to get back into my old sales pitch. As if I'd never stopped doing it.

I clearly remembered my *second* lesson in life.

People *want* to be fooled. Anyone can be taken for a ride.

Catherine hesitated. "Twelve Dalí watercolors . . . on paper . . . that's interesting . . . how much would they come to?" she asked.

Grab, squeeze and—*snòk*, I thought.

Problem was, she didn't have balls.

"Depends," I said, and rolled my eyes. "What kind of watercolors? What size? What does the image represent? I don't have to tell you that a frivolous and idyllic surrealist image sells far better than a dark and brooding landscape that's only surrealist in passing. A couple of days ago, I saw Dalí's *Life Is a Dream* for sale at a private Dalí museum in Cadaqués. Sixteen watercolors on Arches paper, brightly executed and beautifully signed and dated between 1962 and 1967, which is artistically the most prolific and valuable period in Dalí's life. The asking price was something like . . . I don't exactly remember . . . two and a half? Three million? Dollars, of course."

"Can you get those watercolors for me?"

"One? Two?"

"All of them. Sixteen, you said?"

"The whole lot?"

"Yes."

I whistled.

"Three million. Catherine, have you got that kind of money?"

"No. *You* have," she said. "That's exactly what you owe me. Go to your bank. Get your money. Buy those Dalís. I'll come back, say . . . in three days? We're staying for another week at the Princesa Sofia in Barcelona. That's not too far from here, is it?"

"I know the owner of the Princesa Sofia," I said. "His brother is a friend of mine. We went to the Perelada castle for a surrealist evening out. Amanda Lear was there, and tonight Julio Iglesias will perform in the casino. You know Amanda Lear, don't you, Catherine?"

Name-dropping doesn't hurt, I thought.

Catherine was taken aback. "Promise me? You'll definitely get the Dalí watercolors for me?" she asked.

"I'll do my best."

"Promise!"

"I can't."

"Why not?"

"They might be sold."

"You think so?"

"Three, four days is eternity in the art business. Anyway, you can't lose. You either got the Dalí watercolors or you get my money."

"I'd prefer the watercolors," Catherine said. "If they're good."

"They're perfect. When Dalí dies, you'll thank me on your knees."

I waved her out. She walked over to her brand-new car. A black

Maserati with tinted windows. I'd seen a car like that only once, in an Italian Mafia movie.

"*I'll be back.* See you in three days," she said.

"Do me a favor, Catherine, will you? Don't bring your gun."

Ana and the boys were still asleep when I got back into the house.

I locked myself in the bathroom and banged my head against the mirror and cried my eyes out.

In the swimming pool in the moonlight, immersing my head in the dark-green water, I was lost in thought. My dream house was in darkness. The Mediterranean in the distance was steeped in impressionist colors. I was crying silently. I didn't have three million dollars. I didn't have two. I didn't have one. The simple truth is, I had nothing left. I had scraped the bottom of my safe to buy the fast and sporty Alfa Romeo after Ana's battered car had let us down, and frankly, I didn't want to be seen in a yellow Ford Fiesta. That was the last of it. The mountaintop hacienda, a luxury car, the good life. All the investors' money I had creamed off MMC and its clients, it was all gone. For the first time since I had moved in, I noticed that my beautiful swimming pool had become a slimy pond. Maintenance? I couldn't be bothered. I was letting myself go.

The wind was blowing hard, as usual. I feared the long, hard winter and the onslaught of the tramontana. I pulled myself out of the swimming pool and went into the house, dripping wet and shivering, and took my family in my arms.

I love you all, I whispered.

I heard the music swelling, swelling, swelling . . . like background music in one of Xavier Cugat's 1950s Hollywood movies.

I hadn't shaved in four days. I was broke. I was out of a job. I hadn't fled to Spain to spend my life cleaning bathroom tiles with a toothbrush.

"I saw a nice flat in Girona the other day," Ana said. "The view is breathtaking, like a Canaletto painting."

"Buy the view and forget about the flat," I said.

It wasn't all bliss.

"Come on," I said to Teri. "Work to be done."

"What are we gonna do?"

"Make a few Dalís."

"How many?"

"Sixteen."

"How do we do that?"

"Piece of cake. What Dalí can do, we can do better."

"You can't make Dalís," Ana said, dragging on a cigarette. "You're not allowed to. Forgery is a crime in this country."

"It's a crime in *any* country," I replied. "We're not going to *fake* Dalí. We won't make a *genuine genuine* Dalí but no *genuine fake* or *fake fake* Dalí either. Run a bath, will you, Ana? Not too warm, not too cold."

"Are you any good at drawing?"

"No."

"Can you paint?"

"No."

". . . and you're going to make some Dalís?"

"Sixteen."

"How are you going to do that?"

"You'll see."

Next day, I took an old Dalí art book titled *La Vida Es Sueño* from my library. That's Spanish and translates as "Life Is a Dream." It consisted of several surrealist full-page black-on-white reproductions of smudgy ink drawings, no added color and very Dalí-like, with a printed date and a printed signature. A French text was embossed on the first page. The text said, ". . . *dans ce monde, tricheur, rien n'est vérité, rien n'est mensonge . . .*" which translates as, "In this world, you trickster, nothing is the truth, and nothing is a lie." I tore sixteen hard, solid, nonglossy pages loose from the spine.

"Can you do that?" Ana asked, reluctant. She was reading a Spanish newspaper.

"Of course I can. It's *my* book, isn't it?"

As I had done with the signatures I had enlarged years ago, I pinned and glued typical Dalí images to the wall, for inspiration: posters, photographs, postcards, illustrations from books—some still bearing the stamp of the library they were stolen from—as well as newspaper and magazine reproductions of Dalí's most famous museum paintings: *Soft Self-Portrait with Fried Bacon, The Great Masturbator, Soft Construction with Boiled Beans, The Persistence of Memory, Atmospheric Skull Sodomizing a Grand Piano, Burning Giraffe,* and several others. I made sure all the familiar surrealist symbols were there: wooden crutches, fried eggs, a masturbating hand, melting clocks, ever-receding horizons, and a convoy of horses and elephants on long spidery legs.

"What are we doing?" Teri asked.

He was a nice boy. He had the darkest eyes and the blackest hair I'd ever seen in my life. He was smart, too, for a boy his age.

"I'm gonna give you a crash course on how to fake an artwork," I said.

"Is it difficult?"

"Difficult? No, it's not difficult. Easy as pie," I said. "Salvador Dalí does it all the time."

"Did you do it before?"

"I had a client once," I said. "A doctor. He gave me fifty thousand dollars for a small Dalí gouache. I didn't have it, so I made one. Two years later, my client asked me to sell the Dalí gouache at Sotheby's or Christie's, wherever, simply because he loved to see his name on the printed page in the sales catalog. *Provenance: Dr. So-and-So, Brussels.* I had lead in my shoes but I did it, Teri, I went to London and brought it in. My gouache doubled its price, it sold for over a hundred thousand dollars. See, Teri? That's life. That's the art world. It's a world of make-believe. Hot air. We're not doing anything out of the ordinary. We're simply going to fake a fake Dalí."

"What's a gouache?" Teri asked.

I sighed. "A gouache is a watercolor painting with lots of pigment and almost no water," I said.

"Are we going to make a gouache now?"

"No. We're going to dilute the pigment and make watercolors."

I threw a couple of tea bags in the shallow water—breakfast tea is best, but Earl Grey will do—and submerged the hard, solid book pages in the bath and let them soak for up to an hour or more, so that they could absorb the water like a sponge and thicken and puff up. Tea gives the finished artwork a yellowish and distinctively antique look. I took the wet paper out of the water and simply dripped some pigment or colored ink or fast-drying acrylic on it. A few drops of blue, red, and green would do. You can also use color markers. As soon as the pigment came into contact with the wet paper, the paper absorbed the colors and the dye blotted into the most beautiful patches, with a real soft pastel look and wild and angry, as if the tramontana itself had a hand in it. No complicated techniques or excessive brushstrokes. I didn't even use a brush, just dropped some paint on the wet reproductions in black-and-white and that was it.

"Wet on wet works like a charm. Don't be afraid to use your imagination," I said to Teri.

"You can't do this," Ana said as she watched us. "These artworks, they're fake."

"The signatures are real."

"A *printed* signature doesn't make it a real work of art."

"It is what it is. It's art. It can be whatever it wants. Whatever *I* want."

"You're committing fraud," Ana said.

"Andy Warhol has been reproducing Campbell's tomato soup and chicken noodle cans by the hundreds and selling them for tens of thousands of dollars. A tomato soup can, is that art? Or chicken noodle? If I'd paint a thousand cans, I couldn't fetch a peseta for them. Why not? Because my name isn't Andy Warhol. You know, Ana, fine art is worth only what the fool wants to pay for it. Rich people have no idea how they're being fooled. They want a Dalí because it's a Dalí that's also a good investment. A Dalí that makes them look smart and doesn't clash with the furniture. Way back at the time of MMC, no investor client of mine really liked the Dalís I sold them. Do you know where they stuffed them, all their expensive investment Dalís? Well out of sight behind a cupboard in the bedroom or under their bed."

"I still think it's unethical, what you're doing," Ana said.

"It is. I *know* it is. What else can I do?"

"Haven't you got any money left?"

"Nothing. I'm broke. But I don't complain, I'm getting used to being broke."

"Poor man. You could have taken all the Chinese vases in the world."

"Yes. I should have. I had the opportunity. But I didn't."

I didn't feel any guilt. Catherine was driving a Maserati she'd bought from the proceeds of counterfeit luxury handbags. An eye for an eye, I thought. I knew it was unethical, but I felt great. I was back on my old turf, and besides, there was three million dollars at stake here.

The result of my bathtub experiment was a set of perfect wash watercolors over a printed reproduction puffed up with water.

I took a deep breath. "That's it," I said, and smiled, "and now, the finishing touch."

I dropped some giant blots of black Chinese ink on the paper and held each sheet askew under the dripping tap. Then I cut the most colorful butterflies from an old biology manual and glued them onto the Chinese ink. The end result looked like one of Dalí's best surrealist Ampurdán landscapes, from dark blue to bright green and bloodred in color and chock-full with long dark shadows, moonlit trees, and giant butterflies that hovered over the horizon like praying mantis. Suddenly I noticed that some of the sixteen sheets didn't have a printed signature after all. A problem? Not at all. I signed them myself, with a bold and sprawling Dalí signature. I took the dripping wet sheets of paper out in the sun and the wind and hung them on a washing line to dry, using wooden clothes-pegs. At the end of the day, I locked them in a hot butane oven for fifteen minutes, so that the Chinese ink could dry out and crack and flake and age the "artworks" with twenty years at least.

"*Jesus,* Stán! You're a con man," Ana said.

"No, Ana. I'm a businessman."

"You got it wrong, Stán. Life is not a Hollywood movie."

"It is, Ana, it is, if you want life to be a Hollywood movie. Did you see *To Catch a Thief* starring Cary Grant? Don't know its Spanish title. A Hitchcock thriller about a string of jewel robberies along the French Riviera. Police officials have a suspect in mind, a retired cat burglar."

"What is a cat burglar?" Teri asked.

"A high-class jewel thief. He tiptoes like a cat, without a sound. That why he's called a *cat* burglar. The cat burglar chooses to unmask the thief himself. He is smarter than the rest and covers his back. I never was a jewel thief, but years ago, Ana, when I met you, I was a high-class crook. I'm doing now what Cary Grant does in the movie. I'm trying to be smarter than the rest and I'm covering my back."

I didn't want to tell her that technically I owed a former client over three million dollars.

"What happens if you're caught?" said Ana.

I shrugged. What could I say? I'll go to prison, I thought. What's the difference? There's already an Interpol warrant out for my arrest. One day or other, I'll end up in prison anyway.

"Don't you care about your reputation?" asked Ana.

"I do care . . . but I haven't got a reputation anymore."

"You made a bad choice of profession, Stán."

I could hardly protest. "Let's come to an understanding," I pleaded. "I can't change track. It's too late in life for me to become a tap dancer. I didn't mean for this to happen. I'm sorry. I'm really sorry. I'll fix it, if I can. I'll do you a favor. I'll cover *your* back and take all the blame."

"Thank you. I don't need your help. I'll save my own life," Ana said.

I spritzed all sixteen watercolors with hair spray as a fixative.

"What are you going to do with these?" Teri asked.

I smiled. "Sell them?" I said, and grinned.

"You can't do that!"

"Sure I can. I'm the master of my own universe. I can do whatever I want. Wait . . . no! I've got a better idea! I won't sell my Dalí watercolors. I'll exchange them for Dalí's *Last Supper*. That's a three-million-dollar painting in Washington, D.C."

Ana gulped. "But that's . . . that's . . . immoral."

"Exactly."

She turned her back on me and slammed the bathroom door shut.

If you can fool a man once, you can fool him every time, my MMC president used to say. Any man, any woman. Three days later, Catherine was back. She honked the car from the driveway. No knocking on the door, and no gun. I went out, smiling and carrying the rolled-up fake Dalí fakes. She didn't even look at them. Didn't say thank you. She threw them in the back of her Maserati and left. I held my head in my hands and started sobbing. I know, I shouldn't complain: gratitude is not of this world. Catherine I haven't seen since.

The last tourist had gone home. No more smells of suntan oil. Cadaqués and Port Lligat were deserted. The salesperson had closed his souvenir shop for the winter and gone to live in Barcelona. The drizzle of early-morning rain had washed the villages. The cobbled streets smelled sweet and clean. It was getting colder. The sun was pale and wintry and didn't give any warmth. Local fishermen blessed the food on their table before they sat down to eat their soup. A Catalan proverb says, *Menjar be i cagar fort, i no tingues por de la mort.* "Eat well and shit well and you won't have to be afraid of death."

I walked by myself around the perimeter of the house. The sea licked the rocks. A half moon lit the scene. It was a night to remember always. Everyone had gone to bed. My little hacienda was in darkness, the pungent perfume of Mediterranean spices floating in the air, from kitchen to bathroom to the wild country beyond. Paraffin wax candles in earthenware pots flickered on the rim of the swimming pool. It looked as if the water was on fire. So many years had gone by.

I was weary. I was disheveled. Watching television, I caught a Spanish news report showing a wheelchair-ridden Dalí in his Figueres hospital room, gesticulating like a madman to the assembled reporters. Suffering from malnutrition, the anchorman said, Salvador Dalí was on a liquids-only diet. Plastic feeding tubes dangled from his nose. He never ventured outside the hospital. As soon as he got better, he would be treated privately in a wing of the Galatea Tower, an extension of the Dalí Museum within walking distance to the hospital. The film of the impromptu press conference was followed by the opening scene from Buñuel's *Un chien andalou,* scripted by Dalí, in which a woman's eye is slit by a razor. Then came some Spanish archive footage of the artist sporting a red-and-black Catalan beret. Dalí in the prime of his life, with a long sad face, the tips of his mustache twitching like antennae. He was in top form, rolling his *r*'s and dramatically lengthening the pauses between words and sentences.

REPORTER:

Maestro, what is the difference between a Dalí painting and a color photograph?

SALVADOR DALÍ:

Two million dolla*rrr*s!

REPORTER:

Are you the best painter in the world?

SALVADOR DALÍ:

No, Velásquez is. Ze day Dalí paints a pictu*rrr*e as good a*zzz* Velásquez, he will die. So Dalí prefe*rrr*s to paint bad pictu*rrr*es and live longe*rrr*.

REPORTER:

You are the most famous artist in the world, isn't that right?

SALVADOR DALÍ:

No. Dalí i*zzz* ze most famous *mannn* in ze whole wo*rrr*ld!

REPORTER:

You sure? Is this true?

SALVADOR DALÍ:

Dalí i*zzz* a lia*rr* who always tells ze t*rrr*uth.

The film cut back from archive footage to the current press conference in the hospital.

Ana watched the broadcast and listened intently. Teri and Lluís were sound asleep.

DOCTOR ON SPANISH TELEVISION:

We can't make an accurate diagnosis. Psychic depression, perhaps. Señor Dalí is suffering from the disease of being Salvador Dalí.

JOURNALIST:

Dalí wants to commit suicide, his doctors say, but a genius must never die. Dalí will live for our King, for Spain, and for Catalonia.

NURSES:

[Applauding] Da-lí! Da-lí! Da-lí!

Son of a bitch, I thought.

I switched to a German news channel, then zapped to a French channel and its international correspondent in Washington and got the shock of my life.

NEWS ANCHOR:

[Looking straight into the camera, in a booming voice] Each year, we spend billions of dollars on art. Our story tonight is about the hundreds of millions we spend on fraudulent art. For example, the huge fraud involving the works of one of the most famous artists of our time: Salvador Dalí. In recent years, thousands of us, you perhaps, and me, have been conned into buying cheap Salvador Dalí reproductions, basically posters, for thousands of dollars each, when they are actually worth only ten or twenty dollars. These fake and phony mass-produced prints are represented by the sellers as original, valuable lithographs, each one signed by the artist himself. It has been called the biggest art scam of the century. In the studio with me is a coconspirator in the Dalí fraud. He stood accused of lining his own pockets, and his company was charged with tax cheating. He pleaded guilty in exchange for a lenient sentence and faces many years in prison and millions of dollars in fines and forfeitures. His former company, Money Management Counselors, is now defunct.

I almost fell off my chair. The camera zoomed in on my president. There he was, groomed and manicured as always, ever the playboy. I watched in horror.

NEWS ANCHOR:
Your salespeople told your investors that the prints they were buying were limited art editions? . . .

MY PRESIDENT:
That's true.

NEWS ANCHOR:
. . . hand-drawn original lithographs signed by the artist himself?

MY PRESIDENT:
Yes, we believed they were signed by the artist.

NEWS ANCHOR:
Were they?

MY PRESIDENT:
Were they what?

NEWS ANCHOR:
Signed by Salvador Dalí?

MY PRESIDENT:
We don't know.

NEWS ANCHOR:
Anyone could have signed them?

MY PRESIDENT:
Yes.

NEWS ANCHOR:
Where did you get the prints?

MY PRESIDENT:
Our sales executive in charge of our art investment branch bought them from Gilbert Hamon, who runs the Arts, Lettres et Techniques art gallery in Paris.

"It's not an art gallery, sucker!" I shouted. "It's a ware-house!

NEWS ANCHOR:
You charged up to four thousand dollars apiece while you had paid sixty dollars apiece yourself. Is that correct?

MY PRESIDENT:
Right.

NEWS ANCHOR:
Good business. You were marketing Salvador Dalí as a bona fide investment?

MY PRESIDENT:
Correct. The idea was to begin a franchise of McDalí galleries, selling Dalí prints the average middle-class buyer can afford. We marked out doctors and dentists as targets as well as butchers, cheese manufacturers, small privately owned companies, and undertakers because they have money and know nothing about the art market. We told our clients we'd buy back in five years at double the price. For the benefit of our clients, we reappraised the artworks year after year and estimated that they increased twenty to twenty-five percent in value each year. People are greedy. We kept telling our investors the price had gone up and they were under the impression they were getting rich when, in reality, *we* were the only ones getting rich.

NEWS ANCHOR:

You will go to jail for doing that. What about the Dalí artworks themselves?

MY PRESIDENT:

Honestly? They are completely worthless.

"Fucking asshole!" I shouted.

Ana was shocked and angry.

"Can you believe it?" I asked her. "He is tearing my life apart."

I lowered my trousers and turned around and farted right in his face.

What was I doing? I couldn't believe it. I was becoming my worst enemy. Relax, I thought. Breathe. Slowly, slowly. Calm down. I shook my head in disbelief. This is a nightmare, I thought. This is one hell of a nightmare, and I may never wake up again.

NEWS ANCHOR:

Does the artist know about this?

MY PRESIDENT:

Salvador Dalí, you mean?

NEWS ANCHOR:

Yes.

MY PRESIDENT:

Salvador Dalí is the most forged artist in history because *he* is responsible for most of the forging and has *never* tried to hide this fact. Quite the contrary. Dalí has spent his life defrauding the art world all the while confessing he was doing so, only to see the financial value of his paintings soar as a consequence.

"This is a fucking disaster," I groaned.

"Only if it's true," Ana said.

"Of course it's fucking true! Why else would it be on TV?"

I could hardly bear to watch. I wanted to smash the screen.

It was worse than a nightmare. It was a Greek tragedy. The man who discovered me, groomed me, fed me, and taught me everything was now killing me. I sank to the floor like a wet noodle. I'm a prisoner, I can't leave this country, I thought. I haven't got a passport. It's expired and has become void. I'm a *sans-papiers* now. I haven't got any money left from the millions I made. What's gonna happen to me? What's gonna happen to *us*?

NEWS ANCHOR:

Are you telling us that Dalí deliberately set out to dupe art critics, museum curators, and art collectors? Is this a surrealist joke played on us by Salvador Dalí?

MY PRESIDENT:

It is impossible to know whether Dalí is joking or whether he is serious.

NEWS ANCHOR:
Why is that?

MY PRESIDENT:
Because he doesn't know himself.

"Don't!" I shouted. "Don't say that! Not in public! Not on TV! Shut up!"

Because of his fucking investment club, I had been forced to flee my country. I couldn't go back. Not now, not ever. With his dramatic confession on television, my president was making life impossible for me in *this* country, too.

It wasn't over yet. Credits rolled over grainy black-and-white footage of Salvador Dalí entering his studio, cluttered with many paintings in various stages of completion. It's the late fifties, early sixties. There is a Eisenhower magazine photograph in the background. Brushes and pots of linseed oil everywhere. He walks up to an easel, conjures a live squid from his jacket pocket, and slams the squid against the blank canvas.

SALVADOR DALÍ:
Marrrilyn Monrrroe!

I turned off the TV and took two aspirins and an Alka-Seltzer.

"I'm a failure, Ana. I made a mess of my life," I said.

Ana was sobbing. "Don't you feel ashamed? Aren't you sorry?" she asked.

"Yes. I'm sorry . . . for myself," I said. "I'm not sorry for my clients. They got what they deserved. People who buy fine art as a short-term or a long-term investment, they've got money to burn. They're greedy. They're mean. They're selfish. Where does their money come from? No one knows. But every fortune in the world is built on crime. I could have been a millionaire, Ana. Easily. You know that, don't you? Perhaps I should have played it mean and hard and selfish up until the end."

Who is the real con artist? I wondered, not for the first time. Was it Dalí? Or is it me?

Very early the next morning, all hell broke loose. After another short, restless night, I was having breakfast while reading a days-old *International Herald Tribune* I had picked up at a Cadaqués newsagent the previous day. A well-known California art dealer who advised Hollywood celebrities on building their fine art collections was arrested and charged with systematically defrauding well-known people in the movie business over a period of time. A front page article from the *IHT*'s Paris news desk interested me even more. DALÍ DEALER GILBERT HAMON ARRESTED AND LOCKED UP IN THE INFAMOUS LA SANTÉ PRISON, the headline read. I gulped. My legs turned to jelly. The art market was collapsing faster than an old soufflé, I thought.

Squad cars and unmarked police vans drove up the mountain. There was a hard and loud knock on the door. Before I could get up, the door was smashed in, and four Guardia Civil *secretos* stormed in, flashing gilded badges. *Secretos* are under-cover agents.

POLICÍA, it said on each badge.

"Ana! Ana! Call Ramón Guardiola!" I shrieked. "Quick! Call your lawyer!"

"You're under arrest!" the *secretos* shouted. Their breath smelled of garlic.

"Why are you arresting me?"

"Did you ever watch *Miami Vice*?" one of the *secretos* asked. "What a wonderful television series that was. Officers in stiff white shirts and dark suits. You can almost smell the toothpaste they're using. Of course they're holding shotguns." He laughed. "But that's only on television. Reality is quite different, as you'll soon find out."

Lluís woke up, crying, "Papa! Papa!"

The *secretos* handcuffed me and pushed me into the back seat of a gray unmarked squad car behind a scratched screen of bulletproof Plexiglas separating the driver from arrested passengers going berserk.

"Come back, Papa!" That was Lluís crying.

"I'll be back, Lluís, I promise," I said. "I'll always come back."

Ana was dressed in a white bathrobe. She was barefoot. She was crying too. Police reporters and private detectives were crawling around the house.

Slowly, as if it were a silent movie, Ana blew me a kiss.

During the night, a thick fog had descended on the bay and the valley wrapping the Black Mountain in mysteries and veils from centuries past. Suddenly a red sun appeared behind the olive groves. The squad cars took off and raced along the hair-pin bends, slipping and sliding, and turned into the parking lot of the Girona penitentiary an hour later and some sixty kilometers inland. Bored prisoners in the courtyard behind the gate shot cigarette butts in a fountain that gurgled drinking water. Plastic coffee cups littered the courtyard. I was transferred to a van that brought me to the police HQ on the Via Laietana in Barcelona and was taken to a little squalid interrogation room on the ground floor. The stony-faced detective who headed the *Grupo de Obras de Arte* was dressed in a multicolored Hawaiian shirt and a green blazer several sizes too large for his bulky frame. He opened a drawer and dropped a loaded .357 Magnum Smith & Wesson with a walnut grip on the tabletop. I counted six cartridges in the cylinder. That gun could shoot a horse in half, I thought. The grip of a Basque-made Star pistol stuck out of a leather holster on his hip.

"Give me your passport," he barked.

"I haven't got one."

"You haven't got a passport?"

"It expired. I cut it up and flushed the pieces in the toilet."

"Give me your name. Write it down."

He gave me pen and paper and hammered my name into a simple computer keyboard. Minutes later, its screen jumped to life.

"Huh-huh," the detective chuckled. "You're flagged. We've got green, blue, and red flags. You're red flag. *Busca y captura.* That's high risk. We call it red-notice status. Find the suspect, arrest him, and lock him up. A warrant for your arrest and an extradition request are issued through Interpol. Are you a dangerous criminal?"

He pressed a print button, and the printer hammered out Arrest Warrant 27-540S.

"You're under arrest, *amigo* Stán. For suspicion of capital fraud. *Aprobatión indebido de fondos.* Trafficking forged and fraudulent artworks. Mail fraud. Forging artistic work in the United States and Europe."

Still handcuffed, I was brought before an examining magistrate in a sharp suit.

"You want a *pro deo* lawyer to represent you?" the magistrate asked. "For free?"

"Do I need a lawyer?"

"I think so."

"I can't believe it," I said. "This is the world turned upside down. If *I* am on trial, *Dalí* is on trial, *art* is on trial. There are *fake fake* Dalís in half the museums in the world, and Interpol gets *me* for . . . for what?"

"Are you familiar with an undertaker who bought a hundred-thousand-dollar Dalí ink drawing from you?" the examining magistrate asked.

"I am. Swirls and ovals. Fried beans. A 1937 futuristic drawing."

"A hundred thousand. Is that what it is worth?"

"Who knows? What is the value of *any* work of art? The price the sucker wants to pay for it, that's the *real* value of art."

"One hundred thousand dollars is what you *coerced* the undertaker into paying."

"That's what he says? I didn't coerce anyone. He couldn't get his money out fast enough. He loved buying it."

"Why?"

"Because it was a Dalí."

"That's what you pretended it to be. Respected art appraisers consider the drawing worthless. What do you say to that?"

I looked down and collected my thoughts. Bullshit, I thought. That drawing is reproduced in a 1940s edition of *American Weekly* as well as in an old museum catalog and a 1960s art book on Dalí and surrealism. It's as good as a drawing can get. Besides, *respected* art appraisers? I don't know any *respected* art appraisers. They're all part of the racket. That's how they make their money. That's how they get rich. That's how *I* made my money. Hear, see, and speak no evil. Even the international salesrooms sold *fake fake* Dalís.

"Are you familiar with a butcher named—?" the examining magistrate read from his file.

"Yes, yes, I remember," I said nervously. "I emptied his Chinese vase."

"A luxury-handbag manufacturer?"

"Yes," I said. "Counterfeit handbags."

"Are you familiar with a cheese farmer in Luxembourg?"

I swallowed and shut up.

"Is there anything you want to say?" the examining magistrate asked.

"My investor-clients gave me their money wholeheartedly, without any reservation. I didn't steal any family jewels," I replied. "Because of this, I've been in the dock before, in my home country. Your counterpart in Belgium asked me who—in my view—was responsible for the mass of Dalí fakes and forgeries flooding the art market. In all honesty, I don't know, I said. I even made an attempt at cracking a joke. Mafia perhaps, I said, or Ku Klux Klan, maybe Darth Vader. I just didn't know.

"Now I know. My president told me, on television the other day. The mad genius pulling the strings is Dalí himself. Salvador Dalí is the most forged artist in history because *he* is responsible for most of the faking and forging of his own works of art. It is not an excuse, but he has to be given credit for the simple fact that he has never tried to hide this, quite the contrary. Dalí has spent half his life defrauding the art world, all the while confessing he was doing so, only to see the value of his own output soar as a consequence."

The stony-faced detective straightened his back. "Watch your words," he said. "Dalí is Catalan. *I* am Catalan. You're a foreigner in this country. You should have more respect."

"Are you telling us that Dalí has *deliberately* set out to dupe art critics, museum curators, and art collectors?" the examining magistrate asked. "That *all* this is a surrealist joke played on us by the most famous artist in living history?"

"Yes, Your Honor. That's what I'm telling you. On television the other day, I heard my president say that it is impossible to know whether Dalí is joking or whether he is serious. He was damn right. That's a line I wrote years ago in *Panorama* magazine, in an article I dreamed up."

"Why is that?"

"Perhaps Dalí doesn't know himself."

"Is this your closing statement?"

"I'll come to that, Your Honor. For over thirty years, Dalí has swindled art dealers with fake works of art. While I was an art dealer and an investment broker, I used my talents of imagination to swindle my clients out of their hard-earned money. I admit, I knowingly swindled my clients with these fake paintings. It was like a game of poker, but Dalí always had the upper hand. The old fox gave me and my colleagues all over the world a taste of his own medicine."

"Your conclusion?"

"I am innocent."

"That's what they all say."

"My case is closed," I said.

I didn't move. I was numb. The detective removed the handcuffs. A *funcionario* took my fingerprints and gave me a roll of toilet paper and a bottle of gasoline to wipe the black ink off my hands. Then he chalked my name and a serial number on a small blackboard he had fastened to a tripod under my chin and took some photographs.

"Which drugs are you on?" a female doctor asked.

"None."

"Heroin? Cocaine? Crack?"

"I don't take drugs. I'm not a druggie. I don't smoke and I don't drink."

"No *drogas*? What are you doing in prison, then?"

"I got busted," I said.

She took my blood pressure, pumping so hard that she almost squeezed my arm off. I waited my turn on a mark on the floor. The detective pulled a second pair of silver handcuffs from a drawer that was full of pistols and revolvers and fastened the metal grippers around my wrists. I was confined to a small police cell in the basement. It wasn't a cell; it was a dungeon, damp and sinister. Using a lighter, someone had burned a large graffito onto the wall that said, ACHTUNG, PICKPOCKETS. The dungeon was dark and cavernous as a pothole.

No mattress, no blankets, nothing. I'd lived through that once before. There were no ringing telephones at the end of the corridor all night. No toilets were flushed, because there were no toilets. Life came to a standstill.

Roll call at six, the next morning, in the cellar of the police HQ on the Via Laietana.

"Guttierez?"

"*Sí.*"

"Amadeo?"

"*Sí.*"

"Sánchez?"

"*Sí.*"

"Lau . . . Lau . . . Lau . . . Damned foreign names!"

"*Sí.*"

"Montalbàn?"

Silence.

"Montalbàn?"

Montalbàn was slumped on the floor, in a pool of his own shit and vomit.

"*Coño!*" the detective said.

Fuck, in Spanish.

Someone laughed.

Silence again.

At the end of roll call—*recuento* in Spanish—a female prosecutor handed me some faxed transfer documents.

"What are these supposed to be?" I asked.

"You were sentenced to two years behind bars. If you do not oppose extradition, as described in the European Convention that came into law on December 13, 1957, you will immediately be transferred to the Interpol branch in Madrid handling all extradition requests."

"What does *immediately* mean?"

"*Ya,*" the examining magistrate said. "Now."

"We're in Spain," I replied. "In Spain, *ya* does not necessarily mean 'now.' *Ya* could be sometime next year, or maybe *mañana,* tomorrow."

"Unfortunately, that is all too true."

". . . and no one knows when *mañana* will be," I sighed.

I was handed a crumpled fax outlining the warrant for my arrest and was transferred to the infamous La Modelo prison in Barcelona. Two weeks later, I was handcuffed to another prisoner, a Sylvester Stallone look-alike. His eyes were wild and bloodshot, like Rambo and Rocky, and his teeth were ivory flecked with black spots, like dominoes. We were locked into a tiny all-metal cage in an armored Mercedes bus and sent on the road to Madrid. There were no benches or pews or seats in the bus and no windows either. The rusty interior was divided into twenty-four steel two-person cages. Urine slushed in a narrow corridor between the cages. Each cage measured four feet in length and three in width, about five feet high, and had a tiny peephole the size of a Mars Bar at eye-level. Two Guardia Civil officers armed with shotguns, in military uniforms, sat in the back of the Mercedes, next to a filthy shithole in the floor that served as a toilet. All around, the landscape was barren, windswept, and moonlike.

It took this coffin-on-wheels two days to reach our final destination: the high-tech top-security Madrid III Valdemoro prison in the capital's suburbs, a stark penitentiary of glass, steel, and concrete, surrounded by scrubby fig trees and soft, fluffy hills that looked like melting marzipan.

"Leave your brain at the gate," the Sylvester Stallone look-alike said as we entered the prison.

I didn't know he *had* a brain.

Again, blood was dripping from my wrists.

"Lau . . . Lau . . . Laurys . . . never mind . . . prison cell seven!"

I slowly dragged myself along the gallery, counting the cells. Barbed wire on high prison walls. Hollow corridors. Metal doors everywhere. The pungent stink of Spanish cigarettes. There were six cell blocks. Three and four were home to serial killers. Five were professional thieves. Psychopaths were in block six, which had a psychiatric ward. One and two were re-served for foreigners awaiting extradition on behalf of Interpol. On the *patio*—the courtyard—prisoners from all six cell blocks happily mingled. I was in cell block one. I counted the cells in my cell block. In cell number four, two male prisoners were sitting on a lower bunk, holding hands. Number five was empty. In six, a poker game was going on. Seven had a poster glued to the cell door. The girl on the poster displayed a vagina as droopy as a freshwater mussel. Cells one, three, and seven were empty.

I shivered. *"Qué barbaridad."* My limbs were numb and my lips were taut and cold.

I was ushered into cell number seven. It was tiny and incredibly hot. Again the stench of bleach and disinfectant was overwhelming and nauseating. Prison is prison, the world over. The lower bunk on one of the cell's two bunk beds was covered with a yellow foam mattress and starched sheets. Next to the bunk bed, there was a metal sink and an open toilet with no lid. A plastic shopping bag marked PERSONAL HYGIENE NO. 1 was lying on my bunk. The bag contained two pairs of underpants, white cotton socks size 5/7, a white T-shirt, one sponge, one bar of foul-smelling soap, a tube of shaving cream, surgical vinyl gloves, one roll-on deodorant, three disposable plastic Bic razors, a toothbrush, toothpaste, three rolls of toilet paper, and three sealed condoms.

What are the surgical gloves for? I thought.

What are the condoms for?

The next morning, in the corridor before breakfast, a medical assistant distributed the day's first supply of bitter, syrupy methadone in tiny Styrofoam cups to a long line of glassy-eyed junkies. Methadone is a synthetic opioid, used medically in the treatment of narcotic addiction.

"First time in prison is awful," the Stallone look-alike said. "Second time is difficult. Thereafter, it becomes routine."

A junkie prisoner in an all-red tracksuit slowly slipped to the floor, and I rushed to help him.

"A red tracksuit means *drogadicto,* an addict. Don't touch, dangerous," the medical assistant told me.

I listened to the hard sonorous banging of kitchen kettles.

"I'm innocent," a wrinkled old man lamented. "You know what I'm saying, don't you?"

"He's innocent," I said. "So am I. What are we doing here?"

"He used a chain saw to cut his wife and four children to ribbons. Leave him alone; he doesn't remember what happened," the medical assistant said.

On the prison yard, another prisoner fumbled with a transistor radio. Sevillanas—a type of folk music sung in Seville—Isabel Pantoja, Julio Iglesias, some Spanish pop groups and Eros Ramazzotti in Spanish.

Isn't he Italian? I wondered.

"*Madre mía,*" the prisoner groaned, "how I love this music."

I was sitting in the recreation area, writing a letter to Ana and making a drawing for my son. A game of backgammon was played on a handmade plywood board. A blaring TV, no one watching. There were three pay phone booths. Agitated prisoners were shouting into the handsets as if they were in conversation with the other end of the world. A backgammon player rattled the dice in an empty Pepsi can that was cut in half. He pushed his index finger against his left nostril and blew a poisonous phlegm of snot that landed right in the middle of my shoe.

"Snake eyes!" he shouted enthusiastically.

Lunch was served on a metal tray. The cook gave me a metal fork, a spoon, a butter knife, and a paper napkin. Saltcellars on the table were handmade out of empty roll-on deodorant containers. Cold Spanish-style gazpacho soup, three grilled sausages, one hardboiled egg, some olives, and a salad leaf. The egg yolk had the color of black pudding. Sausages tasted like shit. I spat out a morsel, and from in between the lumps of fat wriggled a whole family of slimy gray-green maggots that slowly crept to the rim of my tray.

"Fucking horrible," one of my dinner partners said.

"Boiled shit every day. After a while, even boiled shit tastes like vanilla fudge," Sylvester Stallone said.

"*Fó étvágyat!*" a prisoner from Hungary said.

What does that mean? I wondered. Enjoy this shit?

I could hear the monotonous *tick-tock, tick-tock* of a Ping-Pong ball against a blind wall.

A white-haired black Cuban stopped me on the prison yard. He wanted to know if it was true that I knew Salvador Dalí professionally. His fingers were long and bony and ended in purple fingernails.

"More or less," I replied. "I met him. Once."

He smiled. "Perhaps we can do business," he said. "I'm an international art forger. Modigliani, Picasso, Braque, Chagall, I did them all and better than they could have done it themselves."

"Nice to meet you," I said.

He grabbed a sheet of paper and quickly drew a perfect Dalí soft watch.

"Shall I sign it for you?" the Cuban asked, smiling again.

"*Metadona!*" The cold, metallic voice reverberated through the loudspeaker system. "Methadone distribution!"

A prisoner who proudly called himself Britain's most-wanted fugitive broke his head over a crossword puzzle in an English tabloid. He was dressed in shorts and a red Manchester United football shirt with the name BEST—George Best—and the number seven on the back.

"Singer and catwalk model?" he asked.

No reply.

"Twiggy? Barbra Streisand?"

"Shut up!"

"*Una chica negra?*"

"Yes! Yes! You're close!"

"Grace Jones."

"Right!

"World-famous artist, as seen on TV. Begins with *D*."

"Dracula!"

"Donald Duck!"

"Dalí?"

"Bingo!"

"*Metadona!* Last call!"

A *funcionario* in a dark suit, a shiny toupee on top of his bald head, wandered the corridors. He looked like Sean Connery in an early James Bond movie.

Dali 257

"Double-oh-seven!" Sylvester Stallone bellowed and flashed his flecked teeth.

"*Qué cojones!*"

"What does *that* mean?" the most-wanted British fugitive asked.

There were no bars in the prison chapel, but then there were no windows either. The priest was dressed in faded stonewashed jeans and brown sandals. He hadn't shaved, and he could definitely use a haircut. He had loosely fitted a white Roman dog collar above a black T-shirt that read AC/DC ROCK IN RIO in an antiquated Gothic script. A red-haired Boris Becker look-alike and a Columbian drug baron acted as altar boys.

"Ultimately, who is responsible for our incarceration?" the priest asked, and rolled his eyes.

"The judge, that *hijo de puta!*" a chorus of prisoners shouted.

Hijo de puta is "son of a bitch" in Spanish.

"In silence, we ask for remission of our sins," the priest said.

One single tea light flickered on the altar.

Accompanied by two guitars, the choir sang a hymn and clapped hands rhythmically. Instead of wine as the symbol for Christ's blood, there was half a can of Pepsi. The host—the body of Christ—was a leftover bread roll from the breakfast table. Even before the last hymn had died out, the churchgoers dashed to the familiarity of the prison yard as if they were a bunch of schoolchildren, elated that class was finally over. The prison yard was sticky with phlegm and sputum, ripped condoms, and orange peel. Rolls of toilet paper everywhere. At midday, it was terrifyingly hot, with temperatures soaring to 100 degrees Fahrenheit. We drank nonalcoholic beer and licked on frozen ice cream cones from the prison canteen.

"Did you like the priest?" a nightclub singer from Andalusía asked me.

"He's okay, I think."

"He killed his boyfriend."

Night fell. The wardens made their rounds. Most prisoners were smoking black Spanish and Cuban tobacco. Empty tins served as an ashtray. Cigarette butts instead of sardines. A heavily armed Guardia Civil truck and an army Jeep circled the prison compound, and pink searchlights flooded the eerie, empty prison yard. I polished my toenails with a lump of concrete from the yard and listened to a tiny pocket radio. The radio presenter rounded off his request program with a Willie Nelson song dedicated to prisoners all over the world. *Come and lie down by my side, till the early morning light.* Lights out. Two minutes to midnight. Half-empty toothpaste tubes rolled in toilet paper were set on fire and thrown through the prison bars, as if they were homemade Molotov cocktails.

"*Viva España!*" a dark voice shouted nearby.

"*Buenas noches,*" the wardens said politely, and double-locked the cells.

Another long, hot sleepless night.

At six in the morning, a barking order blasted out of the loud-speakers: *"Lau . . . Lau . . . Stán! Stán Lau . . .* never mind . . . *Al Centro!* You're off! Back home!"

I couldn't believe my ears.

Three and a half months after my arrest, a letter from the attorney-general initiated my release from the high-tech top-security Madrid III Valdemoro prison. In my home country, His Majesty the King had granted me a royal pardon. Don't ask me why. I didn't know. You don't question the King's decisions. I kissed the letter. I kissed it again. His Majesty must have thought I'd suffered enough. He was right. I hadn't been out of Spain and into the world for five long years. I had sneaked past shop windows like a thief in the night. I feared my own mirror image. Wherever I'd spotted a policeman in uniform, I had ducked and crept away. For five long years, I had felt safe only on my mountaintop. There's still justice in the world, I thought, and again kissed the letter. A local judge in Madrid signed my release papers. Instead of the usual black robe that is a symbol of a judge's dignity and impartiality, she was smartly dressed in a fashionable Armani two-piece, as if she were ready to go shopping at any moment. She flipped through my prison file.

"You're an expert on Salvador Dalí? The artist?" she asked.

I nodded. "Sort of, Your Honor," I said.

"I've got an original Dalí at home."

"Have you?"

"Yes. I'm the proud owner of a Dalí print."

"Signed?"

"Yes. A bold signature."

"Numbered?"

"Yes. Signed and numbered."

"Where did you buy the print?"

"On Madison Avenue in New York. We were on holiday, my husband and I. That was a great find."

I was getting itchy and feeling uncomfortable.

"A bargain," the judge said.

"What's the title of the print, Your Honor? Do you remember?"

"*Don Quixote.*"

I sighed. A policeman unlocked my handcuffs.

"You're free to go."

"Great Dalí you've got," I complimented the judge. "A superb investment."

Back home in Cadaqués, sitting outside, I watched the beginnings of another day. Like a ball of fire, the sun simmered over the bare and inhospitable mountains. On the opposite slope from our little hacienda, a publicity firm was erecting road signs and poster billboards for advertising. Bulldozers began breaking the rock and digging ditches. There was a flurry of activity. Soon the first condominiums would adorn the landscape, and peace and tranquillity would be ruined forever. Again, Ana had seen some superb flats in Girona. Since Lluís was growing up fast and needed to go from kindergarten to elementary school, nearby Girona would be a perfect solution for domestic bliss. The city has one of the most beautiful old town centers in Spain, with a lovely Jewish Quarter, and Barcelona and the Pyrenees in comfortable reach. But if I wanted to get away from my mountain, I needed money and I needed it fast. Perhaps I could sell my macho Alfa Romeo. Or my gold Cartier watch. I could sell the villa. To make ends meet while I was in prison, Ana had already sold her father's paintings and some silver tableware that had been in her family for ages. She had put the house in Agullana up for sale. The market was sluggish; there were no immediate takers.

My head was buzzing. I needed some respite and drove to the Perelada castle, where I drowned my sorrow in local pink *cava* while in the casino, Julio Iglesias again crooned Frank Sinatra standards in Spanish. In the tavern, I was sitting at the bar next to a bragging Swedish businessman and his beautiful blond bombshell. They were my age, I guess. He professed to be an art expert. Since he collected nineteenth-century Nordic landscape paintings for fun, as an expensive pastime, he boasted he'd sure as hell never been taken for a ride.

Opportunity came knocking.

"Did you ever buy a surrealist Dalí?" I asked.

"No."

"No Dalí?"

"No, never."

"Why not?"

"Why should I?"

"Dalí is dying."

"Have you got a surrealist Dalí to sell?" he asked.

"Me? Oh, no. I've got nothing to sell."

"Nothing?"

"I'm not a salesperson. I used to be an art dealer, and my only product was Salvador Dalí. I was selling works of art not for their artistic value or their sheer beauty but purely as an investment, which meant that—one day or other—I resold for my clients and always at a profit. The art market is global, you know, with new money from China, India, and Russia joining in and pushing prices up."

I heard myself talk. Tittle-tattle it was, idle words. I recognized the old arguments and my old lies. It was disgusting, but I needed the money. One last trick, I thought. I'll pull one last trick. I wasn't dressed for the part, in faded jeans and a red polo that had seen better days, but there's only one last time, and I'd give it a try anyway.

"You were an art dealer?" the Swedish businessman asked.

"I was. A damned good one. Call Sotheby's. Call Christie's. Ask for me."

"What are you doing now, professionally?"

"Now? Nothing."

Fifteen years of grabbing and pulling balls, that's a lot of balls, I thought.

"How come nothing?"

"I'm enjoying life. I told you, I was good, as an art dealer. I've got money in the bank."

"How old are you?"

"Forty-five," I said.

"What kind of profit did your clients make when you sold their Dalí paintings?" the Swedish businessman asked.

"The sky was the limit."

"At long term?"

"In investments, there is no long term," I said. "We can all be dead tomorrow."

He shrugged. "I don't invest in something I don't know," he said.

Which means he's sitting on his money, I thought.

"Good idea, if you ask me," I said. "Do you trust your bank?"

"Depends."

"On what?"

"Which bank it is."

I sighed. "Ever heard of the Société de Banque Suisse?"

"Sure. That's where I've got one of our business accounts."

"Good. As you know, the Société publishes a monthly newsletter, *Le Mois Économique et Financier,* a trade journal for investment bankers. What did it say a couple of months ago? Art investments far outsell any classical investment. You know what a good Dalí oil on canvas could bring you in today's market?"

"I have no idea. You tell me."

"I won't bullshit you. Salvador Dalí is dying. One man's death is another man's bread. When he dies, his production line stops. The factory grinds to a halt. No more Dalís. No more supply while demand will be as strong as ever and—take my word for it—even stronger. Prices will go through the roof.

Now there's one thing you always have to bear in mind. Sotheby's and Christie's or private art dealers in London and New York or even Stockholm won't give you a Dalí for free, not in a million years. They're not Santa Claus. They charge you a hefty commission. Up to 20%. Why should you pay that? Buy from Dalí directly. He lives around the corner. Costs you no extras. You're here now. Take up the challenge."

Grab, pull, and—*snók!*

The old tricks were coming back like high fever, and I wasn't proud of it.

"That's interesting," his bombshell wife said. She looks like Anita Ekberg stepped out of Fellini's *La Dolce Vita* and pumped up overnight, I thought.

"Have another . . . what do you drink? Brut Rosado?" the Swedish businessman said.

"Is Dalí really such a good investment?" his wife asked.

"You want an investment?" I replied. "Call your stockbroker. Call your banker. Investments go up and down. I don't know about you, but *I* don't want my money to go down. I can tell you this: Whatever Dalí touches, it turns to gold. Dalí is lifelong happiness. You want to experience the happiness money is capable of buying? Talk to me."

"What have you got to sell?"

I suppressed a smile. "I don't sell. I may *advise* you. No strings attached. The question is, what have *you* got to pay?"

"Fifty thousand," the blond bombshell said.

"We're in Spain here. Fifty thousand pesetas? That's chicken feed."

"Dollars, of course. Fifty thousand dollars."

"I'm sorry, folks," I said. "Dalí is not a clearance sale."

"We can make it two hundred. Two hundred thousand dollars. That's as high as we can go," said the blond bombshell.

"Now you talk like a man. I'll arrange for you to have a top-quality masterpiece."

"Who says it's gonna be a masterpiece?"

"I do."

"Is this masterpiece a bargain?"

"A bargain? Are you kidding me? Someone presents you with a bargain, it's stolen, it's a fake. Might be fake *and* stolen. It's a fraud. There are no bargains in the art world."

"I want a *beautiful* Dalí," the wife said.

"Fuck beauty."

They both laughed. "If we buy now, when will we start making a profit?"

"A British investment magazine has calculated that the art of Salvador Dalí has gone up 25.94 percent per year between 1970 and 1975, and that's only for starters. When Dalí dies, prices will skyrocket."

Old clichés. Words-words-words. They still worked the magic.

I was an old fox. I still knew my sales talk by heart.

Time to close. "You know, Dalí is no longer an artist," I said. "He's become a luxury product, like a Louis Vuitton handbag. The rich want to be part of it. They want to been *seen* with their Dalí. To use the language of the stock exchange: Dalí is a blue chip, on a par with IBM and Siemens or Saab and Volvo. A

household name. Dalí is top of the bill. Every Dalí has its certificate of authenticity signed by Dalí or his business manager.
With such a certificate, even a fake Dalí would become a genuine Dalí."

"I want ironclad authentication," the Swedish businessman
said.

No fucking way, I thought.

"When can we get our first Dalí?" the blond bombshell
asked.

"*Your* first Dalí? It's yours already? Depends. When will *your*
money be available?"

"Two hundred thousand?"

"Yes. Dollars."

"A week from now?"

"Perfect. No check accepted. Cash only. Give me a telephone
number where I can reach you. I'll be in touch. Remember: you
don't buy from me. You're buying from Dalí directly. I'm only
the middleman."

"But you will resell and make us a profit?"

"Yep. The moment Dalí dies."

"When will that be?"

"Could be tomorrow, for all I know."

How wonderful it is to make money like this, I thought.

Avida Dollars. *Dollar mad.* For Salvador Dalí, those days were
over. If press reports were to be believed, he had gone into
hibernation. He lived in a no-man's-land between waking and

dreaming, life and death, the past and the hereafter. An indiscreet hospital nurse said he howled for hours, like a caged animal. Another nurse compared him to a plant in a greenhouse. He lacked control of his bladder and bowel movements and wore a diaper that was removed and refreshed three times a day. A Catholic priest had administered the last sacrament to him.

Ana got an urgent call from Ramón Guardiola. He asked her to come to the Galatea Tower immediately. I drove her over to Figueres and waited outside. When she came out, she was over the moon.

"What happened?" I asked as she danced out of the Galatea Tower.

This is what Ana told me.

"How many languages do you speak, Ana?" Ramón Guardiola had kindly asked her when she arrived at their meeting.

"Catalan, Spanish, French, some English—and German, of course."

"German? How come?"

"As a girl, I went to the Swiss School in Barcelona that was an integral part of the German-speaking community in Europe. Official school language was German."

"German? In Barcelona?"

"*Selbstverständlich.*"

"Ana, would you like to work for Salvador Dalí?"

She was taken aback.

"Me? Work for Dalí? What do you mean?"

"Sad as it is, the body of Dalí is a very, very sick body,"

Ramón Guardiola told Ana. "His life has been superactive. Not a day went by without an explosion of his genius. Today Dalí is bored. As long as Gala was alive, she read from German magazines such as *Der Spiegel* and *Bunte* or *Stern* while Dalí was painting. He didn't understand a word of what she read aloud to him, but loved the poetry of the language and the melodious tone of her voice. Its softness comforted him and dampened his angry outbursts. That's why Dalí named Gala his Quatre Cloches, because her voice chimed like four bells."

"What did Dalí call her when he got angry?" asked Ana.

"When he was angry, he said Gala was his Prime Minister."

Ana laughed. "I'd love to work for Dalí," she said. "What would you like me to do?"

"Since you're fluent in German, I'd ask you to come over to the Galatea Tower every day for an hour or two and read from *Stern* or any other German magazine. In German, of course. It doesn't really matter which one. Would you do that for us, Ana? Dalí can also listen to his favorite LP, which is Wagner's *Tristan und Isolde,* while you translate the libretto."

"I know. I've heard Dalí loves it when Wagner sounds like grilled sardines on his old gramophone," Ana replied.

Her sudden connection to Dalí was an amazing stroke of luck.

"Stán? You know who I am from now on?"exclaimed Ana once she had finished her remarkable story. "I am the new Gala! I am Salvador Dalí's Quatre Cloches. Perhaps I'll be his Prime Minister tomorrow!"

That day, the Dalí Museum sent out a press release. It

claimed that the artist had painted over a hundred new canvases since the first manifestation of his illness. According to the press release, the late canvases were said to represent the most sincere expression of surrealist art and should therefore be considered an essential part of Salvador Dalí's oeuvre. Bunkum, I thought, based on what I'd seen and heard. These late canvases, they're Young Dalí and Isidro Bea leftovers.

I still hadn't met Isidro Bea.

Who was he? Where was he?

Ana kept me up to date and told me more about what it was like, visiting Dalí on a daily basis. He had been in a bedroom fire after an accidental short circuit and suffered second-degree burns that covered 18 percent of his body. His hair was scorched away. Sometimes he wore a white furry turban. He was unable to walk, and nurses positioned him in a kind of bedside chair covered in white in an elegant, airy room. His body weight dropped steadily. He never ate solid food. Sometimes he asked for a glass of wine. Four nurses attended Dalí around the clock. The windows in his room were shuttered night and day. Crowds of reporters milled in the lobby of Torre Galatea.

Ana's arrangement with Ramón Guardiola lasted four weeks, until Dalí became too ill even to listen to his Quatre Cloches. Even for Ana, the strain was showing, and it was time to get out. Dalí had hallucinations and made animal noises. He thought he was a snail and crawled around the bedroom floor. Often Dalí howled like a caged and terrified animal. He made pincer motions with his hands and thought he was a lobster.

Every night, I asked Ana, "How was Señor Dalí today?"

Her answer was invariably the same.

"As lifeless as an insect preserved in amber."

Suddenly news came from Ramón Guardiola that the patient was improving. A pacemaker was implanted. His prostate was removed. He allowed the curtains to be opened during the day. The sun was shining in again. Recent portrait photographs of Dalí were circulated to the press, his face heavily made up, like an old movie star. His nurses reported that he stared at a flickering television screen all day long. He was sobbing and hallucinating. His doctors confessed that Dalí was trapped in his fantasies. Their diagnosis: mental deterioration and advanced cerebral sclerosis. His nose tubes were removed. He drank a glass of pink champagne and ate an omelet, though he could barely swallow, since his saliva was thick as mud. When he was given a bath in eau de cologne, it yellowed his few remaining strands of hair and the wreckage of his once-famous mustache.

Llongueras came all the way from Barcelona for a last haircut.

"*Llarg! Llarg!*" Dalí screamed.

Long, long. No haircut for Dalí.

Llongueras combed his hair and touched up the straggly ends of his mustache with a black pencil.

The mystique of Dalí-land is gone, I thought. Years ago, Dalí had been the Muhammad Ali of modern art and the Elvis Presley of his own sex circus. Now he was just another dying man. There was blood in his lungs, and despite the newly implanted pacemaker, he had an irregular heartbeat. On January 23, 1989, the early-morning edition of the local *Diari de Girona* splashed its headline all over the front page. DALÍ HA MORT, in Catalan. "DALÍ HAS DIED." It was premature. Dalí still had to pull his last trick. The old devil looked at the front page, tossed and turned in his bed, and then closed his eyes. A couple of minutes later, but only after he had read his own obituary, Salvador Dalí did at last die.

Outside his museum, a long line of tourists and art lovers mourned his passing. A nearby footwear shop put a pair of old paint-splashed patent-leather Dalí shoes up for sale.

"Shall we go to his funeral?" Ana asked that day.

"No need to," I said. "He won't see us and we won't see him."

It was a cold day for a funeral. Winter in Spain. A flock of chattering green parakeets in nearby orange and lemon trees disturbed the silence. No pink champagne for the mourners. Salvador Dalí was buried in the middle of his own museum, right next to the underground ladies toilet. Every time a lady visitor flushes the toilet, Dalí gets wet feet and turns around in anger.

One more thing to do. I'd promised to phone the Swedish businessman and his beautiful bombshell wife. I postponed and delayed. I can't do this, I thought. I can't do this. I've got Ana and the kids to consider. I can't risk their future. They were born here, they live here, this is their country—if the deal turns sour, their world collapses. *I* had been a fugitive, I don't want *them* to become fugitives, too. It's been enough of a strain; there's an end to everything, and it's never too late to repent and come to your senses. I had to stop being greedy, once and for all. There's more to life than money. There's the sun to enjoy. There's the sea. The mountains. There's Ana to love. There's Lluís and Teri. I was a free man; I was in good health. Why would I risk prison again? For money? For the kick of danger? The rush of adrenaline? Come on, I thought, grow up, don't be silly. I looked in the mirror and saw my former self and didn't like him one single bit. I wanted to forget that man. Erase him from my memory.

Was this what redemption is all about?

My hands were sweaty. On an impulse, I picked up the telephone and dialed the number the Swedish businessman had given me. My legs were shaking. I was nervous all over.

His blond bombshell wife answered the phone. "My dear Stan . . . we've got money for you," she said in a silken voice. "Have you got something for us? Have you got our Dalí?"

"Keep your money," I said.

"Keep it? What about our Dalí?"

"There *is* no Dalí."

"W-W-What did you say?"

"Are you deaf? Hard of hearing? Or what? There is no Dalí!" I shouted. "*There is no Dalí!*"

"But . . . but . . . Dalí died, you know."

"This whole Dalí thing, it's a con," I said. "A scam. A set-up. It always was. An elaborate hoax involving *fake fake* paintings with *fake fake* signatures and *fake fake* certificates of authenticity. I lied to you. I never told you the truth. The truth is, I'm bankrupt. I need money badly and I tried to con you. Forget it and forgive me. I'm sorry. I'm really sorry and I apologize." I slammed the phone down and heaved a sigh of relief. It was finally over. Everything was finally over.

Several months after Dalí's funeral, my little hacienda was put up for sale. I'd cleaned the swimming pool one last time and rinsed the toilets and scaled the bathroom tiles. I removed embers and dead wood from the fireplace. There were Nat King Cole songs on the radio, in Spanish. *Aquellos ojos verdes,* "Those Green Eyes." I was gazing out the window, watching the low afternoon sun reflect in the Mediterranean, when I finally got the call I no longer expected. Isidro Bea on the line. Isidoro in Spanish, Isidro in Catalan. He had an old man's voice, slow, raspy, tired, and guttural. I could tell that he wasn't used to speaking on the telephone. He said he was in Cadaqués to pack up and asked if he could see me before dinner.

I said, "Bar Boia? At six?"

"Good idea. Bar Boia has the best *carajillo* on the Costa Brava."

Almond blossoms lay like powdery snow across the mountain range in the north. When he arrived at the bar, I told Isidro Bea that he looked like a Pablo Picasso stand-in or body double: short, bald, stocky, and suntanned

He laughed. "Señor Dalí always called me his own Picasso for private use," he said.

For old time's sake, I asked for a *cortado,* please, *corto de café,* steamy hot milk and just a drop of coffee. *Amargo,* bitter, no sugar.

"I phoned you a couple of times last year. There was no reply," Isidro Bea said.

"I was away. Nothing special. I was in prison."

"In prison?"

"Yeah."

"Where?"

"Girona, Barcelona, Madrid."

"What a coincidence! Sixty years ago, Señor Dalí was locked up in Girona penitentiary, too. For about two weeks, I believe. He was released without charges."

"Dalí? In Girona prison? You sure? How do you know?"

"Señor Dalí enjoyed recalling his time behind bars."

"What was he in prison for?"

"Don't know. In those days . . . probably had something to do with sodomy," Isidro Bea said. "Señor Dalí was a show-off. He always exaggerated. He pretended that male residents in Cadaqués have erections so hard, they could crack nuts on them." He chuckled. "What I know for a fact—because I've seen them myself—is that there live thousands of lobsters down in the bay. Whenever a cha-cha-cha is played on the jukebox, here in Bar Boia, they rhythmically clap their pincers. Perhaps lobsters have erections so hard you can crack nuts on them, but I wouldn't know about that."

I smiled. "They must, they're Catalan lobsters," I said.

I asked him about Salvador Dalí, and Bea told me he had

been Señor Dalí's number-one assistant since 1955. He was six years younger than Dalí. Originally he was a stage designer. He used to have his own studio with two associates and worked almost exclusively for the Gran Teatre del Liceu, as the Barcelona opera house on the Ramblas is called.

"One day, I don't remember why, probably because the pay was good, I accepted a commission to decorate a ceiling in a private mansion in Palamós on the Costa Brava," Bea told me. "I had to do it in under twenty-four hours, for a wedding party was to be held in the mansion. The design was based on a small painting by Señor Dalí in the collection of the father of the bride. Some surrealist thing with butterflies. I was used to laying out theatrical backdrops, so I immediately started blowing up the butterflies the size of a horse. The job took me only one working day. Señor Dalí was a guest at the wedding party. When he saw his small painting reproduced on the ceiling, enlarged a hundredfold, he was greatly impressed and asked me to work for him, since he was besieged with orders and couldn't cope. Soon I was mapping out Señor Dalí's *Last Supper* and painted every square inch of it. I liked that, because I'm a classical painter and a devout Catholic. Señor Dalí liked it, too—he didn't even highlight it with a surrealist symbol, like a butterfly or a melting clock, he just left it like that—and sold my painting to the National Gallery of Art in Washington, D.C. More postcards of that painting are sold than of all the works by Leonardo da Vinci and Raphael put together. I also made a second and smaller version of Señor Dalí's *Last Supper* with Mia Farrow and Ali MacGraw as two of the twelve apostles. It was the beginning of a fruitful collaboration that lasted for thirty years."

Isidro Bea explained how they worked together. In one instance, Dalí showed him a cover of the French *Paris Match* magazine and cutout images and illustrations of Dalí art books and *Life* magazine. They slid the magazine cover and the cutouts in an overhead slide projector with a very bright lamp that is generally used to display images to an audience and moved the cutouts around to get the right "surrealist" composition. The projector worked like a magic lantern and cast the images like a slide show on a blank artist's canvas. That's how surrealist Dalí paintings were scrambled together.

"I worked very fast, as if it wasn't a painting but a theater backdrop. I pencil-copied the outline and quickly applied the sea and the sky in more or less figurative brushstrokes while Señor Dalí snuggled in his old sofa and added a tiny lobster or some crawling ants as a finishing touch. A second assistant affixed Señor Dalí's signature."

"Where was that?"

"In the secret studio. It was cool there, in summer, and dark. That's where we could use the magic lantern."

"I've been to Dalí's house. I haven't seen a secret studio," I said.

Again, Bea chuckled. "No one has. In fact, there were *two* secret studios. A circular one above the house, at the end of the garden, without any windows so that nobody could ever look in—that studio had a glass roof—and the cool, dark one next to the main entrance to the house. The studios were always locked. Only Señor Dalí and myself had a key."

"Amazing," I said.

"We knew all the tricks," Isidro Bea told me. "Basic rules? Different styles? Perspective? We always found someone who was good at it. My specialty was blowing up a small image into a huge painting. That's where my training as a stage designer came in. If you take a closer look at Señor Dalí's monumental paintings from the late fifties, sixties, and early seventies, you will notice that backgrounds are in the *clars de suc* style, which is Catalan jargon for the technique of thinning oil paint to create a soft and glamorous pastel effect. By God, I worked hard! I slaved like a robot imbued with the spirit of Señor Dalí. I single-handedly painted all the monumental Dalí canvases that are now in major museums the world over: *The Last Supper* in Washington, D.C.; *The Discovery of America by Christopher Columbus* in St. Petersburg, Florida; the *Battle of Tetouan* in the Minami Art Museum in Tokyo; *Railway Station at Perpignan* in the Ludwig Museum in Cologne, Germany; as well as the so-called atomic paintings with objects floating and flying around in space. In fact, from the early sixties onward, Señor Dalí depended entirely on me. To be honest, he had lost his mythical and magical surrealist touch. Soon after his great creative years, in the late twenties and early thirties, Señor Dalí started recycling his own worn-out surrealist images and threw dust in everyone's eyes. I prepared the canvas and worked out the perspective and the architecture of every Dalí painting that is now the pride of a major museum.

You know what I was really good at? Clouds! I've also seen them, those press photographs of Señor Dalí standing on a scaffold in his museum and feverishly painting a mural on the ceiling in the room that is known as the Palace of the Wind. The artist's palette Señor Dalí is holding in his hand is *my* palette. His brushes are *my* brushes. Look at the ceiling, nothing but whirling clouds. *Saint James*: clouds. *The Discovery of America*: clouds. *Last Supper*: clouds. Look at the size of the paintings and see for yourself. *Saint James the Great*: four hundred by three hundred centimeters. *The Discovery of America*: four hundred and ten by two hundred and eighty-four centimeters. *The Last Supper*: one hundred and sixty-seven by two hundred and sixty-eight centimeters. They're blowups, they're theater backdrops, they're stage designs. It took me only a few days to copy every square inch of Señor Dalí's giant *Battle of Tetouan* from a color photograph in *Life* magazine. A giant canvas like *Saint James the Great* I had to finish in a couple of hours because Señor Dalí was pressed for money. On the spot, Lady Beaverbrook bought it for a million dollars. A few days after the sale, I handed Gala my invoice for four days work. It came to a total of seventy-five dollars all included. Gala was avaricious, a penny pincher, and declined to pay my invoice. She gave me fifty dollars, take it or leave it."

"What did Lady Beaverbrook have to say about that?"

"She didn't know. No client of Señor Dalí has ever seen me in person. When an important visitor rang the bell, I had to hide in an alcove under the stairs or was banned for the rest of the day to the secret studio, where I painted Señor Dalí's masterpieces, because that was the only part of the house spacious enough, where we had long, sizable walls. You've been in Señor Dalí's house, you've seen those cramped, pocket-sized rooms and passageways and low, claustrophobic corridors and walk-throughs. Does anyone believe Señor Dalí painted those monumental canvases in his "official" studio? Take *Saint James the Great*, four hundred by three hundred centimeters. 'Dalí needs a larrrge oil on canvas. Do as you please,' Señor Dalí said, and he gave me a picture postcard of the interior of the cathedral of Santiago de Compostella and a handful of scallop shells from the beach. I projected the postcard and the shells together on an oversize canvas—no problem for me, as a stage designer, I was used to working large formats—and smack in the middle, I projected a color photograph that I'd cut out of the *National Geographic* of a white rearing horse rising from the sea and getting up on its hind legs. In the left- and right-hand corner, I painted a portrait of Gala draped under a white cotton sheet that I copied from an old art book in Señor Dalí's library, as well as rocks and cliffs from Cadaqués, Cap de Creus, and Port Lligat copied from a local tourist brochure. That was that, everything carefully mapped out. I did as I pleased. Señor Dalí had visitors every day. The first important and wealthy visitor that day was the wife of a Canadian publishing magnate. She wanted a Dalí painting, no matter what subject, and asked Señor Dalí if he could explain the meaning of *Saint James the Great*. Señor Dalí coughed and said the subject of the painting was the antiexistential idea of the Fatherland and the fruit of the explosion of four petals of a jasmine flower in an atomic

cloud whereby the shells are a metamorphosis of Spanish cas-
tanets that symbolize the birth of Aphrodite of Crete. I was tend-
ing and weeding the garden and pretended to be the gardener.
When I heard Señor Dalí saying that, rolling his *rrr*'s as in Spanish, exaggerating his pronunciation and articulating every syllable, I almost died in a fit of laughter. Because I was always pressed
for time, I used an undercoat of fast-drying industrial paint from
an artist's supply shop in Barcelona. Without blinking an eye,
Señor Dalí told Lady Beaverbrook that he diluted his oil paint
with the poison of a thousand wasps. Rubbish, of course, I used
white spirit, like every other commercial painter in the world.
Lady Beaverbrook was so impressed, though, she bought the
painting on the spot.

"For me, looking back now, there's no difference between a
Salvador Dalí masterpiece and a stage design for an opera
house. When I arrived in Cadaqués thirty years ago, I had a job
to do, and I did it to the best of my ability. Did I fool the art
world? No, not at all. If anyone fooled the art world, Señor Dalí
did. He handed me a handful of cutouts from books and magazines: the Ampurdán landscape with its beautiful skyline, a portrait photograph of his father, a Vermeer painting and a burning
giraffe, and he said, 'Isid*rrr*o, make a one-million-dolla*rrr* mas-
te*rrr*piece for Dalí!' and I started my working day in the secret
studio while Señor Dalí was entertaining his international clientele around the swimming pool, guzzling pink champagne from
Perelada. Late at night, when his clientele was fast asleep in the
one hotel nearby, Señor Dalí would sneak to the secret studio
and add a surrealist icon or two to my painting, like a splendid

butterfly—always butterflies—or one of his world-famous drooping soft watches. Next day, Señor Dalí sold my theater backdrop for a fortune."

"Every year for thirty years, Gala and Dalí left Spain and Cadaqués at the end of summer and spent autumn in Paris and winter in New York," I said. "Were you unemployed for a couple of months?"

"Not at all. Before they set off in their ultraluxurious Cadillac, Señor Dalí's manservant at the wheel, I was given a list of paintings that had to be finished by the time he got back six months later. The list—his 'su*rr*ealist ideas,' Señor Dalí called them—consisted of a thin folder containing doodles and sketches as well as photographs, press clippings, picture postcards, and magazine cutouts. I've heard all these gory stories of Señor Dalí's sex orgies. While he was jerking off in his New York hotel suite, I was doing the slave labor in the secret studio, and when my work was done, I gave the folder with Señor Dalí's surrealist ideas to Captain Moore. None of the sketches or doodles was ever signed. Today, they're sold in fine art galleries all over the word, signed 'Dalí' and dated and beautifully framed."

"Who signed them? Did you?"

"Captain Moore, I guess. I didn't."

Now I chuckled. It didn't surprise me at all. Nothing could surprise me anymore.

"Sometimes Señor Dalí would send me an airmail parcel from New York, outlining new ideas and proposals and suggestions. If a painting was an instant hit, Señor Dalí always asked me to make an exact copy. Painting in duplo, he called it. The prefix *du* in *duplo* refers to the number two. One of my success stories was *Exploding Head of Raphael* that I must have copied at least ten times. They were copies from copies from copies, and they sold like cheesecake. From a visit to Rome, Señor Dalí brought back a tourist brochure with a photograph of the interior of the Pantheon cupola seen from inside out. Using the overhead projector, I flashed the cupola on a blank canvas and outlined its magnificent geometrical architecture. Over the dome, I projected a portrait of Saint Teresa of Avila in such a way that it looked as if the geometrical formation was the skull of the mystic sister nun. That's how I left the painting. 'Saint Terrresa is a sperrrmhead!' Señor Dalí shouted, and with a few quick brushstrokes, he added blobs of sperm ejaculating and spraying and splashing from the detonating and exploding head.

"I was married with two daughters, María and Janina, and was still working part-time as a stage designer, to supplement my income. In 1963, I painted a fresco, a flat piece of theatrical scenery on burlap—three hundred and five by three hundred and forty-five centimeters—for a new production that would premiere in the Barcelona Opera House. At the very last moment, the production was cancelled, and my backdrop was rolled up and stored away until Señor Dalí bought it and retitled my stage design *Galacidalacideoxyribonucleicacid,* his longest title in one word, as he proclaimed proudly. After he ceremoniously signed it, Señor Dalí sold my fresco for half a million dollars."

Isidro Bea shook his head and laughed. "Since I am a practicing Catholic, I refused to work on a Sunday, which for me is the Lord's day. Señor Dalí understood. Instead of working on Sunday, I went to Mass, and after Mass, Señor Dalí and I collected sea urchins in the shallow waters of Cadaqués and Port Lligat.

"In 1972, I fell ill and was hospitalized for several months. Panic! A drama! Captain Moore asked not one but *two* artists to stand in for me: Georges Mathieu, the French abstract expressionist; and a certain Phillips, an American who painted Señor Dalí's *Lincoln in Dalívision* in a New York studio. Captain Moore left after a bitter dispute with Gala, and Señor Dalí's new manager hired Manuel Pujol Baladas to join the team. He was a young man who worked for Walt Disney and was known in the secret studio as Young Dalí because he cleverly imitated Señor Dalí's early surrealist style. All three were interims, Georges Mathieu, Phillips, and Young Dalí, and had a totally different style, but that was not a problem. Whenever clients and museum curators complained that no two recent paintings looked alike, they were told that Señor Dalí was so creative that he continuously invented new styles. I came out of hospital and went back to work. Suddenly there were *four* Dalí substitutes creating surrealist masterpieces in the secret studio: a Frenchman, an American, Young Dalí, and myself. It had become a grotesque comedy."

I shook my head. How amazing, I thought, how amazing but how true.

"Did you know that Señor Dalí even tried to sell his

mustache?" Isidro Bea asked. "Somebody offered him a million dollars. Señor Dalí replied that the selling price was two million. For a million, the buyer could have half his mustache."

"When Dalí died, did he leave you anything?" I asked.

"Oh, yeah. Look at this."

Isidro Bea held up a little silver box. He opened it. Inside on red velvet was Dalí's famously fake mustache fashioned on two hairy drinking straws.

Cypress trees rustled softly. Their long shadows made me nervous.

"Would you like to see the secret studio?" Isidro Bea asked suddenly. "We can walk, if you feel like it. I've got the key."

Down in the valley, the transparent and melancholy twilight colored the dark hills and coves even darker. The sea was calm, like a mirror. We walked to Señor Dalí's private house, past the cemetery where Dalí's father was buried. With their cold light, fireflies lit up the mountain while cicadas chirped endlessly. It was a genuine cricket concert, and I enjoyed it immensely. On a faraway hill, I could hear the faint melody of a Catalan rumba carried on the Mediterranean breeze, erotic and sensual even in the fading light.

The landscape of vineyards was idyllic and miraculously beautiful, the groves drooping with olives, purple and fully ripe and beautifully rounded. It felt like the end of the end of the world. Immaculate swans were drifting on the surface of the sea, only they didn't have lit candles on their backs, as in times past when Señor Dalí was still around. It was a surreal moment, one I would never have encountered anywhere else in the world. In the half dark, I could imagine the faint contours of Dalí's famous sculpture of Christ made of driftwood and the overgrown cypress tree sticking out of the stranded old rowing boat. It was quiet, serene, and isolated.

In the passing moonlight, I recognized the smooth outline of Dalí's egg on top of his sex boudoir. Long gone were those nights, many summers ago, when Señor Dalí was forever farting and snoring with such a roar that he kept the whole village of Cadaqués awake. When some frothy semen slipped from his limousine in a wet dream, he screamed so loudly that he made the bells in the church tower chime in unison.

The garden had gone wild. Loudspeakers were hidden in the oleander bushes.

"Some months ago, I came here with Arturo Caminada—Señor Dalí's manservant—to remove the rubbish dump that had been there for ages," Isidro Bea said. "Under the rotting garbage, we discovered some paintings on wood wrapped up in plastic. They were Señor Dalí's original 1945 oil designs for Alfred Hitchcock's *Spellbound,* starring Ingrid Bergman and Gregory Peck and featuring the famous dream sequence with floating eyes, twisted landscapes, and a faceless man in a tuxedo. Arturo told me that, locking the house for the winter, he found an old key in a cupboard, with a New York warehouse label attached to it. The key was sent to New York. Michael Ward Stout tried it on a walk-in safe Señor Dalí had abandoned half a century ago. The key fit. In the safe were over a thousand long-forgotten *genuine genuine* Dalís."

The high whitewashed walls of Señor Dalí's house clung to

the side of the cliff, cold and lifeless. The house was in darkness. Potted shrubs bordered the walls. Blinds were drawn in the secret studio, next to the main entrance of the house. The small entrance was barricaded with a beautiful antique Spanish door, smeared with oil paint. A glass window was smashed to pieces. The garden stretched as far as the hillside and down toward the sea. In the distance, I could faintly make out the ragged mass of black rocks known as Cap de Creus.

Isidro Bea used his own key to let us into the secret studio. Electricity had been cut off. We hadn't brought a flashlight. I allowed my eyes to get accustomed to the dark and could make out skeletons of stuffed animals and mannequin dolls that hung on the walls. Pots and tubes and blends of paint filled shelves lined with brushes and pencils and color crayons. The easels were empty. There were optical instruments everywhere: the enormous pale green overhead projector, magnifying glasses, mirrors, cameras. . . . The studio was cluttered with outrageously kitsch acquisitions: a plaster cast of the *Venus de Milo,* a Davy Crockett coonskin hat, thirty-two blocks of clay, a miniature Goodyear blimp, Venetian masks, cardboard silhouette displays of a man and a woman, peasants probably, nine or ten feet in height, washed out by sun and rain and wind, paint-smeared sunglasses, canes, an Adidas American football and a 1960s cassette player without any cassettes.

I looked around. Where are they? I wondered. Nothing to be seen, nowhere.

"What are you looking for?" Isidro Bea asked.

"Señor Dalí's dildos," I said.

Bea shook with laughter. "Gala had been playing the roulette tables and lost a fortune," he said. "A member of Señor Dalí's household was furious. His gun drawn, he was target-practicing to let off steam. As a target, he used Señor Dalí's personalized dildos, neatly placed in a row, like bottles on a shelf. He squeezed the trigger and shouted: 'Hitler: *Banggg!* Dead. Kennedy: *Banggg!* Dead. Fidel Castro: *Banggg!* Dead. Mao Tse-tung: *Banggg!* Dead. Mother Teresa: *Banggg!* Dead. Salvador Dalí: *Banggg!* Dead.' The dildos exploded in an orgasm of paint. 'They're all dead now,' he said, and holstered his gun."

"It's rather a mess here," I said.

"An inventory was never drawn up," Isidro Bea said. "There was so much more. The place was cluttered. A shambles. It's all gone. Stolen, probably. Ransacked."

"What are the blocks of clay for?" I asked.

Again, Bea laughed. "Señor Dalí had thirty-two perfectly shaped blond women dressed as angels each sit on a block of wet clay and then made an imprint of their bare bottom," he said. "I transferred the imprints on Arches paper. Señor Dalí signed the imprints and included them in his *Bible* illustrations, just like that, a signature and the imprint of a girl's bare ass. Magically, Señor Dalí's *Bible* got the pope's blessing—"

"Where are they now, those thirty-two bare asses?"

Bea giggled. "—and Captain Moore sold the imprints to the Vatican Museum. That's where they are on permanent exhibition now."

The paintings in the secret studio were all signed. None was authentic or *genuine genuine* or original and undisputed. They were copies of copies of endless copies. None of the paintings bore the distinctive hallmark of Salvador Dalí's 1930s surrealist style. I didn't know who'd painted them, but it certainly wasn't Señor Dalí. Bea told me that one of the half-finished oils on hardboard was called *The Happy Horse* or something like that. It looked awful. In the dim light of the moon through the shutters, I could distinguish a finger-painted rotting carcass on the hardboard, covered with a mass of buzzing flies. The carcass was disintegrating in what looked like the draft of an unfinished Ampurdán countryside.

"This one the four of us did together," Bea said. "Georges Mathieu, Phillips, Young Dalí, and myself. We had a few bottles of wine, that afternoon. We came and attacked the hardboard. You can't be sure it's a horse, can you? It might be a mule or a donkey. But you can certainly see it's rotting away."

The oil paint was still sticky.

Isidro Bea took a brush and some half-empty tubes from a shelf.

"It's your turn," he said.

"Me?"

"*Sí.*"

"I'm not an artist."

"Am I?" Isidro Bea asked.

It seemed like an adventure, a challenge, a wonderful idea at the time. I grabbed the thick brush and smeared some poisonous green slime onto the hardboard.

"Sign it."

"No, I won't."

"Don't be silly."

Why not? I thought. I had been fingerprinted in Girona's penitentiary, in Barcelona's La Modelo prison, and in Interpol's high-tech top-security Madrid III Valdemoro prison—and I pushed my thumb into the sticky remains of the horse or the mule or the donkey or whatever it was, and with the hint of a smile on my lips, I twisted an imaginary Dalí mustache while I gave Bea one of Dalí's trademark wide-eyed looks.

"There can be only one *last* Dalí," I said.

"Let's hope so," Isidro Bea replied. "With a man like Señor Dalí, you never know. Damn, I forgot the certificate of authenticity."

"Señor Dalí had six hundred and sixty-six or perhaps six hundred and seventy-nine different signatures," I said. "A signature for each and every occasion. I wonder which one in the end will be authentic."

"*That* one," Bea said, and pointed his finger at the painting.

There was no signature.

In between the soft hills and naked mountains, milky white and ripe like melting Camembert, I could vaguely see the bell tower through the darkness, and the rocks and cliffs, sculpted into weird shapes by wind and rain and salt lashed from the sea. A herd of impossibly spindly-legged elephants waded through the Mediterranean. In the far distance, a giraffe walked across the vast expanse of emptiness. The giraffe was on fire, flames leaping up its back, until they filled the screen that burned to blackness. However surreal, these were the images we're all familiar with now. I smiled and shook these surreal thoughts and visions from my head.

As we left the garden in Port Lligat, it began snowing.

Epilogue

In the end, Ana and I separated. Things couldn't last, after what I'd been through. I was carrying too much negative baggage and needed to clear my head. Where one door closes, another door opens, as the famous Cervantes wrote four centuries ago. One journey ends where another begins. I got a new passport and split my time between London and my home country. Using my own prison experience for inspiration and background, I started writing crime fiction. I often return to Cadaqués, to be with my son. He is a young man now. We sit at the Bar Boia on the pebble beach, slurping *café con leche* and *cortado* and gazing out at the azure Mediterranean, enjoying the sun, the warmth, and the pleasant smell of freedom in the air, all the while reminiscing about things past and present. Josep had died. So had Captain Moore, rumba-band leader Xavier Cugat, Arturo

Caminada, Ramón Guardiola, Marc Lacroix, Antoni Ribas, and
Andy Warhol. Isidro Bea had died. As he'd predicted, Young Dalí
was sentenced to a long prison term and fled the country, to Mexico. He's a struggling artist again. Boys throw stones in the
crystal-clear water. No more chamber orchestra making music on
the beach and no more white swans drifting lazily on the sea's surface, burning candles on their backs. There is barely a breath of
wind. Clouds hang like frayed bedsheets in the blue sky above the
soft green hills and the jagged edges of rocks and coves. I still
haven't read Malcolm Lowry's *Under the Volcano,* though I've
seen the film, on television. Like pearls, my tears are rolling to the
sea. We listen to the sloshing of the Mediterranean and the constant gurgling of the coffee machine, and suddenly I remember
something Isidro Bea told me the day we met, something I'd forgotten about.

It was during the last period of Señor Dalí's long life. The
small biplane was flying along the coastline and trailing the familiar banner that read, WELCOME TO DALÍ-LAND. The artist himself
was sitting in his garden. He gasped for air and lifted his head. His
watery eyes looked up at the thundering machine in the clear
blue sky.

The old man called up. "Where is Dalí-land?" he gurgled.
"Who is Dalí?"